BEYOND ILLUSION & DOUBT

BOOKS by
His Divine Grace A. C. Bhaktivedanta Swami Prabhupāda

Bhagavad-gītā As It Is
Śrīmad-Bhāgavatam (18 vols.; with disciples)
Śrī Caitanya-caritāmṛta (9 vols.)
The Nectar of Devotion
Kṛṣṇa, the Supreme Personality of Godhead
Teachings of Lord Caitanya
Śrī Īśopaniṣad
The Nectar of Instruction
Easy Journey to Other Planets
Kṛṣṇa Consciousness: The Topmost Yoga System
Perfect Questions, Perfect Answers
Teachings of Lord Kapila, the Son of Devahūti
Transcendental Teachings of Prahlāda Mahārāja
Dialectic Spiritualism
Beyond Illusion and Doubt
Teachings of Queen Kuntī
Kṛṣṇa, the Reservoir of Pleasure
The Science of Self-Realization
The Path of Perfection
Search for Liberation
Life Comes from Life
The Perfection of Yoga
Beyond Birth and Death
On the Way to Kṛṣṇa
Rāja-vidyā: The King of Knowledge
Elevation to Kṛṣṇa Consciousness
Kṛṣṇa Consciousness: The Matchless Gift
The Nārada-bhakti-sūtra (with disciples)
The Mukunda-mālā-stotra (with disciples)
A Second Chance
The Journey of Self-Discovery
The Quest for Enlightenment
The Laws of Nature
Dharma: The Way of Transcendence
Renunciation Through Wisdom
Geetār-gan (Bengali)
Vairāgya-vidyā (Bengali)
Back to Godhead magazine (founder)

A complete catalog is available upon request

The Bhaktivedanta Book Trust
3764 Watseka Ave.
Los Angeles
CA 90034, USA

The Bhaktivedanta Book Trust
P.O. Box 262
Botany, N.S.W.
2019, Australia

The Bhaktivedanta Book Trust
P.O. Box 324
Borehamwood, Herts.
WD6 1NB, U.K.

BEYOND ILLUSION & DOUBT

A Vedic View of Western Philosophy

Articles from
Back to Godhead magazine

His Divine Grace
A. C. BHAKTIVEDANTA
SWAMI PRABHUPĀDA
Founder-Ācārya of the International Society for Krishna Consciousness

THE BHAKTIVEDANTA BOOK TRUST
Los Angeles • London • Stockholm • Bombay • Sydney • Hong Kong

ON THE COVER: Lord Kṛṣṇa expands Himself as the Supersoul in everyone's heart. From Him come all knowledge, the ability to remember, and the power to forget.

ENDPAPERS: From the moment of birth our body continuously changes, but the soul within remains unchanged and finally passes into a new body at death.

Readers interested in the subject matter of this book are invited by the International Society for Krishna Consciousness to correspond with its secretary.

International Society for Krishna Consciousness
3764 Watseka Avenue
Los Angeles, California 90034, USA

Telephone: 1-800-927-4152
http://www.harekrishna.com
e-mail: letters@harekrishna.com

International Society for Krishna Consciousness
P.O. Box 262
Botany, NSW 2019, Australia

International Society for Krishna Consciousness
P.O. Box 324, Borehamwood
Herts., WD6 1NB, England

Telephone: 0181-905 1244
e-mail: bbl@com.bbt.se

Design: Arcita Dāsa
Art: Lord Viṣṇu (detail from a painting) by Jadurāṇī-Devī Dāsī
Illustrations of philosophers: Mahānta Dāsa

First Printing, 1999: 50,000

Printed in Singapore

ISBN 0-89213-326-0

Contents

Introduction

Philosophy? What's that? The word comes from the two Greek words *philo* ("love") and *sophia* ("wisdom"). So philosophy is love of wisdom or knowledge.

Of course, there are many kinds of wisdom and knowledge. Philosophy, however, specifically concerns itself with questions related to the ultimate nature and meaning of experience and reality. As composer Burt Bacharach put it in a famous song, "What's it all about, Alfie?"

In that sense, we are all philosophers, because we all do, from time to time, wonder what it's all about. Perhaps this sense of wonder comes from going camping in the desert and looking up at night and seeing the vast array of stars. Or perhaps it comes from a sense of disappointment. We lose something, or fail to achieve something, and we ask, "Why me?" We pray to God for something, and we don't get it. We see that others get what we want for ourselves. And therefore we ask, "God, are You listening to me, are You really there?" Or perhaps we're confronted with a difficult choice in life, and we wonder, "God, what should I do?" We search for some basis to make a decision. Or sometimes we find that what appeared to be solid and real—a relationship, a position, something—suddenly disappears. And we wonder, "What's real? Is there anything in this world I can really count on?" Or we see things happening around us in ways we can't explain, and we wonder, "Is there any logic, any reason to all this?" Or we hear someone trying to justify himself to us, and we can tell he isn't making any sense. And we question him, "Do you know what you're *saying*?" Whether we know it or not, all these questions we keep asking are philosophical questions.

Philosophy has traditionally been divided into four branches. The first is logic, the study of the formal structure of argument, of how a conclusion properly flows from certain assumptions, premises, and statements. The second branch is metaphysics, the study of the ultimate nature of reality—of

God and the universe and consciousness. The third branch is epistemology, the science of how we know things. And the fourth branch is axiology, the study of values, of ethics, of how we determine what is right and wrong. This branch also includes aesthetics, the study of what is truly beautiful.

In all these areas many questions come up, as we have seen. But how do we find the answers? Western philosophy has relied on individual speculation, which involves taking evidence from our senses and evaluating it with our minds. But this method leaves us with a great deal of uncertainty. After all, our senses are imperfect, and our minds are subject to illusion, mistakes, and the propensity to cheat, to pretend we know something when we really don't. With all these variables, each philosopher tends to come to a different set of answers to the fundamental questions. Indeed, it seems that one really can't be a leading philosopher without saying something substantially different from the philosophers who've come before. This constant overhauling of philosophies throughout Western history can make the study of philosophy very frustrating, especially for people who are consulting philosophers not just to play an intellectual game but to find practical answers to life's most perplexing questions.

There is another approach to philosophy, however. The philosophers of the Vedic civilization of ancient India distinguished two ways of getting at the truth. One is called the ascending path of knowledge, and the other is called the descending path. Western philosophers commonly use the ascending path, the path of speculation. The Vedic philosophers recognized that one who uses this method can never achieve certain knowledge, free from illusion and doubt, because of those pesky imperfect mind and senses. They preferred the descending path of knowledge. Recognizing the existence of a supreme intelligence behind the universe we experience with our senses, the Vedic philosophers accepted that the only way of getting certain answers to ultimate questions is to receive knowledge coming down from the supreme intelligence, God, known by the name Kṛṣṇa.

This knowledge, originating with Kṛṣṇa, has been passed down through a chain of spiritual masters since the beginning of time. There is no need to change it, there is no need to speculate about it. It is perfect knowledge. The duty of a spiritual master is simply to pass this knowledge on to his or her disciples, who in turn become spiritual masters and pass it on to a new generation of disciples. Because this knowledge is not the product of imperfect human minds and senses, it is beyond illusion and doubt.

But we should not blindly accept knowledge from the descending path. It is not dogma. We can test it with logic and reason and discover for ourselves how it is superior to any contrary conclusions arrived at through the speculative method. And by practicing yoga we can experimentally verify the truths received through the descending path. In this particular age, the most highly recommended process of yoga is *bhakti-yoga,* the yoga of devotion to God.

In recent times, the most prominent spiritual master in the line of spiritual masters coming from Kṛṣṇa is His Divine Grace A. C. Bhaktivedanta Swami Prabhupāda (known popularly as Śrīla Prabhupāda). His own spiritual master, His Divine Grace Bhaktisiddhānta Sarasvatī Ṭhākura, asked Śrīla Prabhupāda to spread the methods and conclusions of Vedic philosophy throughout the world.

In the early 1970s, Śrīla Prabhupāda, decided to analyze Western philosophy in light of Vedic philosophy. In a series of tape-recorded conversations, his scholarly disciples Hayagrīva Dāsa and Śyāmasundara Dāsa presented to Śrīla Prabhupāda selections from the teachings of prominent Western philosophers, from Socrates to Carl Jung, and Śrīla Prabhupāda commented upon them. *Beyond Illusion and Doubt* is based on those conversations. All but one of the chapters of *Beyond Illusion*—the one dealing with the philosophy of John Stuart Mill—originally appeared as articles in *Back to Godhead,* the magazine of the Hare Kṛṣṇa movement. Śrīla Prabhupāda founded this magazine in India in

1944, and since then it has become the world's foremost journal dedicated to the teachings of Lord Kṛṣṇa.

We are under no illusion that *Beyond Illusion* presents an exhaustive treatment of Western philosophy. After all, for the most part the philosophers presented here, some of the most prominent in the West, wrote voluminously and created a complex system of thought outlining an original world view. Rather, what you'll find here is a fascinating series of insights into some of their most salient ideas and a concise yet thorough presentation of the basics of *bhakti-yoga*.

You'll read how Śrīla Prabhupāda applauds Socrates' opposition to the Sophists' view that morality is relative—that there is no absolute standard of right and wrong. "The highest duty of man is to care for his soul," Socrates declared; Śrīla Prabhupāda agrees, and explains how.

Excerpts from *Plato's Republic* provide Śrīla Prabhupāda with a context for explaining the Vedic social system, while Aristotle's speculations on God and man come in for some sharp criticism.

Śrīla Prabhupāda notes several similarities between the Vedic view and the ideas of Origen, the father of Christian mysticism—especially concerning reincarnation—but points out that Origen was wrong to believe the soul is created.

Śrīla Prabhupāda shows how ridiculous is Augustine's statement that "Reincarnation is ridiculous," but he approves Aquinas's five proofs for the existence of God.

Kierkegaard was perfectly correct, says Śrīla Prabhupāda, when he wrote that in the highest stage of life a person submits himself to God and obeys Him totally, but he was wrong when he insisted that the truly religious life must entail great suffering.

Schopenhauer recommended that the way to real happiness is to destroy all desire and will and thus reach "nirvāṇa." No, says Śrīla Prabhupāda, desire and will are intrinsic to the soul and must simply be purified of their material focus.

Darwin draws some heavy fire for his evolutionary theory, which ignores God's role in the origin of the species.

"The greatest good for the greatest number" was the slogan of John Stuart Mill's utilitarian philosophy, but Śrīla Prabhupāda asks, "Who will determine what the greatest good is?"

Almost two decades before the fall of the Soviet Union cast Marx's atheistic philosophy into the dustbin of history, Śrīla Prabhupāda points out the fatal flaw in the communist doctrine: everything belongs not to the state but to God, and therefore everything must be used in His service.

Nietzsche extolled the "superman," one who has completely conquered his passions and is dependent on no one; Śrīla Prabhupāda shows how the real superman is the fully self-realized soul who recognizes his complete dependence on God.

Regarding Freud, Śrīla Prabhupāda explains that whatever relief psychoanalysis can give is simply palliative unless the patient recognizes that the root of his problems is his misidentification of the self with the body and his alienation from God.

Quoting the *Bhagavad-gītā,* Śrīla Prabhupāda calls Sartre's existentialism demonic because it ignores the authority and very existence of God and declares man a "useless passion" striving vainly in a purposeless world.

Finally, Śrīla Prabhupāda heartily applauds this statement from Carl Jung's autobiography: "One must be utterly abandoned to God; nothing matters but fulfilling His will. Otherwise, all is folly and meaningless." Unfortunately, Jung never found a qualified guru from whom to learn the science of Kṛṣṇa consciousness.

We are not so unfortunate as Dr. Jung. From *Beyond Illusion and Doubt* and the many other books Śrīla Prabhupāda has left us, as well as from his followers who are faithfully carrying forward his teachings, we can learn the philosophy, practice, and goals of Kṛṣṇa consciousness and make our lives successful.

The Publishers

Editor's note: A native Bengali, Śrīla Prabhupāda learned English in the early part of the twentieth century, when it was common to use only the male pronoun where today we might write "he or she" or "him or her," and similarly to use the word *man* to indicate a human being of either gender. Thus when Śrīla Prabhupāda says "Through this method of self-study, any intelligent man can see that he is not the body," he is not excluding women from this important step in self-realization, nor is he barring them from yoga or God realization when he says, "Through meditation, the yogī sees the Supreme Truth (Kṛṣṇa, or God) within himself."

Chapter ONE

SOCRATES

Socrates (469–399 B.C.) was a thorn in the side of the leaders of ancient Athens, who saw him as a corruptor of young men. The problem was that he was uncompromising in his search for an objective understanding of such moral virtues as justice, courage, and piety, and he passed on this spirit to his students, most notably Plato. And in the process, the leaders contended, he neglected the gods of the state. He taught all who would listen to engage in self-examination and tend to their souls. Even today, many have heard of Socrates' instruction to "know thyself," but what does it mean? Here Śrīla Prabhupāda explains that to really know the self one must know the Supreme Self, Kṛṣṇa.

Disciple: Socrates strongly opposed the Sophists, a group of speculators who taught that the standards of right and wrong and of truth and falsity were completely relative, being established solely by individual opinion or social convention. Socrates, on the other hand, seemed convinced that there was an absolute, universal truth or good, beyond mere speculation and opinion, that could be known clearly and with certainty.

Śrīla Prabhupāda: He was correct. For our part, we accept Kṛṣṇa, God, as the supreme authority, the Absolute Truth. Kṛṣṇa is by definition supreme perfection, and philosophy is perfect when it is in harmony with Him. This is our position. The philosophy of the Kṛṣṇa consciousness movement is religious in the sense that it is concerned with carrying out the orders of God. That is the sum and substance of religion. It is not possible to manufacture a religion. In the *Śrīmad-Bhāgavatam,* manufactured religion is called *kaitava-dharma,* just another form of cheating.

Our basic principle is *dharmaṁ tu sākṣād bhagavat-praṇītam*. The word *dharma* refers to the orders given by God, and if we follow those orders we are following dharma. An individual citizen cannot manufacture laws, since laws are given by the government. Our perfection lies in following the orders of God cent percent. Those who have no conception of God or His orders may manufacture religious systems, but our system is different.

Disciple: The Socratic dialectic usually sought to arrive gradually at an understanding of the essence of a particular moral virtue—for example, self-control, piety, courage, or justice—by examining proposed definitions for completeness and consistency. Socrates wanted to establish more than just a list of universal definitions, however. He tried to show that any particular virtue, when understood in depth, was not different from all the others. The unity of the virtues thus implied the existence of a single absolute good. For Socrates, the goal of life is to rise by means of the intellect to a realization of this absolute good. A person who had attained such knowledge of the good would be self-realized in that he would always do the good without fail. A soul who had thus realized the good was said to be in a healthy or sound state, or to have attained wisdom. Socrates' name for the single absolute good was "knowledge."

Could one say that Socrates was a kind of *jñāna-yogī*?
Śrīla Prabhupāda: Socrates was a *muni*, a great thinker. However, the real truth comes to such a *muni* after many, many births. As Kṛṣṇa says in the *Bhagavad-gītā* [7.19]:

bahūnāṁ janmanām ante jñānavān māṁ prapadyate
vāsudevaḥ sarvam iti sa mahātmā su-durlabhaḥ

"After many births and deaths, one who is actually in knowledge surrenders unto Me, knowing Me to be the cause of all causes and all that is. Such a great soul is very rare."

People like Socrates are known as *jñānavān*, wise men, and after many births they surrender themselves to Kṛṣṇa. They do not do so blindly, but knowing that the Supreme Personality of Godhead is the source of everything. However, this process of self-searching for knowledge takes time. If we take the instructions of Kṛṣṇa directly and surrender unto Him, we save time and many, many births.
Disciple: Socrates terms his method *maieutic*, that is, like that of a midwife. He thought that a soul could not really come to knowledge of the good by the imposition of information from an external source. Rather, such knowledge had to be awakened within the soul itself. The teacher's business is to direct, encourage, and prod a soul until it gives birth to the truth. The *maieutic* method therefore suggests that since the soul is able to bring the truth out of itself, knowledge is really a kind of recollection or remembrance. If so, then there must have been a previous life in which the soul possessed the knowledge it has forgotten. This suggests, then, that the soul (understood as something involving intelligence and memory) exists continuously through many lives and, indeed, is eternal.[1]
Śrīla Prabhupāda: Yes, the soul is eternal. And because the

[1]Scholars disagree about whether Socrates explicitly taught the doctrine of remembrance. Even if the doctrine was Plato's, Plato clearly thought it inherent in Socrates' *maieutic* itself.

soul is eternal, the intelligence, mind, and senses are also eternal. However, they are all now covered by a material coating, which must be cleansed. Once this material coating is washed away, the real mind, intelligence, and senses will emerge. That is stated in the *Nārada-pañcarātra: tat-paratvena nirmalam.* The purificatory process takes place when one is in touch with the transcendental loving service of the Lord and is chanting the Hare Kṛṣṇa *mahā-mantra.* Caitanya Mahāprabhu said, *ceto-darpaṇa-mārjanam:* one must cleanse the heart. All misconceptions come from misunderstanding one's real nature and one's relationship with God. We are all part and parcel of God, yet somehow or other we have forgotten this. Previously we rendered service to God, but now we are rendering service to something illusory. This is *māyā.* Whether we are liberated or conditioned, our constitutional position is to render service. In the material world we work according to our different capacities—as a politician, a thinker, a poet, or whatever. But if we are disconnected from Kṛṣṇa, all of this is *māyā.* When we perform our duty in order to develop Kṛṣṇa consciousness, our duty enables liberation from this bondage.

Disciple: It is interesting that nowadays we find the kind of relativism taught by the Sophists to be again very widespread: "If you believe it, then it's true for you." Socrates took up the task of vigorously combating this position, trying to demonstrate by strong arguments that there must be an absolute truth that is distinguishable from the relative and that must be categorically acknowledged by everyone.

Śrīla Prabhupāda: That is what we are also doing. The Absolute Truth is true for everyone, and the relative truth is relative to a particular position. The relative truth depends on the Absolute Truth, which is the *summum bonum.* God is the Absolute Truth, and the material world is relative truth. Because the material world is God's energy, it appears to be real or true, just as the reflection of the sun in water emits some light. But that reflection is not independent of the sun, and as soon as the sun sets, that light will disappear. The Absolute

Truth is Kṛṣṇa, and this cosmos is relative truth, a manifestation of Kṛṣṇa's external energy. If Kṛṣṇa withdrew His energy, the cosmos would not exist.

In another sense, Kṛṣṇa and Kṛṣṇa's energy are not different. We cannot separate heat from fire; heat is also fire, yet heat is not fire. This is the position of relative truth. As soon as we experience heat, we understand that there is fire. Yet we cannot say that heat is fire. Relative truth is like heat because it stands on the strength of the Absolute Truth, just as heat stands on the strength of fire. Because the Absolute is true, relative truth also appears to be true, although it has no independent existence. A mirage appears to be water because in actuality there is such a thing as water. Similarly, this material world appears attractive because there is actually an all-attractive spiritual world.

Disciple: Socrates held that the highest duty of man was to "care for his soul," that is, to cultivate that healthy state of soul which is true knowledge, the attainment of the good. When a man becomes fixed in such knowledge he will as a matter of course act correctly in all affairs, he will be beyond the dictates of the passions, and he will remain peaceful and undisturbed in every circumstance. Socrates himself seems to have attained such a state, as his own behavior at the time of his death illustrates: he calmly drank the poison hemlock rather than give up his principles. He seems to have realized knowledge of at least some aspect of the Absolute Truth, although we must add that he never spoke of it as a person or gave it a personal name.

Śrīla Prabhupāda: That is the preliminary stage of understanding the Absolute, known as Brahman realization, realization of the impersonal feature. One who advances further attains Paramātmā realization, realization of the localized feature, whereby one realizes that God is everywhere. It is a fact that God is everywhere, but at the same time God has His own abode (*goloka eva nivasaty akhilātma-bhūtaḥ*). God is a person, and He has His own abode and associates. Although He is in His abode, He is present everywhere, within every atom (*andāntara-stha-paramāṇu-cayāntara-stham*). Like other impersonalists, Socrates cannot understand how God, through His potency, can remain in His own abode and simultaneously be present in every atom. The material world is His expansion, His energy (*bhūmir āpo 'nalo vāyuḥ khaṁ mano buddhir eva ca*). Because His energy is expanded everywhere, He can be present everywhere. Although the energy and the energetic are nondifferent, we cannot say that they are not distinct. They are simultaneously one and different. This is the perfect philosophy of *acintya-bhedābheda-tattva,* inconceivable simultaneous oneness and difference of God and His energies.

Disciple: Socrates held that "all the virtues are one thing—knowledge." He saw goodness and knowledge as inseparable. This union of the two seems to reflect features of *sattva-guṇa* as described in the *Bhagavad-gītā.*

Śrīla Prabhupāda: *Sattva-guṇa,* the mode of goodness, is a position from which we can receive knowledge. Knowledge cannot be received from the platform of passion and ignorance. If we hear about Kṛṣṇa, or God, we are gradually freed from the clutches of darkness and passion. Then we can come to the platform of *sattva-guṇa,* and when we are perfectly situated there, we are beyond the lower modes. In the words of *Śrīmad-Bhāgavatam* [1.2.18–19]:

> *naṣṭa-prāyeṣv abhadreṣu nityaṁ bhāgavata-sevayā*
> *bhagavaty uttama-śloke bhaktir bhavati naiṣṭhikī*
>
> *tadā rajas-tamo-bhāvāḥ kāma-lobhādayaś ca ye*
> *ceta etair anāviddhaṁ sthitaṁ sattve prasīdati*

"For one who regularly attends classes on the *Śrīmad-Bhāgavatam* and renders service to the pure devotee, all that is troublesome to the heart is almost completely destroyed, and loving service unto the Personality of Godhead, who is praised with transcendental songs, is established as an irrevocable fact. As soon as irrevocable loving service is established in the heart, the effects of nature's modes of passion and ignorance, such as lust, desire, and hankering, disappear from the heart. Then the devotee is established in goodness, and he becomes completely happy."

This process may be gradual, but it is certain. The more we hear about Kṛṣṇa, the more we become purified. Purification means freedom from the attacks of greed and passion. Then we can become happy. From this platform of purity, known as the *brahma-bhūta* platform, we can realize ourselves and then realize God. So before realizing the Supreme Good, we must first come to the platform of *sattva-guṇa,* goodness. Therefore we have regulations prohibiting illicit sex, meat-eating, intoxication, and gambling. Ultimately we must transcend even the mode of goodness through *bhakti.* Then we become liberated, gradually develop love of God, and regain our original state (*muktir hitvānyathā rūpam svarupeṇa vyavasthitiḥ*). This means giving up all material engagements and rendering full service to Kṛṣṇa. Then we attain the state where *māyā* cannot touch us. If we keep in touch with Kṛṣṇa, *māyā* has no jurisdiction. This is perfection.

Disciple: Socrates took the oracular *gnothi seauton,* "know thyself," to enjoin "care of the soul." Care of the soul, as we have seen, involved an intense intellectual endeavor, a kind of introspective contemplation or meditation. It gradually purified the self, detaching it more and more from the body and its passions. Thus through the contemplative endeavor entailed by "know thyself," a person attained knowledge and self-control, and with that he also became happy.

Śrīla Prabhupāda: Yes, that is a fact. Meditation means analyzing the self and searching for the Absolute Truth. That is described in the Vedic literatures: *dhyānavasthita-tad-gatena manasā paśyanti yaṁ yoginaḥ.* Through meditation, the yogī sees the Supreme Truth (Kṛṣṇa, or God) within himself. Kṛṣṇa is there. The yogī consults with Kṛṣṇa, and Kṛṣṇa advises him. *Dadāmi buddhi-yogaṁ tam.* When one is purified, he is always seeing Kṛṣṇa within himself. This is confirmed in the *Brahma-saṁhitā* [5.38]:

premāñjana-cchurita-bhakti-vilocanena
santaḥ sadaiva hṛdayeṣu vilokayanti
yaṁ śyāmasundaram acintya-guṇa-svarūpaṁ
govindam ādi-puruṣaṁ tam ahaṁ bhajāmi

"I worship the primeval Lord, Govinda, who is always seen by the devotee whose eyes are anointed with the pulp of love. He is seen in His eternal form of Śyāmasundara, situated within the heart of the devotee." Thus an advanced saintly person is always seeing Kṛṣṇa. In this verse, the word *śyāmasundara* means "blackish but at the same time extraordinarily beautiful." Being the Supreme Personality of Godhead, Kṛṣṇa is of course very beautiful. The word *acintya* means that He has unlimited inconceivable qualities. Although He is situated everywhere, as Govinda He is always dancing in Vṛndāvana with the *gopīs.* There He plays with His friends and sometimes, acting as a naughty boy, teases His mother. These pastimes of the Supreme Person are described in the *Śrīmad-Bhāgavatam.*

Disciple: As far as we know, Socrates himself had no teacher in philosophy. Indeed, he refers to himself as "self-made." Do you believe that one can be self-taught? Can genuine self-knowledge be attained through one's own meditation or introspection?

Śrīla Prabhupāda: Yes. Ordinarily everyone thinks according to the bodily conception. If I begin to study the different parts of my body and seriously begin to consider what I am, I will gradually arrive at the study of the soul. If I ask myself, "Am I this hand?" the answer will be "No, I am not this hand. Rather, this is my hand." I can thus continue analyzing each part of the body and discover that all the parts are mine but that I am different. Through this method of self-study, any intelligent man can see that he is not the body. This is the first lesson of the *Bhagavad-gītā* [2.13]:

dehino 'smin yathā dehe kaumāraṁ yauvanaṁ jarā
tathā dehāntara-prāptir dhīras tatra na muhyati

"As the embodied soul continuously passes, in this body, from boyhood to youth to old age, the soul similarly passes into another body at death. A sober person is not bewildered by such a change."

At one time I had the body of a child, but now that body no longer exists. Nonetheless, I am aware that I possessed such a body; therefore from this I can deduce that I am something other than the body. I may rent an apartment, but I do not identify with it. The body may be mine, but I am not the body. By this kind of introspection, a man can teach himself the distinction between the body and the soul.

As far as being *completely* self-taught, according to the *Bhagavad-gītā* and the Vedic conception, life is continuous. Since we are always acquiring experience, we cannot actually say that Socrates was self-taught. Rather, in his previous lives he had cultivated knowledge, and this knowledge was simply continuing. That is a fact. Otherwise, why is one person intelligent and another ignorant? This is due to continuity of life through the process of transmigration of the soul.

Disciple: Socrates believed that through intellectual endeavor a person can attain knowledge or wisdom, which is nothing else but the possession of all the virtues in their unity. Such a person always acts in the right way and thus is happy. Therefore the enlightened man is meditative, knowledgeable, and virtuous. He is also happy because he acts properly.

Śrīla Prabhupāda: Yes, that is confirmed in the *Bhagavad-gītā* [18.54]. *Brahma-bhūtaḥ prasannātmā na śocati na kāṅkṣati:* when one is self-realized, he immediately becomes happy, joyful (*prasannātmā*). This is because he is properly situated. A person may labor a long time under some mistaken idea, but when he finally comes to the proper conclusion, he becomes very happy. He thinks, "Oh, what a fool I was, going on so long in such a mistaken way!" Thus a self-realized person is happy.

Happiness means that one no longer has to think of attaining material things. For instance, Dhruva Mahārāja told the Lord, *svāmin kṛtārtho 'smi varaṁ na yāce:* "Having seen You, my Lord, I don't want any material benediction." Prahlāda Mahārāja also said, "My Lord, I don't want material benefits. I have seen my father—who was such a big materialist that even the demigods were afraid of him—destroyed by You within a second. Therefore I am not after these things."

So real knowledge means that one no longer hankers for anything. The *karmīs, jñānīs,* and yogīs are all hankering after something. The *karmīs* want material wealth, beautiful women, and good positions. If one is not hankering for what one does not have, he is lamenting for what he has lost. The *jñānīs* are also hankering, expecting to become one with God and merge into His existence. And the yogīs are hankering after some magical powers to befool others into thinking that they have become God. In India some yogis convince people that they can manufacture gold and fly in the sky, and foolish people believe them. Even if a yogī can fly, what is his great achievement? There are many birds flying. What is the difference? An intelligent person can understand this. If a person says that he will walk on water, thousands of fools will come to see him. People will even pay ten rupees just to see a man bark like a dog, not thinking that there are many dogs barking anyway. In any case, people are always hankering and lamenting, but the devotee is fully satisfied in the service of the Lord. He doesn't hanker for anything, nor does he lament.

Disciple: Through *jñāna-yoga,* the search for truth, Socrates may have realized Brahman. Could he have also realized Paramātmā?

Śrīla Prabhupāda: Yes.

Disciple: But what about the realization of Bhagavān, Kṛṣṇa? I thought that Kṛṣṇa can be realized only through *bhakti-yoga,* devotional service.

Śrīla Prabhupāda: Yes, one cannot enter into Kṛṣṇa's abode without being His pure devotee. Kṛṣṇa states this in the *Bhagavad-gītā* [18.55]: *bhaktyā mām abhijānāti.* "One can understand Me as I am only by devotional service." Kṛṣṇa never says that He can be understood by *jñāna-yoga, karma-yoga,* or *aṣṭāṅga-yoga.* The personal abode of Kṛṣṇa is especially reserved for the *bhaktas,* and the *jñānīs,* yogīs, and *karmīs* cannot go there.

Disciple: Now, although Socrates described himself as "self-made," he believed not only in the value of insight or meditation but also in the idea that knowledge can be imparted from one person to another. He therefore believed in the role of a guru, or teacher, which he himself was for many people.

Prabhupāda: Yes, this is the standard Vedic principle—that to learn the truth one must approach a guru, or spiritual master. In the *Bhagavad-gītā* [4.34] Kṛṣṇa gives the same instruction:

tad viddhi praṇipātena paripraśnena sevayā
upadekṣyanti te jñānaṁ jñāninas tattva-darśinaḥ

"Just try to learn the truth by approaching a spiritual master. Inquire from him submissively and render service unto him. The self-realized souls can impart knowledge unto you because they have seen the truth." Here "seen the truth" means the spiritual master is constantly seeing the Lord within his heart. In other words, within his heart he can constantly see the Supreme Lord as the Supersoul and take advice from Him. In the *Bhagavad-gītā* [10.10] Kṛṣṇa confirms that He enlightens the pure devotee from within: *dadāmi buddhi-yogaṁ tam.* "I give him intelligence." These are the qualifications of a real spiritual master.

So, it seems that Socrates would give his disciples a chance to develop their understanding. That is a good process, and it is natural. It is just like when a father teaches his child to walk. First of all he helps the child, taking his hand: "Now walk, walk. Let me see how you walk." Although the child sometimes falls down, the father will encourage, "Oh, you are doing very nicely. Now stand up again and walk." Similarly, a genuine spiritual master gives his disciple a chance to develop his intelligence so he can think properly how to go back home, back to Godhead.

Disciple: What does it mean to "think properly how to go

back home, back to Godhead"?
Śrīla Prabhupāda: To always think of Kṛṣṇa. We should act in such a way that we have to think of Kṛṣṇa all the time. For instance, we are discussing Socratic philosophy in order to strengthen our Kṛṣṇa consciousness. Therefore the ultimate goal is Kṛṣṇa; otherwise we are not interested in criticizing or accepting anyone's philosophy. We are neutral.
Disciple: So the proper use of intelligence is to guide everything in such a way that we become Kṛṣṇa conscious?
Śrīla Prabhupāda: That's it. Without Kṛṣṇa consciousness, we remain on the mental platform. Being on the mental platform means hovering. On that platform, we are not fixed. It is the business of the mind to accept this and reject that, but when we are fixed in Kṛṣṇa consciousness we are no longer subjected to the mind's acceptance or rejection.
Disciple: Right conduct then becomes automatic?
Śrīla Prabhupāda: Yes, as soon as the mind wanders, we should immediately drag it back to concentrate on Kṛṣṇa. While chanting, our mind sometimes wanders far away, but when we become conscious of this, we should immediately bring the mind back to hear the sound vibration of "Hare Kṛṣṇa." That is called *yoga-abhyāsa,* the practice of yoga. We should not allow our mind to wander elsewhere. We should simply chant and hear the Hare Kṛṣṇa mantra; that is the best yoga system.
Disciple: Socrates could have avoided the death penalty if he had compromised his convictions. He refused to do this and so became a martyr for his beliefs.
Śrīla Prabhupāda: It is good that he stuck to his point yet regrettable that he lived in a society in which he could not think independently. Therefore he was obliged to die. In that sense, Socrates was a great soul because although he appeared in a society that was not very advanced, he was still such a great philosopher.

Chapter TWO

PLATO

Plato (428?–347 B.C.) was one of the most creative and influential thinkers in Western philosophy. The chief student of Socrates, he founded the Academy in Athens in 387 B.C., beginning an institution that continued for almost a thousand years and came to be known as the first European university. There are some striking similarities between Plato's ideal state and the one Kṛṣṇa outlines in the Bhagavad-gītā. *But, as Śrīla Prabhupāda points out, Plato erred in his conception of the soul and of the goal of education.*

Disciple: In the *Republic,* Plato's major work on political theory, Plato wrote that society can enjoy prosperity and harmony only if it places people in working categories or classes according to their natural abilities. He thought people should find out their natural abilities and use those abilities to their fullest capacity—as administrators, as military men, or as craftsmen. Most important, the head of state should not be an average or mediocre man. Instead, society should be led by a very wise and good man—a "philosopher king"—or by a group of very wise and good men.

Śrīla Prabhupāda: This idea appears to be taken from the *Bhagavad-gītā,* where Kṛṣṇa says that the ideal society has four divisions: *brāhmaṇas, kṣatriyas, vaiśyas,* and *śūdras.* These divisions come about by the influence of the modes of nature. Everyone, both in human society and in animal society, is influenced by the modes of material nature [*sattva-guṇa, rajo-guṇa,* and *tamo-guṇa,* or goodness, passion, and ignorance]. By scientifically classifying men according to these qualities, society can become perfect. But if we place a man in the mode of ignorance in a philosopher's post, or put a philosopher to work as an ordinary laborer, havoc will result.

In the *Bhagavad-gītā* Kṛṣṇa says that the *brāhmaṇas*—the most intelligent men, who are interested in transcendental knowledge and philosophy—should be given the topmost posts, and under their instructions the *kṣatriyas* should work. The administrators should see that there is law and order and that everyone is doing his duty. The next section is the productive class, the *vaiśyas,* who engage in agriculture and cow protection. And finally there are the *śūdras,* common laborers who help the other sections. This is Vedic civilization—people living simply, on agriculture and cow protection. If you have enough milk, grain, fruit, and vegetables, you can live very nicely.

The *Śrīmad-Bhāgavatam* compares the four divisions of society to the parts of the body—the head, the arms, the belly, and the legs. Just as all parts of the body cooperate to keep the body fit, in the ideal state all sections of society cooperate under the leadership of the *brāhmaṇas.* Comparatively, the head is the most important part of the body, since it gives directions to the other parts. Similarly, the ideal state functions under the directions of the *brāhmaṇas,* who are not personally interested in political affairs or administration because they have a higher duty. At present the Kṛṣṇa consciousness movement is training *brāhmaṇas.* If the administrators take our advice and conduct the state in a Kṛṣṇa conscious way, there will be an ideal society throughout the world.

Disciple: How does modern society differ from the Vedic ideal?

Śrīla Prabhupāda: Now there is large-scale industrialization, which means exploitation of one person by another. Such industry was unknown in Vedic civilization—it was unnecessary. In addition, modern civilization has taken to slaughtering and eating animals, which is barbarous. It is not even human.

In Vedic civilization, when a person was unfit to rule he was deposed. For instance, King Vena proved to be an unfit king. He was simply interested in hunting. Of course, *kṣatriyas* are allowed to hunt, but not whimsically. They are not allowed to kill many birds and beasts unnecessarily, as King Vena was doing and as people do today. At that time the intelligent *brāhmaṇas* objected and immediately killed him with a curse. Formerly, the *brāhmaṇas* had so much power that they could kill simply by cursing; weapons were unnecessary.

At present, however, because the head of the social body is missing, it is a dead body. The head is very important, and our Kṛṣṇa consciousness movement is attempting to create some *brāhmaṇas* who will form the head of society. Then the administrators will be able to rule very nicely under the instructions of the philosophers and theologians—that is, under the instructions of God-conscious people. A God-conscious *brāhmaṇa* would never advise opening slaughterhouses. But now, the many rascals heading the government allow animal slaughter. When Mahārāja Parīkṣit saw a degraded man trying to kill a cow, he immediately drew his sword and said, "Who are you? Why are you trying to kill this cow?" He was a real king. Nowadays, unqualified men have taken the presidential post. And although they may pose themselves as very religious, they are simply rascals. Why? Because under their noses thousands of cows are being killed, while they collect a good salary. Any leader who is at all religious should resign his post in protest if cow slaughter goes on under his rule. Since people do not know that these administrators are rascals, they are suffering. And the people are also rascals because they are voting for these bigger rascals. It is Plato's view that the government should be ideal, and this is the ideal: The saintly philosophers should be at the head of the state; according to their advice the politicians should rule; under the protection of the politicians, the productive class should protect the cows and provide the necessities of life; and the laborer class should help. This is the scientific division of society that Kṛṣṇa advocates in the *Bhagavad-gītā* [4.13]: *cātur-varṇyaṁ mayā sṛṣṭaṁ guṇa-karma-vibhāgaśaḥ.* "According to the three modes of material nature and the work ascribed to them, the four divisions of human society were created by Me."

Disciple: Plato also observed social divisions. However, he advocated three divisions. One class consisted of the guardians, men of wisdom who governed society. Another class consisted of the warriors, who were courageous and who protected the rest of society. And the third class consisted of the artisans, who performed their services obediently and worked only to satisfy their appetites.

Śrīla Prabhupāda: Yes, human society does have this threefold division, also. The first-class man is in the mode of goodness, the second-class man is in the mode of passion, and the third-class man is in the mode of ignorance.

Disciple: Plato's understanding of the social order was based on his observation that man has a threefold division of intelligence, courage, and appetite. He said that the soul has these three qualities.

Śrīla Prabhupāda: That is a mistake. The soul does not have any material qualities. The soul is pure, but because of his contact with the different qualities of material nature, he is "dressed" in various bodies. This Kṛṣṇa consciousness movement aims at removing this material dress. Our first instruction is "You are not this body." It appears that in his practical understanding Plato identified the soul with the bodily dress, and that does not show very good intelligence.

Disciple: Plato believed that man's position is marginal—between matter and spirit—and therefore he also stressed the development of the body. He thought that everyone should be educated from an early age, and that part of that education should be gymnastics—to keep the body fit.

Śrīla Prabhupāda: This means that in practice Plato very strongly identified the self as the body. What was Plato's idea of education?

Disciple: To awaken the student to his natural position—whatever his natural abilities or talents are.

Śrīla Prabhupāda: And what is that natural position?

Disciple: The position of moral goodness. In other words, Plato thought everyone should be educated to work in whatever way is best suited to awaken his natural moral goodness.

Śrīla Prabhupāda: But moral goodness is not enough, because simple morality will not satisfy the soul. One has to go above morality—to Kṛṣṇa consciousness. Of course, in this material world morality is taken as the highest principle, but there is another platform, which is called the transcendental (*vasudeva*) platform. Man's highest perfection is on that platform, and this is confirmed in *Śrīmad-Bhāgavatam*. However, because Western philosophers have no information of the *vasudeva* platform, they consider the material mode of goodness to be the highest perfection and the end of morality. But in this world even moral goodness is infected by the lower modes of ignorance and passion. You cannot find pure goodness (*śuddha-sattva*) in this material world, because pure goodness is the transcendental platform. To come to the platform of pure goodness, which is the ideal, one has to undergo austerities (*tapasā brahmacaryeṇa śamena ca damena ca*). One has to practice celibacy and control the mind and senses. If one has money, one should distribute it in charity. Also, one should always be very clean. In this way one can rise to the platform of pure goodness.

There is another process for coming to the platform of pure goodness, and that is Kṛṣṇa consciousness. If one becomes Kṛṣṇa conscious, all good qualities automatically develop in him. Automatically he leads a life of celibacy, controls his mind and senses, and has a charitable disposition. In this Age of Kali, people cannot possibly be trained to engage in austerity. Formerly, a *brahmacārī* would undergo austere training. Even though he might be from a royal or learned family, a *brahmacārī* would humble himself and serve the spiritual master as a menial servant. He would immediately do whatever the spiritual master ordered. The *brahmacārī* would beg alms from door to door and bring them to the spiritual master, claiming nothing for himself. Whatever he earned he would give to the spiritual master, because the spiritual master would not spoil the money by spending it for sense gratification—he would use it for Kṛṣṇa. This is austerity. The *brahmacārī* would also observe celibacy, and because he followed the directions of the spiritual master, his mind and senses were controlled.

Today, however, this austerity is very difficult to follow, so Śrī Caitanya Mahāprabhu has given the process of taking to Kṛṣṇa consciousness directly. In this case, one need simply chant Hare Kṛṣṇa, Hare Kṛṣṇa, Kṛṣṇa Kṛṣṇa, Hare Hare/ Hare Rāma, Hare Rāma, Rāma Rāma, Hare Hare and follow the regulative principles given by the spiritual master. Then one immediately rises to the platform of pure goodness.

Disciple: Plato thought the state should train citizens to be virtuous. His system of education went like this: For the first three years of life, the child should play and strengthen his body. From three to six, the child should learn religious stories. From seven to ten, he should learn gymnastics; from ten to thirteen, reading and writing; from fourteen to sixteen, poetry and music; from sixteen to eighteen, mathematics. And from eighteen to twenty, he should undergo military drill. From twenty to thirty-five, those who are scientific and philosophical should remain in school and continue learning, and the warriors should engage in military exercises.

Śrīla Prabhupāda: Is this educational program for all men, or are there different types of education for different men?

Disciple: No, this is for everyone.

Śrīla Prabhupāda: This is not very good. If a boy is intelligent and inclined to philosophy and theology, why should he be

forced to undergo military training?
Disciple: Well, Plato said that everyone should undergo two years of military drill.
Śrīla Prabhupāda: But why should someone waste two years? No one should waste even two days. This is nonsense—imperfect ideas.
Disciple: Plato said this type of education reveals what category a person belongs to. He had the right idea that one belongs to a particular class according to his qualification.
Śrīla Prabhupāda: Yes, that we also say, but we disagree that everyone should go through the same training. The spiritual master should judge the tendency or disposition of the student at the start of his education. He should be able to see whether a boy is fit for military training, administration, or philosophy, and then he should fully train the boy according to his particular tendency. If one is naturally inclined to philosophical study, why should he waste his time in the military? And if one is naturally inclined to military training, why should he waste his time with other things? Arjuna belonged to a *kṣatriya* family. He and his brothers were never trained as philosophers. Droṇācārya was their master and teacher, and although he was a *brāhmaṇa,* he taught them *Dhanur Veda* [military science], not *brahma-vidyā. Brahma-vidyā* is theistic philosophy. No one should be trained in everything; that is a waste of time. If one is inclined toward production, business, or agriculture, he should be trained in those fields. If one is philosophical, he should be trained as a philosopher. If one is militaristic, he should be trained as a warrior. And if one has ordinary ability, he should remain a *śūdra,* or laborer. This is stated by Nārada Muni in *Śrīmad-Bhāgavatam: yasya yal-lakṣaṇaṁ proktam.* The four classes of society are recognized by their symptoms and qualifications. Nārada Muni also says that one should be selected for training according to his qualifications. Even if one is born in a *brāhmaṇa* family, he should be considered a *śūdra* if his qualifications are those of a *śūdra.* And if one is born in a *śūdra* family, he should be accepted as a *brāhmaṇa* if his symptoms are brahminical. The

spiritual master should be expert enough to recognize the tendencies of the student and immediately train him in that line. This is perfect education.

Disciple: Plato believed that the student's natural tendency wouldn't come out unless he practiced everything.

Śrīla Prabhupāda: No, that is wrong. Because the soul is continuous, everyone has some tendency from his previous birth. I think Plato didn't realize this continuity of the soul from body to body. According to the Vedic culture, right after a boy's birth astrologers should calculate what category he belongs to. Astrology can help if there is a first-class astrologer. Such an astrologer can tell what line a boy is coming from and how he should be trained. Plato's method of education was imperfect because it was based on speculation.

Disciple: Plato observed that a particular combination of the three modes of nature is acting in each individual.

Śrīla Prabhupāda: Then why did he say that everyone should be trained in the same way?

Disciple: Because he claimed that the person's natural abilities will not manifest unless he is given a chance to try everything. He saw that some people listen primarily to their intelligence, and he said they are governed by the head. He saw that some people have an aggressive disposition, and he said such courageous types are governed by the heart—by passion. And he saw that some people, who are inferior, simply want to feed their appetites. He said these people are animalistic, and he believed they are governed by the liver.

Śrīla Prabhupāda: That is not a perfect description. Everyone has a liver, a heart, and all the bodily limbs. Whether one is in the mode of goodness, passion, or ignorance depends on one's training and on the qualities he acquired during his previous life. According to the Vedic process, at birth one is immediately given a classification. Psychological and physical symptoms are considered, and generally it is ascertained from birth that a child has a particular tendency. However, this tendency may change according to circumstances, and if one does not fulfill his assigned role, he can be transferred to another class. One may have had brahminical training in a previous life, and he may exhibit brahminical symptoms in this life, but one should not think that because he has taken birth in a *brāhmaṇa* family he is automatically a *brāhmaṇa.* A person may be born in a *brāhmaṇa* family and be a *śūdra.* It is a question not of birth but of qualification.

Disciple: Plato also believed that one must qualify for his post. His system of government was very democratic. He thought everyone should be given a chance to occupy the different posts.

Śrīla Prabhupāda: Actually, we are the most democratic because we are giving everyone a chance to become a first-class *brāhmaṇa.* The Kṛṣṇa consciousness movement is giving even the lowest member of society a chance to become a *brāhmaṇa* by becoming Kṛṣṇa conscious. *Caṇḍālo 'pi dvija-śreṣṭho hari-bhakti-parāyaṇaḥ:* Although one may be born in a family of *caṇḍālas,* as soon as he becomes God conscious, Kṛṣṇa conscious, he can be elevated to the highest position. Kṛṣṇa says that everyone can go back home, back to Godhead. *Samo 'haṁ sarva-bhūteṣu:* "I am equal to everyone. Everyone can come to Me. There is no hindrance."

Disciple: What is the purpose of the social orders and the state government?

Śrīla Prabhupāda: The ultimate purpose is to make everyone Kṛṣṇa conscious. That is the perfection of life, and the entire social structure should be molded with this aim in view. Of course, not everyone can become fully Kṛṣṇa conscious in one lifetime, just as not all students in a university can attain the Ph.D. degree in one attempt. But the idea of perfection is to pass the Ph.D. examination, and therefore the Ph.D. courses should be maintained. Similarly, an institution like the Kṛṣṇa consciousness movement should be maintained so that at least some people can attain the ultimate goal, Kṛṣṇa consciousness, and so that everyone can approach it.

Disciple: So the goal of the state government should be to help everyone become Kṛṣṇa conscious?

Śrīla Prabhupāda: Yes, Kṛṣṇa consciousness is the highest goal. Therefore, everyone should help this movement and take advantage of it. Regardless of his work, everyone can come to the temple. The instructions are for everyone, and *prasādam* is distributed to everyone. Therefore, there is no difficulty. Everyone can contribute to this Kṛṣṇa consciousness movement. The *brāhmaṇas* can contribute their intelligence, the *kṣatriyas* their charity, the *vaiśyas* their grain, milk, fruits, and flowers, and the *śūdras* their bodily service. By such joint effort, everyone can reach the same goal—Kṛṣṇa consciousness, the perfection of life.

Disciple: In a very famous allegory in the *Republic,* Plato describes representatives of humanity chained in a dark cave and able to see only shadows cast by the light of a fire. One person breaks free and sees the outside world, and he returns to the cave to tell the people there that they are living in darkness. But the cave-dwellers consider him crazy.

Prabhupāda: This is just like our story of Dr. Frog. He had never gone out of his dark well, so he thought, "Here is everything." When he was told about the vast Atlantic Ocean, he could not conceive of a body of water so expansive.

Similarly, those who are in the dark well of this material world cannot conceive of the light outside, in the spiritual world. But that world is a fact. Suppose someone has fallen into a well and he cries out, "I have fallen into this well! Please save me!" Then a man outside drops down a rope and calls, "Just catch hold of this rope and I will pull you out!" But no, the fallen man has no faith in the man outside and does not catch hold of the rope. Similarly, we are telling everyone in the material world, "You are suffering. Just take up this Kṛṣṇa consciousness and all your suffering will be relieved." Unfortunately, people refuse to catch hold of the rope, or they do not even admit they are suffering.

But one who is fortunate will catch hold of the rope of Kṛṣṇa consciousness, and then the spiritual master will help him out of this dark world of suffering and bring him to the illuminated, happy world of Kṛṣṇa consciousness.

Chapter THREE

ARISTOTLE

Aristotle (384–322 B.C.) was Plato's leading student and the teacher of Alexander the Great. Although he was one of the most brilliant minds of ancient Greece, pioneering in such fields as astronomy, meteorology, biology, and zoology, Aristotle could still only guess about the nature of God. As Śrīla Prabhupāda says here, "By speculation Aristotle may have known something about God, but our point is that we can know everything about God from God Himself."

Disciple: Aristotle constructed a system of abstract notions and principles—"matter," "form," and "privation"; "potency" and "act"; the ten categories; the four kinds of causes; and so on—which he tried to show were universal in scope, capable of explicating reality on all levels. He wanted to show how all of reality is thus intelligible.

Aristotle thought of the cosmos as a hierarchy. At the bottom is prime or pure matter, which possesses no intelligible essence, or "form"; it is pure potency, without actuality. And at the top is God, the unmoved mover of the whole system, who is pure actuality (He is all that He could ever be), sheer form, pure intelligible, intellectual essence, with no tinge of matter or potentiality. In between are the changing substances compounded of matter and form—the elements, minerals, plants, animals, humans, and the ethereal intelligences that move the stars. The higher up the scale you go, the more form predominates over matter. In this way, Aristotle rejected the separation between the world of forms and the world of matter that characterized the philosophy of his teacher, Plato.

One modern philosopher has observed that Aristotle's conception of God was motivated entirely by dispassionate rational concerns—no extraneous ethical or religious interests influenced his idea—and that this did not go far toward producing an idea of God available for religious purposes.

Śrīla Prabhupāda: By speculation Aristotle may have known something about God, but our point is that we can know everything about God from God Himself. This is not a question of "religion." It is simply a matter of the best process to know God. When we learn about God from God Himself, then our knowledge is perfect. In the *Bhagavad-gītā* [7.1] Kṛṣṇa says,

mayy āsakta-manāḥ pārtha yogaṁ yuñjan mad-āśrayaḥ
asaṁśayaṁ samagraṁ māṁ yathā jñāsyasi tac chṛṇu

"Now hear, O son of Pṛthā, how by practicing yoga in full consciousness of Me, with mind attached to Me, you can know Me in full, free from doubt." This is the process of Kṛṣṇa consciousness. Of course, we may speculate about God, and if we simply think of God that will help us to some extent. If we are in darkness, we may speculate and concoct ideas about the sun. This is one kind of knowledge. But if we actually come into the sunlight, our knowledge is complete. We may contemplate the sun in darkness, but the best process is to come into the sunshine and see for ourselves.

Disciple: Aristotle understood substance to be a composite of "form" and "matter." "Form" is the essence of a substance, that by which it is what it is, its actuality. "Matter," for Aristotle, is not a kind of stuff; rather it designates the failure of a substance to be fully informed. In other words, matter is a substance's potentiality for development toward form, or its disintegration away from form. God is perfect: He is pure form, without potentiality or matter. But man is a combination of matter and form. Since man is form and matter, he is imperfect, less than fully real or realized. This imperfection is inherent, being located in matter or potentiality.

Śrīla Prabhupāda: That is nonsense. Man is not made of matter but is covered by matter. Man is made of spirit. If God is spirit, man is also spirit. In the Bible it is also said that "man is made in the image of God"; therefore man is originally perfect. A person is generally healthy, but if he falls into a diseased condition, it is not his inherent imperfection. It is something external that has attacked a healthy man. According to his original nature, the living entity is healthy, or in other words, pure spirit.

Disciple: Although Aristotle criticized the Platonic separation between matter and form, his evaluation of these two was much like that of his teacher. Matter for Aristotle is unknowable and unintelligible, of no intrinsic worth; it is the cause of imperfection, change, and destruction. Form alone is the object of knowledge, the really real, the unchangeable and enduring; it alone endows the world with meaning, intelligibility, and intrinsic purpose.

Śrīla Prabhupāda: This means that the Supreme Absolute must have form. *Īśvaraḥ paramaḥ kṛṣṇaḥ sac-cid-ānanda-vigrahaḥ.* The word *vigrahaḥ* indicates form. That form is not dead but is the activating spirit. Kṛṣṇa's form is *sac-cid-ānanda:* eternal, fully cognizant, and blissful. Our bodies are neither fully cognizant nor fully blissful, but Kṛṣṇa's body is. He knows past, present, and future, and He is always happy. Our knowledge is limited, and we are always full of anxieties.

Disciple: For Aristotle, form gives changing things an immanent goal or purpose—entelechy. Therefore all matter has some form for its actualization. The world is an unfolding of phenomena realizing themselves. In other words, nature is driven by purpose.

Śrīla Prabhupāda: We agree with this. According to the *Padma Purāṇa,* there are 8,400,000 varieties of living forms, and none of them are accidental. According to one's karma, one receives a particular form. Lord Brahmā receives his form according to his karma, and the dog or cat receives its form according to its karma. There is no question of accident. Nature unfolds in accordance with a plan, by virtue of which these various forms are existing. *Yas 'tv indra-gopam athavendram aho sva-karma-bandhānurūpa-phala-bhājanam ātanoti.* From Indra down to the *indra-gopa,* a microscopic germ, all living entities are working out the results of their karma. If one's karma is good, he attains a higher form; if it is not good, he attains a lower form.

There is a process of evolution. The living entity passes from one species to another, from fish to trees to vegetables to insects to birds, beasts, and humans. In the human form, the result of evolution is fully manifest. It is like a flower unfolding from a bud. When the living entity attains the human form, his proper duty is to understand his lost relationship with God. If he misses this opportunity, he may regress. Aristotle is correct, therefore, when he says that everything has a purpose. The whole creative process aims at bringing the living entity back home, back to Godhead.

Disciple: Does every living entity eventually come to that point?

Śrīla Prabhupāda: As a human being, you can properly utilize your consciousness, or you can misuse it. That is up to you. Kṛṣṇa gives Arjuna instructions and then tells him that the decision is up to him. Under the orders of Kṛṣṇa, nature has brought you through so many species. Now, as a human, you can choose whether to return to God or again endure the cycle of birth and death. If you are fortunate, you make the proper choice according to the instructions of the spiritual master and Kṛṣṇa. Then your life is successful.

Disciple: Aristotle sees a hierarchy of forms extending from minerals, vegetables, and animals up to human beings and ultimately God, who is pure form and pure act. God is devoid of all potentiality or materiality.
Śrīla Prabhupāda: Of course there is a hierarchy. And the individual soul transmigrates from one form to another. That is a fact. But who is to say that the next form you attain is closer to perfection? If you have a human form this life, there is no guarantee that you will get a higher form in the next. You accept another form just as you accept another suit of clothes. Those clothes may be valuable, or of no value whatsoever. You get your clothes according to the price you pay, and you accept a form according to your work. Similarly, you bring about your own form, and you enjoy or suffer according to your work.

In any case, a material form is never perfect, because it undergoes six changes. It is born, it grows, it stays for a while, it leaves some by-products, it dwindles, and then it vanishes. When your form vanishes, you have to take on another form, which also undergoes the same processes. When a form vanishes, it decomposes, and its various elements return to nature. Water returns to water, earth returns to earth, air returns to air, and so forth.
Disciple: Aristotle's God is the unmoved mover. He is perfect, and He wants nothing. He does not have to actualize Himself, because He is completely actualized.
Śrīla Prabhupāda: We agree that God is all-perfect. Parāśara Muni defines God as the totality of wisdom, strength, wealth, fame, beauty, and renunciation. Kṛṣṇa possesses all these qualities in full, and when He was present on earth everyone could see He was all-perfect. A perfect person can rule others, and we accept the leadership of a person according to his degree of perfection. If one is not somewhat wise, beautiful, wealthy, and so forth, why should we accept him as a leader? And one who is supremely perfect in all these qualities is the supreme leader. That is natural. Since Kṛṣṇa is supremely perfect, we should accept Him as our leader.

Disciple: God is pure form or actuality, without matter or potentiality. But for Aristotle, form without matter means thought. Therefore, he considered God to be entirely mind or intellect (*nous*) and the divine life to be the life of the mind. God's perfection requires this.
Śrīla Prabhupāda: When he said that God is mind, what did he mean? Did he have some conception of God's personality? God must be a person; otherwise how could He think?
Disciple: Aristotle said that God's activity was thought, and that His thought had itself as its sole object: God's thinking is *noesis noeseos,* thinking of thinking. Thus His nature is self-contemplation.
Śrīla Prabhupāda: Does this mean that when one is perfect he engages in no activity? Does God simply sit down and meditate? If so, what is the difference between God and a stone? A stone simply sits; it has no activity. How is inactivity perfection? Kṛṣṇa never meditates, yet when He speaks He delivers perfect knowledge. Kṛṣṇa enacts various pastimes: He fights with demons, protects His devotees, dances with the *gopīs,* and delivers words of enlightenment. There is no question of sitting like a stone and engaging in "self-contemplation."
Disciple: But is it not possible to meditate while acting?
Śrīla Prabhupāda: Certainly, but God doesn't have to meditate. Why should He? He is perfect. One meditates to come from the imperfect stage to the perfect stage. Since God is perfect to begin with, what business does He have meditating? Everything is simply actualized by His will alone.

Aristotle recommends that a man should meditate to become perfect. This meditation presupposes imperfection. Contemplation is recommended for conditioned living entities, but we should understand that God is never conditioned or imperfect. He is so powerful that whatever He desires or wills immediately comes into being. This information is given in the *Vedas. Parāsya śaktir vividhaiva śrūyate.* God's multi-energies are so powerful that everything is immediately actualized as soon as He desires.
Disciple: But what about the meditations of the Buddha?

Śrīla Prabhupāda: Buddha's mission was different. He was setting an example for miscreants who were engaged in mischievous activities. He was recommending that they sit down and meditate, just as you tell a mischievous child to sit in a corner and be quiet.
Disciple: Aristotle never really says that we should end our activities. But he does say that we should contemplate God.
Śrīla Prabhupāda: That is our process. *Śravaṇaṁ kīrtanaṁ viṣṇoḥ smaraṇam.* One should always think of Kṛṣṇa. Kṛṣṇa consciousness means remembering Kṛṣṇa and acting for Him. When you sweep Kṛṣṇa's temple, you remember Kṛṣṇa. When you cook for Kṛṣṇa, you remember Kṛṣṇa. When you talk about Kṛṣṇa, you remember Kṛṣṇa. This is the process Kṛṣṇa Himself recommends in the *Bhagavad-gītā* [6.47]:

yoginām api sarveṣāṁ mad-gatenāntar-ātmanā
śraddhāvān bhajate yo māṁ sa me yuktatamo mataḥ

"Of all yogīs, the one with great faith who always abides in Me, thinks of Me within himself, and renders transcendental loving service to Me—he is the most intimately united with Me in yoga and is the highest of all. That is My opinion."
Disciple: Aristotle reasons that if God were to know changing things, it would entail change in God Himself. Thus it seems that Aristotle's God has no knowledge of the world. This means that He cannot return the love He receives. He neither loves nor cares for mankind.
Śrīla Prabhupāda: What kind of God is this? If one knows nothing of God, one should not speak of God. God certainly reciprocates with His devotees. As we offer our love to God, He responds and cooperates accordingly. In the *Bhagavad-gītā* [4.11] Kṛṣṇa says,

ye yathā māṁ prapadyante tāṁs tathaiva bhajāmy aham
mama vartmānuvartante manuṣyāḥ pārtha sarvaśaḥ

"As all surrender unto Me, I reward them accordingly.

Everyone follows My path in all respects, O son of Pṛthā." When we fully surrender to God in loving service, we can actually understand God's nature.

Disciple: According to Aristotle, God causes motion in the world not actively but by being the object of desire. He moves the world the way the beloved moves the lover. In spite of His being the supreme object of thought and desire, there is no mention of His being a person. On the contrary, He seems to be merely a sort of consciousness that has no object save itself.

Śrīla Prabhupāda: It appears that Aristotle is a Māyāvādī, an impersonalist. One has to speculate if one does not receive perfect knowledge from God Himself.

Disciple: But at least the idea of God's moving the world by attraction shows that Aristotle had some idea of God as all-attractive.

Śrīla Prabhupāda: Unless God is all-attractive, how can He be God? Therefore the word *kṛṣṇa,* which means "all-attractive," is the perfect name for God. God attracts everyone. In Vṛndāvana He attracts His parents, the cowherd boys and girls, the animals, the fruits and flowers, the trees—everything. Even the water was attracted to Kṛṣṇa. The Tenth Canto of *Śrīmad-Bhāgavatam* describes how the water of the river Yamunā would become stunned in ecstasy and stop flowing as soon as she saw Kṛṣṇa.

Disciple: Aristotle had the idea that God was totally unified, without duality. In what way would you say that God's thought and His activity are one?

Śrīla Prabhupāda: God need only think of a thing in order for that thing to be created or actualized. God's thinking, feeling, willing, and acting are the same. Because we are imperfect, when we think of something it may or may not happen. But whenever God thinks of something, it takes place. Because Kṛṣṇa thought that the Battle of Kurukṣetra should take place, there was no stopping it. At first Arjuna declined to fight, but Kṛṣṇa plainly told him that whether he fought or not, almost all the warriors there were destined to die. He therefore told Arjuna to become His instrument and take the credit for killing them. No one can check what God decides. It doesn't matter whether you help God or not, but it is in your interest that you become His instrument.

Disciple: Aristotle said that a person is happiest and most like the divine himself when he performs his activities in such a way that he is always contemplating "things divine."

Śrīla Prabhupāda: Yes, that is the process of *bhakti,* devotional service. But unless one is a devotee, how can he constantly think of God? Śrīla Rūpa Gosvāmī gives the example of a married woman who has a paramour. She performs her household chores very nicely, but she is always thinking, "When will my lover come at night?" So if it is possible to think of an ordinary person all the time, why not God? It is simply a question of practice, of developing your attraction for Him. Then, despite engaging in so many different types of work, you can think of God incessantly.

Now, Aristotle may have some vague conception of God, but he has no clear idea of Kṛṣṇa's personality. We can think concretely of God because we receive information from Vedic literature that God is a person and He acts in a certain way. In the *Bhagavad-gītā* it is stated that impersonalists experience a great deal of trouble because they have no clear idea of God. If you have no conception of God's form, your attempt to realize God will be very difficult.

Disciple: For Aristotle, God is known by speculative reason, not by revelation.

Śrīla Prabhupāda: We are all limited, and God is unlimited; therefore we cannot understand God by our limited sensory powers. Consequently, God must be known by revelation. As the *Padma Purāṇa* states, *ataḥ śrī-kṛṣṇa-nāmādi na bhaved grāhyam indriyaiḥ.* It is not possible to know God by mental speculation. But when we engage in His service, He reveals Himself. As Kṛṣṇa Himself says in the *Bhagavad-gītā* [7.25],

nāhaṁ prakāśaḥ sarvasya yoga-māyā-samāvṛtaḥ
mūḍho 'yaṁ nābhijānāti loko mām ajam avyayam

"I am never manifest to the foolish and unintelligent. For them I am covered by My internal potency, and therefore they do not know that I am unborn and infallible." It is a fact that unless God reveals Himself, He is not known. Therefore He appears, and great authorities like Vyāsadeva, Nārada, Śukadeva Gosvāmī, Rāmānujācārya, Madhvācārya, and Caitanya Mahāprabhu—great scholars and transcendentalists—accept Him as He reveals Himself. Arjuna saw God face to face, and he accepted Him. When we are freed of ignorance by our service to God, God reveals Himself.

Chapter FOUR

ORIGEN

Origen of Alexandria (A.D. 185?–254?) was one of the most influential founders of the Christian Church and ranks among the most prolific writers and teachers in the history of the Church. Known as the father of Christian mysticism, he taught reincarnation, a doctrine that later Church authorities rejected. Though many of Origen's teachings seem to derive from the Vedic literatures, Śrīla Prabhupāda notes here that Origen was mistaken to think that the soul was created at some point.

Disciple: Origen is generally considered the founder of formal Christian philosophy because he was the first to attempt to establish Christianity on the basis of philosophy as well as faith. He believed that the ultimate spiritual reality consists of the supreme, infinite person, God, as well as individual personalities. Ultimate reality may be defined as the relationships of persons with one another and with the infinite person Himself. In this view, Origen differs from the Greeks, who were basically impersonalists.

Śrīla Prabhupāda: Our Vedic conception is almost the same. Individual souls, which we call living entities, are always present, and each one of them has an intimate relationship with the Supreme Personality of Godhead. In material, conditioned life, the living entity has forgotten this relationship. By rendering devotional service, he attains the liberated position and at that time revives his relationship with the Supreme Personality of Godhead.

Disciple: Origen ascribed to a doctrine of the Trinity, in which God the Father is supreme. God the Son, called the *Logos,* is subordinate to the Father. It is the Son who brings the material world into existence. That is, God the Father is not the direct creator; rather, it is the Son who creates directly, like Lord Brahmā. The third aspect of the Trinity is the Holy Spirit, who is subordinate to the Son. According to Origen, all three of these aspects are divine and co-eternal. They have always existed simultaneously as the Trinity of God.

Śrīla Prabhupāda: According to the *Vedas,* Kṛṣṇa is the original Personality of Godhead. As He confirms in the *Bhagavad-gītā: ahaṁ sarvasya prabhavaḥ.* "I am the source of all spiritual and material worlds." [*Bhagavad-gītā* 10.8] Whether you call this origin the Father or the Holy Spirit, it doesn't matter. The Supreme Personality of Godhead is the origin. According to the Vedic conception, there are two types of expansions: God's personal expansions, called *viṣṇu-tattva,* and His partial part-and-parcel expansions, called *jīva-tattva.* There are many varieties of personal expansions: *puruṣa-avatāras, manvantara-avatāras, līlā-avatāras, yuga-avatāras,* and so on. For the creation of this material world, the Lord expands as Brahmā, Viṣṇu, and Maheśvara (Śiva). Viṣṇu is a personal expansion, and Brahmā is a *jīva-tattva* expansion. Between the personal *viṣṇu-tattva* expansions and the *jīva-tattva* expansions is a kind of intermediate expansion called Śiva, or Maheśvara. The material ingredients are given, and Brahmā creates each universe. Viṣṇu maintains the creation, and Lord Śiva annihilates it. It is the nature of the external potency to be created, maintained, and dissolved. More detailed information is given in the *Śrīmad-Bhāgavatam* and *Caitanya-caritāmṛta*.

In any case, the *jīvas,* or living entities, are all considered sons of God. They are situated in one of two positions: liberated or conditioned. Those who are liberated can personally associate with the Supreme Personality of Godhead, and those who are conditioned within this material world have forgotten the Supreme Lord. Therefore they suffer here in different bodily forms. They can be elevated, however, through the practice of Kṛṣṇa consciousness under the guidance of the *śāstras* and the bona fide guru.

Disciple: Origen believed that it is through the combined working of divine grace and man's free will that the individual soul attains perfection, which consists of attaining a personal relationship with the infinite person.

Śrīla Prabhupāda: Yes, and that is called *bhakti-mārga,* the path of devotional service to the Supreme Personality of Godhead, Bhagavān. The Absolute Truth is manifested in three features: Brahman, Paramātmā, and Bhagavān. Bhagavān is the personal feature, and the Paramātmā, situated in everyone's heart, may be compared to the Holy Spirit. The Brahman feature is present everywhere. The highest perfection of spiritual life includes the understanding of the personal feature of the Lord. When one understands Bhagavān, one engages in His service. In this way, the living entity is situated in his original constitutional position and is eternally blissful.

Disciple: Origen considered that just as man's free will precipitated his fall, man's free will can also bring about his salvation. Man can return to God by practicing material detachment. Such detachment can be made possible by help from the *Logos,* the Christ.

Śrīla Prabhupāda: Yes, that is also our conception. The fallen soul is transmigrating within this material world, up and down in different forms of life. When his consciousness is sufficiently developed, he can be enlightened by God, who gives him instructions in the *Bhagavad-gītā.* Through the spiritual master's help, he can attain full enlightenment. When he understands his transcendental position of bliss, he automatically gives up material bodily attachments. Then he attains freedom. The living entity attains his normal, constitutional position when he is properly situated in his spiritual identity and engaged in the service of the Lord.

Disciple: Origen believed that all the elements found in the material body are also found in the spiritual body, which he called the "interior man." Origen writes: "There are two men in each of us. . . . As every exterior man has for homonym the interior man, so it is for all his members, and one can say that every member of the exterior man can be found under this name in the interior man." Thus for every sense that we possess in the exterior body, there is a corresponding sense in the interior body, or spiritual body.

Śrīla Prabhupāda: The spirit soul is now within this material body, but originally the spirit soul had no material body. The spiritual body of the spirit soul is eternally existing. The material body is simply a coating of the spiritual body. The material body is cut, like a suit, according to the spiritual body. The material elements—earth, water, air, fire, etc.—become like a clay when mixed together, and they coat the spiritual body. It is because the spiritual body has a shape that the material body also takes a shape. In actuality, the material body has nothing to do with the spiritual body; it is but a kind of contamination causing the suffering of the spirit soul. As soon as the spirit soul is coated with this material contamination, he identifies himself with the coating and forgets his real spiritual body. That is called *māyā,* ignorance or illusion. This ignorance continues as long as we are not fully Kṛṣṇa conscious. When we become fully Kṛṣṇa conscious, we understand that the material body is but the external coating and that we are different. When we attain this uncontaminated understanding, we arrive at what is called the *brahma-bhūta* platform. When the spirit soul, which is Brahman, is under the illusion of the material bodily conditioning, we are on the *jīva-bhūta* platform. *Brahma-bhūta* is attained when we no longer identify with the material body but with the spirit soul within. When we come to this platform, we become joyful.

brahma-bhūtaḥ prasannātmā na śocati na kāṅkṣati
samaḥ sarveṣu bhūteṣu mad-bhaktiṁ labhate parām

"One who is thus transcendentally situated at once realizes the Supreme Brahman and becomes fully joyful. He never laments or desires to have anything. He is equally disposed toward every living entity. In that state he attains pure devotional service unto Me." [*Bhagavad-gītā* 18.54] A person in this position sees all living entities as spirit souls; he does not see the outward covering. When he sees a dog, he sees a spirit soul covered by the body of a dog. This state is also described in the *Bhagavad-gītā:*

vidyā-vinaya-sampanne brāhmaṇe gavi hastini
śuni caiva śva-pāke ca paṇḍitāḥ sama-darśinaḥ

"The humble sages, by virtue of true knowledge, see with equal vision a learned and gentle *brāhmaṇa,* a cow, an elephant, a dog, and a dog-eater [outcaste]." [*Bhagavad-gītā* 5.18] When one is in the body of an animal, he cannot understand his spiritual identity. This identity can best be realized in a human civilization in which the *varṇāśrama* system is practiced. This system divides life into four *varṇas* (*brāhmaṇa, kṣatriya, vaiśya,* and *śūdra*) and four *āśramas* (*brahmacārī, gṛhastha, vānaprastha,* and *sannyāsa*). The highest position is that of a *brāhmaṇa-sannyāsī,* a platform from which one may best realize his original constitutional position, act accordingly, and thus attain deliverance, or *mukti. Mukti* means understanding our constitutional position and acting accordingly. Conditioned life, a life of bondage, means identifying with the body and acting on the bodily platform. On the *mukti* platform, our activities differ from those enacted on the conditioned platform. Devotional service is rendered from the *mukti* platform. If we engage in devotional service, we maintain our spiritual identity and are therefore liberated, even though inhabiting the conditioned, material body.

Disciple: Origen also believed that the interior man, or the spiritual body, has spiritual senses that enable the soul to taste, see, touch, and contemplate the things of God.

Śrīla Prabhupāda: Yes. That is devotional life.

Disciple: During his lifetime, Origen was a famous teacher and was very much in demand. For him, preaching meant explaining the words of God and no more. He believed that a preacher must first be a man of prayer and must be in contact with God. He should not pray for material goods but for a better understanding of the scriptures.

Śrīla Prabhupāda: Yes, that is a real preacher. As explained in Vedic literatures: *śravaṇaṁ kīrtanam.* First of all, we become perfect by hearing. This is called *śravaṇam.* When we are thus situated by hearing perfectly from an authorized person, our next stage begins: *kīrtanam,* preaching. In this material world, everyone is hearing something from someone else. In order to pass examinations, a student must hear his professor. Then, in his own right, he can become a professor himself. If we hear from a bona fide spiritual master, we become perfect and can become real preachers. We should preach about Kṛṣṇa for Kṛṣṇa, not for any person within this material world. We should hear and preach about the Supreme Person, the transcendental Personality of Godhead. That is the duty of a liberated soul.

Disciple: As far as contradictions and seeming absurdities in scripture are concerned, Origen considered them to be stumbling blocks permitted to exist by God in order for man to pass beyond the literal meaning. He writes that "everything in scripture has a spiritual meaning, but not all of it has a literal meaning."

Śrīla Prabhupāda: Generally speaking, every word in scripture has a literal meaning, but people cannot understand it properly because they do not hear from the proper person. They interpret instead. There is no need to interpret the words of God. Sometimes the words of God cannot be understood by an ordinary person; therefore we may require the transparent medium of the guru. Since the guru is fully cognizant of the words spoken by God, we are advised to receive the words of the scriptures through the guru. There is no ambiguity in the words of God, but due to our imperfect knowledge, we sometimes cannot understand. Not understanding, we try to interpret, but because we are imperfect, our interpretations are also imperfect. The purport is that the words of God, the scriptures, should be understood from a person who has realized God.

Disciple: Origen did not believe that the individual soul has been existing from all eternity. It was created. He writes: "The rational natures that were made in the beginning did not always exist; they came into being when they were created."

Śrīla Prabhupāda: That is not correct. Both the living entity and God are simultaneously eternally existing, and the living entity is part and parcel of God. Although eternally existing, the living entity is changing his body. *Na hanyate hanyamāne śarīre.* [*Bhagavad-gītā* 2.20] One body after another is being created and destroyed, but the living being himself exists eternally. So we disagree when Origen says that the soul is created. Our spiritual identity is never created. That is the difference between spirit and matter. Material things are created, but spirit is without beginning:

> *na tv evāhaṁ jātu nāsaṁ na tvaṁ neme janādhipāḥ*
> *na caiva na bhaviṣyāmaḥ sarve vayam ataḥ param*

"Never was there a time when I did not exist, nor you, nor all these kings; nor in the future shall any of us cease to be." [*Bhagavad-gītā* 2.12]

Disciple: Origen differed from later Church doctrine in his belief in transmigration. Although he believed that the soul was originally created, he also believed that it transmigrated because it could always refuse to give itself to God. So he saw the individual soul as possibly rising and falling perpetually on the evolutionary scale. Later Church doctrine held that one's choice for eternity is made in this one lifetime. As Origen saw it, the individual soul, falling short of the ultimate goal, is reincarnated again and again.

Śrīla Prabhupāda: Yes, that is the Vedic version. Unless one is liberated and goes to the kingdom of God, he must transmigrate from one material body to another. The material body grows, remains for some time, reproduces, grows old, and becomes useless. Then the living entity has to leave one body for another. Once in a new body, he again attempts to fulfill his desires, and again he goes through the process of dying and accepting another material body. This is the process of transmigration.

Disciple: It is interesting that neither Origen nor Christ rejected transmigration. It wasn't until Augustine that it was denied.

Śrīla Prabhupāda: Transmigration is a fact. A person cannot wear the same clothes all his life. Our clothes become old and useless, and we have to change them. Similarly, at death we have to change our old and useless bodies. The living being is eternal, but he has accepted a material body for sense gratification, and such a body cannot endure perpetually. All of this is thoroughly explained in the *Bhagavad-gītā:*

dehino 'smin yathā dehe kaumāraṁ yauvanaṁ jarā
tathā dehāntara-prāptir dhīras tatra na muhyati

"As the embodied soul continuously passes, in this body, from boyhood to youth to old age, the soul similarly passes into another body at death. A sober person is not bewildered by such a change." [*Bhagavad-gītā* 2.13]

śarīraṁ yad avāpnoti yac cāpy utkrāmatīśvaraḥ
gṛhītvaitāni saṁyāti vāyur gandhān ivāśayāt

"The living entity in the material world carries his different conceptions of life from one body to another as the air carries aromas. Thus he takes one kind of body and again quits it to take another." [*Bhagavad-gītā* 15.8]

So, this process of transmigration will continue until one attains liberation and goes back home, back to Godhead.

Chapter FIVE

AUGUSTINE

Most religious scholars regard Augustine (A.D. 354–430) as the main father of the Roman Catholic church and one of the leading formulators of Christian philosophy. He wrote, "Reincarnation is ridiculous. . . . There is no such thing as a return to this life for the punishment of souls. . . ." Read Śrīla Prabhupāda's response below.

Disciple: Augustine considered the soul to be spiritual and different from the material body—but he also believed that the soul did not exist before the body's birth. He thought that the soul is simply the superior part of the person and the body the inferior part. He also thought that the soul attains immortality only after God creates it. At death, Augustine said, the soul goes on to live eternally.
Śrīla Prabhupāda: But if the soul is created, how is it immortal? How is it eternal? How can the soul sometimes not be eternal?
Disciple: Well, first of all, Augustine considered that because

of Adam's fall, all men are subject to the death of the body. In addition, Augustine believed that while God destines some men to enjoy everlasting happiness after death, He destines others to undergo everlasting suffering. In other words, Augustine said that some people endure both physical death—when the soul abandons the body—and "soul-death"—when God abandons the soul. Thus, when one is damned he faces not only physical death but also "soul-death."

Śrīla Prabhupāda: Figuratively speaking, when one forgets his identity as a servant of God, he undergoes a kind of death—but actually the soul is eternal. So, what Augustine calls "soul-death" is actually forgetfulness of God. Of course, until one acquires freedom from material existence, one is "spiritually dead," even though still existing in the material form. Forgetfulness of one's real identity is a kind of death, because only when one is alive to God consciousness is he actually alive. In any case, the soul is eternal and survives the annihilation of the body.

Disciple: Augustine would consider that in some cases the forgetful stage is everlasting, that God eternally abandons the damned soul to eternal perdition.

Śrīla Prabhupāda: This is not so. Our consciousness can always be revived, and that is the conviction of this Kṛṣṇa consciousness movement. A man is unconscious when he is sleeping, but if you call him again and again, the sound of his name enters his ear, and he awakens. Similarly, this process of chanting the Hare Kṛṣṇa mantra awakens one to spiritual consciousness. Then one can return to his normal, spiritual life.

Of course, one may be "eternally abandoned" in the sense that one may remain forgetful for millions of years. It may *seem* eternal, but actually one's spiritual consciousness can be revived at any moment by good association, by the method of hearing and chanting about Kṛṣṇa. Devotional service therefore begins with *śravaṇam*—hearing. In the beginning especially, hearing is very important. If one hears the truth from a self-realized soul, one can awaken to spiritual life and remain spiritually alive in devotional service.

Disciple: Augustine rejected the idea that the material bodies in this world are like prisons for the punishment of sin.

Śrīla Prabhupāda: The soul is essentially part and parcel of God, but in this material world the soul is factually imprisoned in different types of bodies. In the *Bhagavad-gītā* [14.4] Śrī Kṛṣṇa says:

sarva-yoniṣu kaunteya mūrtayaḥ sambhavanti yāḥ
tāsāṁ brahma mahad yonir ahaṁ bīja-pradaḥ pitā

"It should be understood that all species of life, O son of Kuntī, are made possible by birth in this material nature, and that I am the seed-giving father." From material nature—the mother—different species are coming. The living entities are found in earth, water, air, and even fire. The individual souls, however, are part and parcel of the Supreme Lord, who impregnates them within this material world. The living entity then comes out into the material world through the womb of some mother. It appears that the soul is coming out of matter, but the soul is not composed of matter. The soul, always part and parcel of God, simply assumes different types of bodies according to his pious or impious activities and desires. The desires of the soul actually determine higher or lower bodies. But in any case the soul is the same. It is therefore said that those who are advanced in spiritual consciousness see the same quality of soul in each and every body, whether it is the body of a dog or a *brāhmaṇa*.

Disciple: Also, Śrīla Prabhupāda, Augustine considered the soul to be created to inhabit only one particular body, which he felt was a gift from God. Augustine thus rejected reincarnation or transmigration. He wrote, "Let these Platonists stop threatening us with reincarnation as a punishment for our souls. . . . Reincarnation is ridiculous. . . . There is no such thing as a return to this life for the punishment of souls. . . . If our creation, even as mortals, is due to God, how can the return to bodies, which are gifts of

God, be punishment?" In other words, if the body is a gift of God, how can it also be a punishment?

Śrīla Prabhupāda: Does he think that when someone takes the body of a hog or a similar lower creature, that is not punishment? Why does one person get the body of King Indra or Lord Brahmā and another the body of a pig or insect? How does he explain the body of a pig? If the body is a gift from God, it can also be a punishment from God. When one is rewarded, he gets the body of a Brahmā or an Indra, and if he is punished he gets the body of a pig.

Disciple: So the degree of punishment or suffering depends on the kind of body one has?

Śrīla Prabhupāda: Yes. There are many people who are well situated, and there are others who are suffering. Suffering and enjoyment take place according to one's body. That is explained in the *Bhagavad-gītā* [2.14]:

mātrā-sparśās tu kaunteya śītoṣṇa-sukha-duḥkha-dāḥ
āgamāpāyino 'nityās tāṁs titikṣasva bhārata

"O son of Kuntī, the nonpermanent appearance of happiness and distress, and their disappearance in due course, are like the appearance and disappearance of winter and summer seasons. They arise from sense perception, O scion of Bharata, and one must learn to tolerate them without being disturbed." A man may perceive cold very acutely, while a fish may not perceive it. So the perception is relative to the body. Thus the body is a source of suffering and enjoyment—or we may consider it as punishment and reward.

Disciple: What about the human body? Is that a gift or a punishment?

Śrīla Prabhupāda: It is both. In the human form of life, as in other forms, material nature punishes the living entity with so much suffering. But at the same time you can consider human life a gift—because in the human form we can approach God. We should think that if God has given us this body for our punishment, it is His mercy, because by undergoing His punishment willingly and practicing Kṛṣṇa consciousness, we may become purified and progress toward God. Devotees think in this way. Although the body is a form of punishment, they consider it a reward—because by undergoing the punishment, they are progressing toward God realization. Even when the body is given by God for our correction, it can thus be considered a gift.

Disciple: According to Augustine, the physical body precedes the spiritual. He writes, "If there is a natural [physical] body, there is also a spiritual body . . . but it is not the spiritual that comes first, but the physical, and then the spiritual."

Śrīla Prabhupāda: No. Every living entity has an eternal spiritual body, which exists before he takes on a material body. As we said, entering the material body is a kind of punishment. Every soul is eternally part and parcel of God, but because of some sinful activity, the living entity comes into this material world. In the Bible it is said that due to disobedience to God, Adam and Eve lost paradise and had to come into the material world. The soul belongs to the paradise in heaven—the planets of Kṛṣṇa—but somehow or other he falls within this material world and takes on a material body. According to one's activities one is elevated or degraded—as a demigod, human being, animal, or plant. In any case, the soul is always aloof from the material body. This is confirmed by the Vedic literatures. Our actual, spiritual life is revived when we are freed from material contamination, or, in other words, from reincarnation.

Disciple: Augustine conceived of a spiritual world in which all the souls would be in bliss and would be eternally loving and glorifying God. They would still possess freedom of will, but sin would have no power to tempt them.

Śrīla Prabhupāda: Yes, sin cannot touch one who remains in contact with God. According to our desires, we associate with the modes of material nature and acquire different types of bodies. Nature, the agent of Kṛṣṇa, affords us facilities by giving us a material body, which is like a machine. When a son insists, "Father, give me a bicycle," the affectionate father complies. This is similar to our relationship with Kṛṣṇa, as He explains in the *Bhagavad-gītā* [18.61]:

īśvaraḥ sarva-bhūtānāṁ hṛd-deśe 'rjuna tiṣṭhati
bhrāmayan sarva-bhūtāni yantrārūḍhāni māyayā

"The Supreme Lord is situated in everyone's heart, O Arjuna, and is directing the wanderings of all living entities, who are seated as on a machine made of the material energy." The supreme father, Kṛṣṇa, is within the core of everyone's heart. As the living entity desires, the father supplies a body manufactured by material nature. This body is destined to suffer, but the spiritual bodies in the Vaikuṇṭhas are not subject to birth, old age, disease, or death or the threefold miseries. The spiritual bodies are eternal and full of knowledge and bliss.

Disciple: Augustine seems to admit the transcendence and omnipresence of God, but he seems at the same time to reject His existence as the localized Paramātmā [Supersoul] accompanying each individual soul. He writes, "God is not the soul of all things but the maker of all souls."

Śrīla Prabhupāda: Then how is God omnipresent? The Paramātmā is described as the all-pervading Supersoul both in the *Brahma-saṁhitā* and the *Bhagavad-gītā*. Besides the verse I have just mentioned, elsewhere in the *Bhagavad-gītā* [13.23] Kṛṣṇa says:

upadraṣṭānumantā ca bhartā bhoktā maheśvaraḥ
paramātmeti cāpy ukto dehe 'smin puruṣaḥ paraḥ

"Yet in this body there is another, a transcendental enjoyer, who is the Lord, the supreme proprietor, who exists as the overseer and permitter, and who is known as the Supersoul." The Supersoul is also present within every atom: *viṣṭabhyāham idaṁ kṛtsnam ekāṁśena sthito jagat*. "With a single fragment of Myself I pervade and support this entire universe." [*Bhagavad-gītā* 10.42] So God's all-pervading Paramātmā feature cannot be denied.

Disciple: For Augustine, the human mind and soul—he called it the "reasonable soul"—were one and the same.
Śrīla Prabhupāda: No, they are different. The soul is placed in various bodies that have different ways of thinking, feeling, and willing—different minds. For instance, a dog's mind is not equal to that of a human being, but this is not to say that a dog does not have a soul. So the mind differs according to the body, but the soul always remains the same.
Disciple: Well, because he lumped together the soul and the mind, Augustine held that the souls of animals are not the same as the eternal, "reasonable" souls of human beings. In this way he could justify animal-killing. He wrote, "Indeed, some people try to stretch the prohibition 'Thou shalt not kill' to cover beasts and cattle, and make it unlawful to kill any such animal. But then, why not include plants and anything rooted in and feeding on the soil? . . . Putting this nonsense aside, we do not apply 'Thou shalt not kill' to plants, because they have no sensation; or to irrational animals that fly, swim, walk, or creep, because they are linked to us by no association or common bond. By the creator's wise ordinance they are meant for our use, dead or alive. It only remains for us to apply the commandment 'Thou shalt not kill' to man alone—oneself and others."
Śrīla Prabhupāda: The Bible says, "Thou shalt not kill"—without qualification. Of course, our Vedic philosophy does admit that one living entity serves as food for another. That is a natural law. As stated in the *Śrīmad-Bhāgavatam,* those animals who have hands eat animals without hands. And the four-legged animals eat animals that cannot move, as well as vegetables. So the weak are food for the strong. One must eat an animal or a vegetable—whatever the case, one must inevitably eat some living entity. It thus becomes a question of selection. However, our Kṛṣṇa consciousness philosophy does not teach us to select our food on the basis that plant life is less sensitive than animal life, or that animal life is less sensitive than human life. We consider all human beings, animals, and plants to be living entities, spirit souls.

So, apart from vegetarian or nonvegetarian diets, we are basically concerned with *kṛṣṇa-prasādam,* food offered to Kṛṣṇa with love and devotion. We simply take the remnants of whatever Kṛṣṇa eats. In the *Bhagavad-gītā* [9.26] Śrī Kṛṣṇa says:

patraṁ puṣpaṁ phalaṁ toyaṁ yo me bhaktyā prayacchati
tad ahaṁ bhakty-upahṛtam aśnāmi prayatātmanaḥ

"If one offers Me with love and devotion a leaf, a flower, a fruit, or water, I will accept it." This is our philosophy. We are concerned with taking the remnants of Kṛṣṇa's food, which we call *prasādam,* mercy.

Since we want to act on the level of loving devotion to Kṛṣṇa, we have to find out what He wants and offer Him only that. We cannot offer Him anything undesirable or unasked for. So meat, fish, and eggs cannot be offered to Kṛṣṇa. If He desired such things He would have said so. Instead, He clearly requests that leaves, fruit, flowers, and water be given to Him. Therefore we should understand that He will not accept meat, fish, or eggs. Vegetables, grains, fruits, milk, and water are the proper foods for human beings and are prescribed in this verse by Lord Kṛṣṇa Himself. Whatever else we might wish to eat cannot be offered to Him, since He will not accept it, and thus we cannot be acting on the level of loving devotion to Kṛṣṇa if we eat such foods.

Disciple: Concerning peace, Augustine writes: "Peace between a mortal man and his Maker consists in ordered obedience, guided by faith, under God's eternal law. . . ."

Śrīla Prabhupāda: Yes. Peace means coming in contact with the Supreme Personality of Godhead. A man in ignorance thinks that he is the enjoyer of this world, but when he contacts the Supreme Personality of Godhead, the supreme controller, he understands that God is the enjoyer. A servant supplies the needs of his master, and we are servants meant to supply enjoyment to God. Actually God has no needs to fulfill, yet He enjoys the company of His servants, who in turn enjoy His company. A servant is very happy when he receives a good master, and a master is happy to acquire a very faithful servant. This is the relationship between the individual soul and God, and when this relationship is destroyed, it is said that the individual soul exists in *māyā,* or illusion. When the relationship is restored, the individual is situated in his spiritual consciousness—Kṛṣṇa consciousness—by which he understands that the Supreme God is the actual enjoyer and that we are His servants. God is the actual enjoyer and proprietor as well as the Supreme Being. When we understand God's transcendental qualities, we become happy and attain peace.

Chapter SIX

AQUINAS

Thomas Aquinas (1225–1274) was the leading Christian philosopher of the middle ages. He led an austere life as a celibate monk, writing prolifically and teaching widely. Here Śrīla Prabhupāda explains that while many of his ideas agree with the teachings of the Bhagavad-gītā *and other Vedic literatures, his claim that God created the universe out of nothing is untenable.*

Disciple: Thomas Aquinas compiled the entire Church doctrine in *Summa Theologiae,* which constitutes the official philosophy of the Roman Catholic Church. Aquinas did not make Augustine's sharp distinction between the material and spiritual worlds, or between secular society and the city of God. For him, both material and spiritual creations have their origin in God. At the same time, he admits that the spiritual world is superior to the material.
Śrīla Prabhupāda: When we speak of "material world," we refer to that which is temporary. Some philosophers, like the

Māyāvādīs, claim that the material world is false, but we Vaiṣṇavas say it is temporary or illusory. It is a reflection of the spiritual world, but in itself it has no reality. We therefore compare the material world to a mirage in the desert. In the material world there is no happiness, but the transcendental bliss and happiness existing in the spiritual world are reflected here. Foolish people chase after this illusory happiness, forgetting the real happiness that is in spiritual life.

Disciple: Aquinas agreed with these statements of Anselm and Abelard: "I believe in order that I may understand" and "I understand in order that I may believe." Thus reason and revelation complement each other as a means to truth.

Śrīla Prabhupāda: Since human reason is not perfect, revelation is also needed. The truth is attained through logic, philosophy, and revelation. According to the Vaiṣṇava tradition, we arrive at the truth through the guru, the spiritual master, who is accepted as the representative of the Absolute Truth, the Personality of Godhead. He transmits the message of the truth because he has seen the Absolute Truth through the disciplic succession. If we accept the bona fide spiritual master and please him by submissive service, by virtue of his mercy and pleasure we can understand God and the spiritual world by revelation. Therefore every day we offer our respects to the guru with this prayer:

yasya prasādād bhagavat-prasādo
yasyāprasādān na gatiḥ kuto 'pi
dhyāyan stuvaṁs tasya yaśas tri-sandhyaṁ
vande guroḥ śrī-caraṇāravindam

"By the mercy of the spiritual master one receives the benediction of Kṛṣṇa. Without the grace of the spiritual master, one cannot make any advancement. Therefore, I should always remember and praise the spiritual master, offering respectful obeisances unto his lotus feet at least three times a day." [*Gurv-aṣṭaka* 8] We can understand God if we please the spiritual master, who carries the Lord's message without speculation. It is stated: *sevonmukhe hi jihvādau svayam eva sphuraty adaḥ.* [*Padma Purāṇa*] When we engage our senses in the Lord's service, the Lord reveals Himself.

Disciple: For Aquinas, God is the only single essence that consists of pure form. He felt that matter is only a potential and, in order to be real, must assume a certain shape or form. In other words, the living entity has to acquire an individual form in order to actualize himself. When matter unites with form, the form gives individuality and personality.

Śrīla Prabhupāda: Matter in itself has no form; it is the spirit soul that has form. Matter is a covering for the actual form of the spirit soul. Because the soul has form, matter appears to have form. Matter is like cloth that is cut to fit the body. In the spiritual world, however, everything has form: God and the spirit souls.

Disciple: Aquinas believed that only God and the angels have nonmaterial form. There is no difference between God's form and God's spiritual Self.

Śrīla Prabhupāda: Both the individual souls and God have form. That is real form. Material form is but a covering for the spiritual body.

Disciple: Aquinas set forth five basic arguments for God's existence: first, God necessarily exists as the first cause; second, the material world cannot create itself but needs something external, or spiritual, to create it; third, because the world exists, there must be a creator; fourth, since there is relative perfection in the world, there must be absolute perfection underlying it; and fifth, since the creation has design and purpose, there must be a designer who planned it.

Śrīla Prabhupāda: We also honor these arguments. Also, without a father and mother, children cannot be brought into existence. Modern philosophers do not consider this strongest argument. According to the *Brahma-saṁhitā,* everything has a cause, and God is the ultimate cause:

īśvaraḥ paramaḥ kṛṣṇaḥ sac-cid-ānanda-vigrahaḥ
anādir ādir govindaḥ sarva-kāraṇa-kāraṇam

"Kṛṣṇa, who is known as Govinda, is the supreme controller. He has an eternal, blissful, spiritual body. He is the origin of all. He has no other origin because He is the prime cause of all causes." [*Brahma-saṁhitā* 5.1]

Disciple: Augustine also states that the relative perfection we find here necessitates an absolute perfection.

Śrīla Prabhupāda: Yes, the spiritual world is absolute perfection, and this temporary material world is but a reflection of that spiritual world. Whatever perfection we find in this material world is derived from the spiritual world (*janmādy asya yataḥ*). According to the *Vedānta-sūtra,* whatever is generated comes from the Absolute Truth.

Disciple: Today, some scientists even admit Aquinas's argument that since nothing can create itself in this material world, something external, or spiritual, is required for initial creation.

Śrīla Prabhupāda: Yes, a mountain cannot create anything, but a human being can give form to a stone. A mountain may be very large, but it remains a stone incapable of giving shape to anything.

Disciple: Unlike Plato and Aristotle, Aquinas maintained that God created the universe out of nothing.

Śrīla Prabhupāda: No. The universe is created by God, certainly, but God and His energies are always there. You cannot logically say that the universe was created out of nothing.

Disciple: Aquinas would contend that since the material universe could not have arisen out of God's spiritual nature, it had to be created out of nothing.

Śrīla Prabhupāda: Material nature is also an energy of God's. As Kṛṣṇa states in the *Bhagavad-gītā:*

> *bhūmir āpo 'nalo vāyuḥ khaṁ mano buddhir eva ca*
> *ahaṅkāra itīyaṁ me bhinnā prakṛtir aṣṭadhā*

"Earth, water, fire, air, ether, mind, intelligence, and false ego—all together these eight constitute My separated material energies." [*Bhagavad-gītā* 7.4] All of these energies

emanate from God, and therefore they are not unreal. They are considered inferior because they are God's separated material energies. The sound that comes from a tape recorder may sound exactly like the original person's voice. The sound is not the person's voice itself, but it has come from the person. If one cannot see where the sound is coming from, one may suppose that the person is actually speaking, although the person may be far away. Similarly, the material world is an expansion of the Supreme Lord's energy, and we should not think that it has been brought into existence out of nothing. It has emanated from the Supreme Truth, but it is the inferior, separated energy. The superior energy is found in the spiritual world, which is the world of reality. In any case we cannot agree that the material world has come from nothing.
Disciple: Well, Aquinas would say that it was created by God out of nothing.
Śrīla Prabhupāda: You cannot say that God's energy is nothing. His energy is exhibited and is eternally existing with Him. God's energy must be there. If God doesn't have energy, how can He be God?

na tasya kāryaṁ karaṇaṁ ca vidyate
na tat-samaś cābhyadhikaś ca dṛśyate
parāsya śaktir vividhaiva śrūyate
svābhāvikī jñāna-bala-kriyā ca

"The Supreme Lord has no duty to perform, and no one is found to be equal to or greater than Him, since everything is done naturally and systematically by His multifarious energies." [*Śvetāśvatara Upaniṣad* 6.8] God has multi-energies, and the material energy is but one. Since God is everything, you cannot say that the material universe comes from nothing.
Disciple: Like Augustine, Aquinas believed that sin and man are concomitant. Because of Adam's original sin, all human beings require salvation, which can be obtained only through God's grace. But the individual has to assent by his free

will for God's grace to function.
Śrīla Prabhupāda: Yes, we call that assent *bhakti,* devotional service. As stated in the *Padma Purāṇa:*

ataḥ śrī-kṛṣṇa-nāmādi na bhaved grāhyam indriyaiḥ
sevonmukhe hi jihvādau svayam eva sphuraty adaḥ

"The material senses cannot appreciate Kṛṣṇa's holy name, form, qualities, and pastimes. When a conditioned soul is awakened to Kṛṣṇa consciousness and renders service by using his tongue to chant the Lord's holy name and to taste the remnants of His food, the soul's consciousness becomes purified, and gradually Kṛṣṇa reveals who He really is."

Bhakti is our eternal engagement, and when we engage in our eternal activities, we attain salvation, or liberation. When we engage in false activities, we are in illusion, *māyā*. *Mukti,* liberation, means remaining in our constitutional position. In the material world, we engage in many different activities, but they all refer to the material body. In the spiritual world, the spirit engages in the Lord's service, and this is salvation.
Disciple: Aquinas considered sins to be both venial and mortal. A venial sin is one that can be pardoned, but a mortal sin cannot. A mortal sin stains the soul.
Śrīla Prabhupāda: When a living entity disobeys the orders of God, he becomes sinful. He is then put into this material world, and that is his punishment. He either rectifies himself by good association or undergoes transmigration. By taking on one body after another, he is subjected to the tribulations of material existence. The soul is not stained, but he can participate in sinful activity. As soon as we are in contact with the material nature, we come under the clutches of the material world:

prakṛteḥ kriyamāṇāni guṇaiḥ karmāṇi sarvaśaḥ
ahaṅkāra-vimūḍhātmā kartāham iti manyate

"The spirit soul bewildered by the influence of false ego

thinks himself the doer of activities that are in actuality carried out by the three modes of material nature." [*Bhagavad-gītā* 3.27] As soon as the living entity enters the material world, he loses his own power. He is completely under the clutches of material nature. Oil never mixes with water, but it may be carried away by the waves.

Disciple: Aquinas felt that the monastic vows of poverty, celibacy, and obedience give a direct path to God, but he did not think that these austerities were meant for the masses of men. He looked on life as a pilgrimage through the world of the senses to the spiritual world of God, from imperfection to perfection, and the monastic vows are meant to help us on this path.

Śrīla Prabhupāda: Yes, according to the Vedic instructions, we must take to the path of *tapasya,* voluntary self-denial. *Tapasā brahmacaryeṇa*. *Tapasya,* or austerity, begins with *brahmacarya,* celibacy. We must first learn to control the sex urge. That is the beginning of *tapasya.* We must control the senses and the mind, and then we should give everything that we have to the Lord's service. By following the path of truth and remaining clean, we can practice yoga. In this way, it is possible to advance toward the spiritual kingdom.

All of this can be realized, however, by engaging in devotional service. If we become devotees of Kṛṣṇa, we automatically attain the benefits of austerities without having to make a separate effort. By one stroke, devotional service, we can acquire the benefits of all the other processes.

Disciple: Aquinas did not believe in a soul per se as being divorced from a particular form. God did not create a soul capable of inhabiting any body or form; rather, He created an angelic soul, a human soul, and an animal soul, or a plant soul. Here again, we find the conception of the soul's creation.

Śrīla Prabhupāda: The soul is not created but is eternally existing along with God. The soul has the independence to turn from God, in which case he becomes like a spark falling from a great fire. Such a separated spark loses its illumination. In any case, the individual soul is always there. The master and

His servants are there eternally. We cannot say that the parts of a body are separately created. As soon as the body is present, all the parts are there with it. The soul is never created, and it never dies. This is confirmed in the very beginning of the *Bhagavad-gītā:*

na jāyate mriyate vā kadācin
nāyaṁ bhūtvā bhavitā vā na bhūyaḥ
ajo nityaḥ śāśvato 'yaṁ purāṇo
na hanyate hanyamāne śarīre

"For the soul there is neither birth nor death at any time. He has not come into being, does not come into being, and will not come into being. He is unborn, eternal, ever-existing, and primeval. He is not slain when the body is slain." [*Bhagavad-gītā* 2.20] It may appear that the soul comes into existence and dies, but this is because he has accepted the material body. When the soul is liberated, he doesn't have to accept another material body. He can return home, back to Godhead, in his original spiritual body.

The soul was never created but is always existing with God. If we say that the soul was created, the question may be raised whether or not God, the Supreme Soul, was also created. Of course, this is not the case. God is eternal, and His parts and parcels are also eternal. The difference is that God never accepts a material body, whereas the individual soul, being but a small particle, sometimes succumbs to the material energy.

Disciple: Is the soul eternally existing with God in a spiritual form?

Śrīla Prabhupāda: Yes.

Disciple: So the soul has a form that is incorruptible. Then what kind of form is the material body?

Śrīla Prabhupāda: The material body is an imitation. It is false. Because the spiritual body has form, the material body, which is a coating, takes on form. As I have already explained, a cloth originally has no form, but a tailor can cut the cloth to fit a form. In actuality, this material form is illusory.

Matter originally has no form. It takes on form for a while as a body, and when the body becomes old and useless, the matter returns to its original position. In the *Bhagavad-gītā* [18.61] the body is compared to a machine. The soul has his own form of spirit, but he is given a machine made of matter, the body, which he uses to wander throughout the universe, attempting to enjoy himself.

Disciple: Aquinas considered that sex is meant exclusively for the begetting of children, and that the parents are responsible for giving their children a spiritual education.

Śrīla Prabhupāda: That is also the Vedic injunction. You should not beget children unless you can liberate them from the cycle of birth and death:

gurur na sa syāt sva-jano na sa syāt
pitā na sa syāj jananī na sā syāt
daivaṁ na tat syān na patiś ca sa syān
na mocayed yaḥ samupeta-mṛtyum

"One who cannot deliver his dependents from the path of repeated birth and death should never become a spiritual master, a father, a husband, a mother, or a worshipable demigod." [*Śrīmad-Bhāgavatam* 5.5.18]

Disciple: Aquinas argued that sex for reasons other than propagation is "repugnant of the good of nature, which is the conservation of the species."

Śrīla Prabhupāda: The conservation of the species doesn't enter into it. Illicit sex is sinful because it is for sense gratification instead of for begetting children. Sense gratification in any form is sinful.

Disciple: Concerning the state, Aquinas, like Plato, believed in an enlightened monarchy, but in certain cases he felt it unnecessary for man to obey human laws if they are opposed to human welfare and are instruments of violence.

Śrīla Prabhupāda: Yes, but first of all we must know what our real welfare is. Unfortunately, as materialistic education advances, we are missing the aim of life. Life's aim is declared openly in the *Vedānta-sūtra: athāto brahma-jijñāsā.* Life is meant for understanding the Absolute Truth. Vedic civilization is based on this principle, but modern civilization has deviated and is devoting itself to that which cannot possibly relieve us from the tribulations of birth, old age, disease, and death. So-called scientific advancement has not solved life's real problems. Although we are eternal, we are presently subjected to birth and death. In this age of quarrel (Kali-yuga), people are slow to learn about self-realization. People create their own way of life, and they are unfortunate and disturbed.

Disciple: Aquinas concludes that if the laws of God and man conflict, we should obey the laws of God.

Śrīla Prabhupāda: Yes. We can also obey the man who obeys the laws of God. It is useless to obey an imperfect person. That is the blind following the blind. If the leader does not follow the instructions of the supreme controller, he is necessarily blind, and he cannot lead. Why should we risk our lives by following blind men who believe that they are knowledgeable but are not? We should instead decide to take lessons from the Supreme Person, Kṛṣṇa, who knows everything perfectly. Kṛṣṇa knows past, present, and future, and what is for our benefit.

Disciple: For Aquinas, all earthly powers exist only by God's permission. Since the Church is God's emissary on earth, the Church should control secular power as well. He felt that secular rulers should remain subservient to the Church, which should be able to excommunicate a monarch and dethrone him.

Śrīla Prabhupāda: World activities should be regulated so that God is the ultimate goal of understanding. Although the Church, or the *brāhmaṇas,* may not directly carry out administrative activities, the government should function under their supervision and instructions. That is the Vedic system. The administrators, the *kṣatriyas,* used to take instructions from the *brāhmaṇas,* who could deliver a spiritual message. It is mentioned in the *Bhagavad-gītā* [4.1] that millions of years ago Kṛṣṇa instructed the sun-god in the yoga of the

Bhagavad-gītā. The sun-god is the origin of the *kṣatriyas*. If the king follows the instructions of the *Vedas* or other scriptures through the *brāhmaṇas,* or through a bona fide church, he is not only a king but a saintly person as well, a *rājarṣi*. The *kṣatriyas* should follow the orders of the *brāhmaṇas,* and the *vaiśyas* should follow the orders of the *kṣatriyas.* The *śūdras* should follow the instructions of the three superior orders.
Disciple: Concerning the beauty of God, Aquinas writes: "God is beautiful in Himself and not in relation to some limited terminus. . . . It is clear that the beauty of all things is derived from the divine beauty. . . . God wishes to multiply His own beauty as far as possible, that is to say, by the communication of His likeness. Indeed, all things are made in order to imitate divine beauty in some fashion."
Śrīla Prabhupāda: Yes, God is the reservoir of all knowledge, beauty, strength, fame, renunciation, and wealth. God is the reservoir of everything, and therefore whatever we see that is beautiful emanates from a very minute part of God's beauty. This Kṛṣṇa declares in the *Bhagavad-gītā* [10.41]:

yad yad vibhūtimat sattvaṁ śrīmad ūrjitam eva vā
tat tad evāvagaccha tvaṁ mama tejo-'ṁśa-sambhavam

"Know that all opulent, beautiful, and glorious creations spring from but a spark of My splendor."
Disciple: Concerning the relationship between theology and philosophy, Aquinas writes: "As sacred doctrine is based on the light of faith, so is philosophy founded on the natural light of reason. . . . If any point among the statements of the philosophers is found contrary to faith, this is not philosophy but rather an abuse of philosophy, resulting from a defect in reasoning."
Śrīla Prabhupāda: Yes, that is correct. Because of material, conditioned life, every man is defective. The philosophy of defective people cannot help society. Perfect philosophy comes from one who is in contact with the Supreme Lord, and such philosophy is beneficial. Speculative philosophers

base their beliefs on imagination.

Disciple: Aquinas concluded that divine revelation is absolutely necessary because very few men can arrive at the truth through the philosophical method. It is a path full of errors, and the journey takes a long time.

Śrīla Prabhupāda: Yes, that's a fact. We should directly contact the Supreme Person, Kṛṣṇa, who has complete knowledge. We should understand His instructions and try to follow them.

Disciple: Aquinas believed that the author of sacred scripture can be only God Himself, who can not only "adjust words to their meaning, which even man can do, but also adjust things in themselves." Also, scriptures are not restricted to one meaning. In this, Aquinas seems to differ from the official Catholic doctrine, which admits only the Pope's interpretation. For him, the scriptures may contain many meanings according to our degree of realization.

Śrīla Prabhupāda: The meaning is one, but if we are not realized, we may interpret many meanings. We present the *Bhagavad-gītā* as it is, without interpretation or motive. We cannot change the words of God. Unfortunately, many interpreters of scripture have spoiled the God consciousness of society. For example, it is stated in both the Bible and the *Bhagavad-gītā* that God created the universe, and that is a fact. One may conjecture that God created the universe out of some chunk, or whatever, but we should not interpret scripture in this way. In the *Gītā* [10.8] Lord Kṛṣṇa states, *ahaṁ sarvasya prabhavo mattaḥ sarvaṁ pravartate:* "I am the source of all spiritual and material worlds. Everything emanates from Me." If it is a fact that everything is an emanation of God's energy, why should we accept a second meaning or interpretation? What is the possible second meaning?

Disciple: Well, in the Bible it is stated that after creating the universe, God walked through paradise in the afternoon. Aquinas would consider this to have an interior, or metaphorical, meaning.

Śrīla Prabhupāda: If God can create, He can also walk,

speak, touch, and see. If God is a person, why is a second meaning necessary? What could it possibly be?
Disciple: Impersonal speculation.
Śrīla Prabhupāda: If God is the creator of all things, He must be a person. Things appear to come from secondary causes, but actually everything is created by the supreme creator.
Disciple: Aquinas seems to have encouraged individual interpretation. He writes: "It belongs to the dignity of divine scripture to contain many meanings in one text, so that it may be appropriate to the various understandings of men for each man to marvel at the fact that he can find the truth that he has conceived in his own mind expressed in divine scripture."
Śrīla Prabhupāda: No. If one's mind is perfect, he may give a meaning, but, according to our conviction, if one is perfect, why should he try to change the words of God? And if one is imperfect, what is the value of his change?
Disciple: Aquinas doesn't say "change."
Śrīla Prabhupāda: Interpretation means change. If man is imperfect, how can he change the words of God? If the words can be changed, they are not perfect, and people will doubt whether they are spoken by God or by an imperfect person.
Disciple: The many different Protestant faiths resulted from such individual interpretation. It's surprising to find this viewpoint in Aquinas.
Śrīla Prabhupāda: As soon as you interpret or change the scripture, the scripture loses its authority. Then another man will come and interpret things in his own way. Another will come and then another, and in this way the original purport of the scripture is lost.
Disciple: Aquinas believed that it is not possible to see God in this life. He writes: "God cannot be seen in His essence by one who is merely man, except he be separated from this mortal life. . . . The divine essence cannot be known through the nature of material things."
Śrīla Prabhupāda: What does he mean by divine essence? For us, God's divine essence is personal. When one cannot conceive of the Personality of Godhead, he sees the imper-

sonal feature everywhere. When one advances further, he sees God as the Paramātmā within his heart. That is the result of yoga meditation. Finally, if one is truly advanced, he can see God face to face. When Kṛṣṇa came, people saw him face to face. Christians accept Christ as the son of God, and when he came, people saw him face to face. Does Aquinas think that Christ is not the divine essence of God?

Disciple: For a Christian, Christ must be the divine essence.

Śrīla Prabhupāda: And didn't many people see him? Then how can Aquinas say that God cannot be seen?

Disciple: It's difficult to tell whether Aquinas is basically impersonalist or personalist.

Śrīla Prabhupāda: That means he is speculating.

Disciple: He writes about the personal feature in this way: "Because God's nature has all perfection and thus every kind of perfection should be attributed to Him, it is fitting to use the word 'person' to speak of God; yet when used of God it is not used exactly as it is of creatures but in a higher sense. . . . Certainly the dignity of divine nature surpasses every nature, and thus it is entirely suitable to speak of God as a 'person.'" Aquinas is no more specific than this.

Śrīla Prabhupāda: Christ is accepted as the son of God, and if the son can be seen, why can't the Father be seen? If Christ is the son of God, who is God? In the *Bhagavad-gītā,* Kṛṣṇa says, *ahaṁ sarvasya prabhavaḥ:* "Everything is emanating from Me." Christ says that he is the son of God, and this means that he emanates from God. Just as he has his personality, God also has His personality. Therefore we refer to Kṛṣṇa as the Supreme Personality of Godhead.

Disciple: Concerning God's names, Aquinas writes: "Yet since God is simple and subsisting, we attribute to Him simple and abstract names to signify His simplicity, and concrete names to signify His subsistence and perfection, although both these kinds of names fail to express His mode of being, because our intellect does not know Him in this life as He is."

Śrīla Prabhupāda: One of God's attributes is being. Similarly, one of His attributes is attraction. God attracts everything. The word *kṛṣṇa* means "all-attractive." What, then, is wrong with addressing God as Kṛṣṇa? Because Kṛṣṇa is the enjoyer of Rādhārāṇī, His name is Rādhikā-ramaṇa. Because He exists, He is called the Supreme Being. In one sense, God has no name, but in another sense He has millions of names according to His activities and attributes.

Disciple: Aquinas maintains that although the names apply to God to signify one reality, they are not synonymous because they signify that reality under diverse aspects.

Śrīla Prabhupāda: God's names are there because He has different features and activities.

Disciple: But Aquinas asserts that no name belongs to God in the same sense that it belongs to creatures.

Śrīla Prabhupāda: The names of creatures are also derived from God. For instance, God appeared as the boar incarnation, and therefore a devotee may be named Varāha dāsa, which means "servant of God in His boar incarnation." This name is not created; it refers to the activities of God.

Disciple: Aquinas believed that names of God that imply relation to creatures are predicated of God temporarily. He writes: "Though God is prior to the creature, still, because the signification of 'Lord' includes the idea of a servant and vice versa, these two relative terms, Lord and servant, are simultaneous by nature. Hence God was not 'Lord' until He had a creature subject to Himself. . . . Thus names which import relation to creatures are applied to God temporarily, and not from eternity, since God is outside the whole order of creation."

Śrīla Prabhupāda: God is always existing as the Lord, and His servants are existing everlastingly with Him. How can He be the Lord without a servant? How can it be that God has no servants?

Disciple: Well, the contention is that creatures were created at one point in time, and before that, God must have been by Himself.

Śrīla Prabhupāda: That is a material idea. It is the material world that is created, not the spiritual world. The spiritual world and God are existing everlastingly. The bodies of creatures in this material world are created, but God is always in the spiritual world with countless servants. According to our philosophy, there is no limit to the number of living entities. Those who do not like to serve are put into this material world. As far as our identity as servants is concerned, that is eternal, whether we are in the material world or the spiritual world. If we do not serve God in the spiritual world, we come down into the material world to serve the illusory energy of God. In any case, God is always the master, and the living entity is always the servant.

Disciple: Aquinas felt that the less determinate God's name is, the more universal and absolute it is. He therefore believed that the most proper name for God is "He who is."

Śrīla Prabhupāda: Why? If God is active and has created the entire universe, what is wrong in addressing Him according to His activities and attributes?

Disciple: Aquinas claims that the very essence of God is the sheer fact of His being, the fact that He is.

Śrīla Prabhupāda: He is, certainly, but "He is" means that He is existing in His abode with His servants, playmates, hobbies, and paraphernalia. Everything is there. We must ask what is the meaning or nature of His being.

Disciple: It seems Aquinas was basically an impersonalist.

Śrīla Prabhupāda: No. He could not determine whether God is personal or impersonal. His inclination was to serve God as a person, but he had no clear conception of His personality. Therefore he speculated.

Disciple: Do the *Vedas* have anything like "He who is"?

Śrīla Prabhupāda: *Oṁ tat sat* is impersonal. This mantra, however, can also be extended as *oṁ namo bhagavate vāsudevāya*. The word *vāsudeva* means "one who lives everywhere," and refers to Bhagavān, the Supreme Personality of Godhead. God is both personal and impersonal, but the impersonal feature is secondary. According to Bhagavān Śrī Kṛṣṇa in the *Bhagavad-gītā* [14.27]:

brahmaṇo hi pratiṣṭhāham amṛtasyāvyayasya ca
śāśvatasya ca dharmasya sukhasyaikāntikasya ca

"And I am the basis of the impersonal Brahman, which is immortal, imperishable, and eternal and is the constitutional position of ultimate happiness." What is the purport to that?
Devotee [reading]: "The constitution of Brahman is immortality, imperishability, eternity, and happiness. Brahman is the beginning of transcendental realization. Paramātmā, the Supersoul, is the middle, the second stage in transcendental realization, and the Supreme Personality of Godhead is the ultimate realization of the Absolute Truth."
Śrīla Prabhupāda: That is divine essence.

Chapter SEVEN

KIERKEGAARD

The Danish philosopher Sören Kierkegaard (1813–1855) is generally regarded as the father of existentialism. His concern with individual existence, choice, and commitment profoundly influenced modern Western theology and philosophy. Here Śrīla Prabhupāda challenges his idea that the deeply religious life must involve intense suffering.

Disciple: Sören Kierkegaard, a devout Christian, believed that religious truth is not innate within man and that man must therefore receive this truth from God. But he thought that God would overawe us if He Himself came to teach. Therefore Kierkegaard said that God comes instead as His own servant in human form. For a Christian, this teacher is Jesus Christ.

Śrīla Prabhupāda: Generally people are on the animal platform. But when a person's consciousness becomes somewhat advanced, he can be educated in the understanding of God through the teachings of spiritual authorities. That is the Vedic system. In the human form the living entity is sometimes very inquisitive and wants to understand God. That inquisitiveness is technically called *brahma-jijñāsā,* interest in the Absolute, which is possible only in the human form of life.

Now, if one is actually anxious to know about God, he has to approach a guru, who is God's servant and His representative. Unless one approaches a bona fide guru, he cannot understand the nature of God, or man's relationship with Him. So accepting a guru is not a fashion but a necessity. However, a guru is not a person who simply manufactures gold or juggles words just to attract foolish people and make money. An actual guru is one who is fully trained in the ocean of spiritual knowledge, or Vedic knowledge. Vedic words are not ordinary material sound vibrations. They are completely spiritual. The Hare Kṛṣṇa *mahā-mantra,* for instance, is a purely spiritual sound. Once a person is fully trained in the ocean of spiritual sound, he becomes a guru and is no longer interested in material life. In fact the definition of the word *guru* is "one who is no longer interested in material things." He has taken shelter of the Supreme Lord, and his material desires have completely ceased. One should approach such a bona fide guru, surrender unto him, serve him, and then question him about God and our relationship with God.

Disciple: Is Kierkegaard correct in maintaining that man would be overawed if God, as He is, came to teach? Didn't Kṛṣṇa, as He is, come to teach the *Bhagavad-gītā*?

Śrīla Prabhupāda: Kṛṣṇa came as He is, but people misunderstood Him because He appeared as a human being. Consequently, they could not surrender to Him. Therefore Kṛṣṇa came later as a devotee, Śrī Caitanya Mahāprabhu, to teach men how to approach God. Caitanya Mahāprabhu taught the very same philosophy that Kṛṣṇa taught in the *Bhagavad-gītā*. But instead of coming as Kṛṣṇa, Lord Caitanya came as Kṛṣṇa's devotee. Rūpa Gosvāmī appreciated Caitanya Mahāprabhu as the most munificent incarnation, because He gives not only Kṛṣṇa but also pure love of Kṛṣṇa (*namo mahā-*

vadānyāya kṛṣṇa-prema-pradāya te). In exchange for Himself, Kṛṣṇa demands full surrender from the devotee. But Caitanya Mahāprabhu, without making any demands, gave pure love of Kṛṣṇa. Because we are all His sons, Kṛṣṇa—the Supreme Lord—is affectionate toward us. He sees us rotting in this material world, and He comes Himself—or He comes as His devotee—and leaves His instructions. Kṛṣṇa is always anxious to enlighten the human beings and show them how to return home, back to Godhead.

Disciple: Kierkegaard thought that the ordinary man does not wish to have a personal relationship with God. Kierkegaard wrote, "The truth is that there are no longer men living who could bear the pressure and weight of having a personal God."

Śrīla Prabhupāda: Yes, a personal God makes demands, just as Kṛṣṇa demands in the *Bhagavad-gītā* [9.34]:

man-manā bhava mad-bhakto mad-yājī māṁ namaskuru
mām evaiṣyasi yuktvaivam ātmānaṁ mat-parāyaṇaḥ

"Engage your mind always in thinking of Me, become My devotee, offer obeisances to Me, and worship Me. Being completely absorbed in Me, surely you will come to Me." This is God's demand. And if we carry it out we attain perfection. *Tyaktvā dehaṁ punar janma naiti mām eti:* Kṛṣṇa clearly states here that when a devotee gives up his material body he does not accept another—he returns back to Godhead in his original, spiritual body.

Disciple: Kierkegaard observed three basic stages in life: the aesthetic stage, the ethical stage, and the religious stage. In the first stage—the aesthetic stage—a person may be either a hedonist in search of sensual pleasure or an intellectual interested in philosophical speculation. Kierkegaard says that both are uncommitted. Neither has any ultimate goal in life.

Śrīla Prabhupāda: How can a philosopher have no ultimate goal?

Disciple: Kierkegaard says that people on this platform are not really philosophers but simply mental speculators. They become bored with themselves, and their lives become empty of meaning and full of despair.

Śrīla Prabhupāda: Despair is a result of impersonalism and voidism. Impersonalists and voidists must necessarily be overcome by despair, because they are always disgusted with their lives and because they do not know the goal of life. When one has no goal he becomes disappointed, and that disappointment is the cause of despair.

Disciple: Kierkegaard sees this despair as the first stepping-stone toward self-realization. Understanding that the aesthetic life ends in despair, in hopelessness, a person abandons this type of life for the next stage.

Śrīla Prabhupāda: We agree with this. After a person has worked very hard and still has not attained peace and prosperity, he may become disgusted and begin to inquire about self-realization. At this point he may begin to ask, "What is the purpose of life?" As we have mentioned before, that inquisitiveness is called *brahma-jijñāsā,* inquiry into the ultimate truth of life. Such an inquiry is natural, and it is necessary for further development.

Disciple: According to Kierkegaard, to attain self-realization we must confront certain choices—we must become aware that life is an "either/or" proposition. Realizing this, we advance to the second stage—the ethical stage. At this point we take an active part in *dealing with* life rather than aimlessly taking pleasure from life. We may act piously or attempt humanitarian deeds.

Śrīla Prabhupāda: But what is the ultimate *goal* of these decisions? Why should people become moral? Simply to feed the poor and open hospitals?

Disciple: For Kierkegaard, the important thing is not so much what one chooses, but that one makes the choice. Through choosing one discovers his own integrity.

Śrīla Prabhupāda: But it is not clear how a person can make the *right* decision. One man may choose to slaughter others, and another man may choose to help others. Or a man may give charity to others and yet at the same time encourage killing animals. For instance, on the one hand Vivekananda advocated feeding the poor, but on the other hand he suggested feeding them with Mother Kālī's *prasādam*—the flesh of bulls. So what kind of ethics is that? What is the value of ethics if it is based on imperfect knowledge?

Disciple: Kierkegaard did not give so much importance to the basis of the decision.

Śrīla Prabhupāda: But if one's decision is not based on truth, what is its value? You must go further than the mere making of decisions. You must know which is the *proper* decision to make.

Disciple: Kierkegaard would say that by turning inward you would naturally make the proper decision. This "turning inward" entails self-knowledge

Śrīla Prabhupāda: But of what value is that inwardness? You may simply think, "I will protect my brother by killing someone." What is the ethics involved? You must have some standard by which to make the right decision.

Disciple: Kierkegaard's standard would be "choose yourself."

Śrīla Prabhupāda: But without *knowing* yourself, how can you *choose* yourself? And how can you know yourself unless you inquire from someone who knows the self and the Supreme Self perfectly? That means you must inquire from a bona fide spiritual master. Most people think they are their body. What kind of self-knowledge is this? *Yasyātma-buddhiḥ kuṇape tri-dhātuke:* "If one thinks he is his body, he is no better than an ass." What is the value of an ass's philosophy?

Disciple: Kierkegaard's philosophy emphasizes the *act* of deciding. The decision itself is not so important.

Śrīla Prabhupāda: But unless we know the aim of life, how can we make the right decision? It is simply childish to say that by choosing either this or that we become enlightened. A child chooses this or that—sometimes he plays with one toy and sometimes with another—but where is his enlightenment? Animals also make decisions. The ass decides to eat a morsel of grass and work all day carrying a load of laundry. If

the basis of our decision is not important, why not decide for unrestricted sense gratification?
Disciple: Kierkegaard would say that unrestricted sense gratification leads to boredom, and ultimately to despair.
Śrīla Prabhupāda: But if you think that sense gratification is the aim of life, then it is not boring to you. If you choose according to your whims, you can make any decision.
Disciple: Kierkegaard would say that we should choose not by whim but by an inward, objective, passionate search. Then the truth will naturally emerge.
Śrīla Prabhupāda: But a Bowery bum may make a passionate decision to purchase a bottle of whiskey as soon as he gets some money.
Disciple: Kierkegaard would say that in his decision there is no commitment to a higher ethic. There is simply the desire for sense gratification. If his decision were made on the ethical level, he would take up a good cause and act on that basis.
Śrīla Prabhupāda: But such "good causes" are relative. You may consider one thing to be a good cause, and I may consider another. Who will ultimately decide?
Disciple: Kierkegaard believed that if we begin to anticipate death, we will make the right decisions. In other words, we should act in such a way that we consider each act to be our last. In this way, he believed, the truth will emerge.
Śrīla Prabhupāda: Every man should think, "I do not wish to die, but death is overcoming me. What is the cause of this? What should I do?" No one wants to die, but death overcomes everyone. No one wants to be diseased, but diseases are inevitable. These are real human problems that cannot be solved simply by making some whimsical decision. We should decide, "I do not wish to suffer, but suffering is coming upon me. Now I must find a solution to this problem." This is the real decision we have to make. We must decide to put a permanent end to suffering—to birth, old age, disease, and death. We should understand that the body exists for a few years and then is doomed to perish. We should also understand that the body is external and that we should not make

our decisions on the basis of the body. Rather, we should make our decisions on the basis of the soul.

Disciple: For Kierkegaard, the third and highest stage of life is the religious stage. On this platform a man submits himself to God and obeys God totally.

Śrīla Prabhupāda: In other words, this is the stage of Kṛṣṇa consciousness. We agree that Kṛṣṇa consciousness is the topmost stage of life.

Disciple: Kierkegaard thought that in the religious stage, there is intense suffering—suffering comparable to that of Job.

Śrīla Prabhupāda: Why is this? If one is Kṛṣṇa conscious, why should he suffer?

Disciple: Kierkegaard was a Christian, and he emphasized the importance of suffering. The Bible says that Christ suffered for our sins, and Kierkegaard believed that the process of overcoming sin involves suffering.

Śrīla Prabhupāda: But that is a wrong theory. If Christ is God or the son of God, why should he suffer? What kind of God is subjected to suffering? Why should either God or man suffer? The whole point is that if there is suffering, you must put an end to it.

Disciple: For Kierkegaard, religious commitment is epitomized by inward suffering.

Śrīla Prabhupāda: No. Suffering arises because we identify with the body. When a person's car is damaged in an automobile accident, he may not actually be injured, but because he identifies himself with matter—with his car—he suffers. Similarly, the spirit soul is riding within the car of the material body, and because the spirit soul identifies himself with the body, he suffers when the body is injured or becomes sick or dies. But because the Kṛṣṇa conscious man is always in full knowledge and is always transcendental to the material world, he never suffers. Whether we suffer or not depends on our knowledge.

Disciple: But doesn't austerity involve suffering?

Śrīla Prabhupāda: No. For one advanced in knowledge, there is no suffering. Of course, there may be some bodily pain, but a person in knowledge understands that he is not the body. Therefore, why should he suffer? He thinks, "Let me do my duty. Hare Kṛṣṇa." That is the advanced stage of Kṛṣṇa consciousness. Suffering is due to ignorance.

Disciple: But don't we have to give up bodily comforts to serve God?

Śrīla Prabhupāda: Rūpa and Sanātana Gosvāmīs were high government ministers, but they abandoned their material opulence to bestow mercy upon the common people. So they wore only loincloths and slept under a different tree every night. Of course, foolish people might say that they were suffering, but actually they were merged in the ocean of transcendental bliss. They simply engaged their minds in thought of Kṛṣṇa's pastimes with the *gopīs.* And from day to day they wrote books about these pastimes. There was no question of their suffering, although a fool may think, "Oh, these men were ministers, high government officials, and they were so comfortable with their families and homes. Now they have no home, and they are going about in loincloths, eating very little." A materialist would think the Gosvāmīs were suffering. But they were not suffering—they were enjoying.

Disciple: Many of the Christian monks and ascetics emphasized suffering. They thought to abandon worldly life means to abandon pleasure and take on suffering.

Śrīla Prabhupāda: This shows that they have a poor fund of knowledge. They have developed this philosophy after the demise of Jesus Christ. It is more or less concocted.

Disciple: Aside from suffering, Kierkegaard emphasized the importance of love in the religious life. In his book *Works of Love,* Kierkegaard considered God to be the hidden source of all love. He wrote: "A man must love God in unconditional obedience and in adoration. It would be ungodliness if any man dared to love himself in this way, or dared to permit another man to love him in this way. . . . You must love God in unconditional obedience even if that which He demands of you may seem injurious to you. . . . for God's wisdom is in-

comparable with respect to our own."
Śrīla Prabhupāda: That is also the instruction of the *Bhagavad-gītā.* God demands that we give up all our plans, as well as the plans of others, and accept His plan:

sarva-dharmān parityajya māṁ ekaṁ śaraṇaṁ vraja
ahaṁ tvāṁ sarva-pāpebhyo mokṣayiṣyāmi mā śucaḥ

"Abandon all varieties of religion and just surrender unto Me. I shall deliver you from all sinful reactions. Do not fear." [*Bhagavad-gītā* 18.66] If we fully depend on Kṛṣṇa, the Supreme Personality of Godhead, He will guide us back to Him.
Disciple: In defining love, Kierkegaard said, "Love is a matter of conscience, and hence it is not a matter of impulse and inclination; nor is it a matter of emotion, nor a matter for intellectual calculation. . . . Christianity really knows only one kind of love: spiritual love."
Śrīla Prabhupāda: Yes, love in the material world is impossible, because in the material world everyone is interested only in his own sense gratification. The love experienced between a man and a woman is not actually love but lust, because both parties are interested only in their own sense gratification. Love means that one does not think of his own sense gratification but of the sense gratification of his beloved. That is pure love. But that pure love is not possible in the material world. When we speak of love in the material world, we are actually misusing the word. Lustful desires take the place of real love.

But we do see examples of pure love in the Vedic descriptions of Vṛndāvana village. There the men, women, animals, fruits, flowers, water, and everything else exist only for the sake of loving Kṛṣṇa. They are not interested in any return from Kṛṣṇa. Now, that is real love (*anyābhilāṣitā-śūnyam*). On the other hand, if we love God with some motive, that is material love. Pure love means that we are simply interested in satisfying the desires of the Supreme Personality of Godhead. Thus real love—individual, collective, or any other kind—applies only to God. Kṛṣṇa, the Supreme Personality of Godhead, is the supreme object of love, and this love can be expressed through admiration, service, or friendship. Or we can love Him as our child or conjugal lover. There are five basic relationships expressing true love of Godhead.

Disciple: For Kierkegaard, love of God is the decisive factor, and from it stems love of our neighbor. He wrote, "If you love God above all else, then you also love your neighbor, and in your neighbor every man. . . . To help another man to love God is truly to love the other man; to be helped by another man to love God is truly to be loved."

Śrīla Prabhupāda: This is the basis of our Kṛṣṇa consciousness movement. We are learning how to love God, and we are teaching the same principle to the whole world. If love of God is taught by a religion, that religion should be considered first class—be it Christian, Hindu, Muslim, or whatever. The test of a religion is this: "Have the followers learned how to love God?" God is the center of love, and since everything is God's expansion, the lover of God is a lover of everyone. A lover of God does not discriminate by thinking only man should be loved and given service. No. He is interested in all living entities, regardless of the forms in which they happen to be existing. A lover of God loves everyone, and his love reaches everyone. When you water the root of a tree, you are nourishing all the parts of the tree—the trunk, branches, twigs, and leaves. When you give food to the stomach, you are satisfying the entire body. And when you love God, you love everyone and everything.

Disciple: Sören Kierkegaard lamented the disintegration of Christianity as an effective form of worship and considered modern Christendom to be a kind of sickness—a corruption of Christ's original message.

Śrīla Prabhupāda: Christianity is Christianity. You cannot call it modern or ancient, nor can you say God is modern or ancient. Either a person is a Christian, or he is not. In other words, either he follows the orders of Christ, or he doesn't. If he does not follow the tenets of his religion, how can he claim to belong to that religion? This is applicable to all religions. For instance, there are many so-called Hindus who do not believe in anything, yet they consider themselves Hindus and *brāhmaṇas*. This is insulting.

Disciple: Concerning the purpose of prayer, Kierkegaard wrote in his *Journals,* "The true success in prayer is not when God hears what is prayed for, but when the person praying continues to pray until *he* hears what God wills."

Śrīla Prabhupāda: Yes, that is very nice. Through prayer one becomes qualified to understand God, to talk with God, and to receive His directions. As stated in the *Bhagavad-gītā* [10.10]:

teṣāṁ satata-yuktānāṁ bhajatāṁ prīti-pūrvakam
dadāmi buddhi-yogaṁ taṁ yena mām upayānti te

"To those who are constantly devoted to serving Me with love, I give the understanding by which they can come to Me." Our ultimate goal is to give up this material world and go back home, back to Godhead. Prayer is just one form of service. There are nine kinds of devotional service that we can perform, as explained by Prahlāda Mahārāja in the *Śrīmad-Bhāgavatam* [7.5.23]:

śravaṇaṁ kīrtanaṁ viṣṇoḥ smaraṇaṁ pāda-sevanam
arcanaṁ vandanaṁ dāsyaṁ sakhyam ātma-nivedanam

"Hearing about the transcendental name, form, qualities, paraphernalia, and pastimes of the Lord; chanting about these things; remembering them; serving the lotus feet of the Lord; offering the Lord respectful worship with incense, flowers, water, and so on; offering prayers to the Lord; becoming His servant; considering the Lord one's best friend; and surrendering everything unto Him—these nine activities constitute pure devotional service."

Whether you perform all nine processes or some of them or only one of them, you can progress in spiritual life. For example, when a Christian or a Muslim offers prayers, his service is as good as the Hindu's service to the Deity in the temple. God is within, and when He sees that we are sincerely serving Him, He takes charge and gives us directions by which we can swiftly approach Him. God is complete in Himself; He is not hankering after our service. But if we offer Him service, we can become purified. When we are completely purified, we can see God and talk with Him. We can receive His instructions personally, just as Arjuna did in the *Bhagavad-gītā.*

Disciple: For Kierkegaard, faith in God develops when the soul is "willing to stand transparent before God in his full integrity."

Śrīla Prabhupāda: Standing transparent before God means engaging in God's service. But to engage in God's service we must understand that we are His parts and parcels. Just as each part of the body engages in the service of the entire body, so every living entity is meant to engage in the service of God, Kṛṣṇa. As soon as you engage in Kṛṣṇa's service, you are self-realized. That is *mukti,* liberation from the miseries of material life. The fruitive workers, mental speculators, and yogīs are trying to realize the self, but because they are not engaged in rendering service to the Supreme Self, Kṛṣṇa, they are not liberated. We are therefore teaching Kṛṣṇa consciousness for the ultimate self-realization of everyone.

Disciple: But Kierkegaard sees self-realization arising out of the expression of the will. He thought that the more self-realized a person is, the more powerful is his will and the better he is able to make proper decisions.

Śrīla Prabhupāda: But if you are part and parcel of the whole, you have to take decisions from the whole. You cannot make your own decisions. The finger does not make decisions for the entire body. The only decision you have to make is the decision to serve Kṛṣṇa—the orders come from Him. Kṛṣṇa ordered Arjuna to fight, and at the end of the *Bhagavad-gītā* Arjuna decided to abide by Kṛṣṇa's will. This is the only choice we have: either to abide by Kṛṣṇa's will or to defy His

will. After we decide to obey Kṛṣṇa, Kṛṣṇa or His representative makes all the other decisions.
Disciple: Then what is the meaning of full will?
Śrīla Prabhupāda: Full will means to surrender to Kṛṣṇa fully—to obey the orders of the Supreme absolutely.
Disciple: Concerning despair, Kierkegaard thought that despair can actually bear fruit in that it can lead one to desire a genuine life of self-realization. In other words, despair can be a springboard to higher consciousness.
Śrīla Prabhupāda: In Sanskrit this is called *nirāśaṁ paramaṁ sukham:* "When one despairs, that is a great happiness." When a person despairs, it means that everything is finished, all responsibility is gone, and he is relieved. Out of despair Arjuna was thinking of becoming a mendicant. When we despair of all happiness in material life, we may then turn to spiritual life. Sometimes Kṛṣṇa smashes all of our material resources so that, out of despair, we may fully engage in His devotional service. In other words, when we want to become God conscious but at the same time, out of strong attachment, we want material enjoyment, Kṛṣṇa will sometimes wreck us materially. At such times we often think that He is being unkind to us, and we despair. We don't realize that this is Kṛṣṇa's mercy—that He is removing all impediments so that we can fully and absolutely surrender.

Once Indra, the Lord of heaven, was forced to take on the body of a hog, and he had to come down to earth as that lowly animal. As a hog, Indra had a hog wife, hog children, and so on. After some time Lord Brahmā came down and told him, "My dear Indra, you were once the Lord of heaven. You once possessed great opulence. Now that you are a hog, you have forgotten your previous exalted position. Please leave this filthy life and come with me." Yet despite Brahmā's pleadings, Indra was not convinced. He said, "Why should I go with you? I am very happy. I have my wife, children, and home." Seeing that Indra had become very much attached to his hog existence, Brahmā began to kill all his hog children. Finally, Brahmā killed Indra's hog wife. When Indra saw that

his wife was killed, he despaired: "Oh, you have killed my whole family!" Only then did Indra agree to go back to the heavenly kingdom with Lord Brahmā. Similarly, Kṛṣṇa sometimes creates a situation in which the living entity will despair and, out of despair, turn to Him and fully surrender to Him.
Disciple: So faith grows out of despair ?
Śrīla Prabhupāda: Yes, to strengthen our faith in God, we have to give up all hope of happiness in this material life. We have to despair of material happiness.
Disciple: Concerning individuality, Kierkegaard wrote, "God is the origin and wellspring of all individuality. . . . [This individuality] is the gift of God through which He permits me to be, and through which He permits everyone to be."
Śrīla Prabhupāda: This idea is explained in the *Kaṭha Upaniṣad* [2.2.13]: *nityo nityānāṁ cetanaś cetanānām.* God is a living being, and we are also living beings. Just as He is eternal, we are also eternal. But the difference is that whereas *qualitatively* we are the same, *quantitatively* we are different. God is infinite, and the living entities are infinitesimal. Therefore, all the living entities are being maintained by God. We are all individual and eternal parts of God, so our natural position is to serve Him and to love Him.
Disciple: Kierkegaard thought that each of us is in a constant state of becoming.
Śrīla Prabhupāda: Becoming what? What is the goal? The goal is Kṛṣṇa. Thus in the *Bhagavad-gītā* [7.7] Kṛṣṇa says,

mattaḥ parataraṁ nānyat kiñcid asti dhanañjaya
mayi sarvam idaṁ protaṁ sūtre maṇi-gaṇā iva

"O conqueror of wealth, there is no truth superior to Me. Everything rests upon Me, as pearls are strung on a thread." Kṛṣṇa is the ultimate truth—the supreme goal—and completeness means coming to Kṛṣṇa consciousness.
Disciple: But even when a person becomes fully Kṛṣṇa conscious and is in association with Kṛṣṇa, won't he still experience the process of becoming?

Śrīla Prabhupāda: No. The becoming process ends. There are, however, spiritual varieties. Everything is complete in the spiritual world, but the living entity enjoys varieties of service to Kṛṣṇa. Sometimes he sees Kṛṣṇa as a cowherd boy, sometimes as Yaśodā's child, sometimes as Rādhārāṇī's consort. Sometimes Kṛṣṇa is in Vṛndāvana, sometimes in Mathurā. There are many spiritual varieties, but everything is complete in itself—there is no question of becoming. One reaches the point where he is simply enjoying variety—that's all.

Disciple: What is the difference between enjoying spiritual variety and enjoying material variety?

Śrīla Prabhupāda: It is artificial to try to enjoy material variety. Material variety is like a plastic flower. A plastic flower has no aroma, so the enjoyment of a plastic flower cannot be the same as the enjoyment of a real flower. It is not satisfying. It is simply artificial, a bluff.

Disciple: Whereas Hegel emphasized speculative thought, Kierkegaard emphasized action. Kierkegaard saw freedom in proper action.

Śrīla Prabhupāda: Yes, spiritual life means proper action. It is improper to think that when we attain the perfectional stage we become inactive. That is the impersonalistic, Māyāvāda theory. Māyāvādīs contend that the living entity is like a jug. A jug makes some sound only as long as it is not full of water. Similarly, the Māyāvādīs say, when we become spiritually "full" we are "silent," or inactive. But from the *Bhagavad-gītā* we understand that the soul is never inactive. When inactivity *is* recommended, this simply means that we should not speak or act foolishly. If we cannot talk intelligently, we had better stop talking. But you cannot equate that inactivity with perfection.

Disciple: Kierkegaard felt that truth is relative and subjective. He thought we could discover truth through personal, individual reflection, which he called "inward passion."

Śrīla Prabhupāda: Truth is truth, and it is absolute. You may manufacture many relative truths, but the Absolute Truth is one. If you have no knowledge of the Absolute Truth, you emphasize relative truths. You may have "inward passion" or whatever, but if you do not know the ultimate goal, you may be misled. It is all right to say that passion leads to truth. But passion means activity. Where will your activity end? What is the purpose of your activity? You may drive your car, but if you do not know where to go, what is the point? You are simply wasting your energy. Of course, you may say, "I do not know where to go, but that doesn't matter. Simply let me start my car and go." But is this a very good proposal?

Disciple: For Kierkegaard it is not *what* is done that counts, but *how* it is done.

Śrīla Prabhupāda: This is a dog's obstinacy.

Disciple: This is the kind of subjectivity that is always uncertain. And uncertainty creates anxiety.

Śrīla Prabhupāda: Yes. One who does not know life's aim will always be in anxiety.

Disciple: For Kierkegaard, this anxiety and uncertainty are dispelled by what he called the "leap of faith."

Śrīla Prabhupāda: Yes, but you must make your leap toward a *goal.* Unless you know the goal, the fixed point, your action and energy may be misdirected.

Disciple: Kierkegaard saw the goal as God. He felt that after passing through the aesthetic and ethical stages of life we should then use all our energy to reach God through Jesus Christ.

Śrīla Prabhupāda: That is a good position. That is our process—to approach God through the bona fide spiritual master. But it is not necessary to pass through any lower stages. If you can reach God through Jesus Christ, why not take to God immediately? Our process is that you must surrender yourself to the spiritual master in order to understand the highest truth. In the *Bhagavad-gītā* [4.34] Kṛṣṇa says,

tad viddhi praṇipātena paripraśnena sevayā
upadekṣyanti te jñānaṁ jñāninas tattva-darśinaḥ

"Just try to learn the truth by approaching a spiritual master. Inquire from him submissively and render service unto him. The self-realized souls can impart knowledge unto you because they have seen the truth." This is the process. It is not that we continue on our own way, hoping to take the right path through experience. If you do not know the right direction, your endeavors will be frustrated. This material world is like a vast ocean, and in the middle of the vast ocean you do not know where to direct your ship. If you simply have a ship without a captain, you will go one way and then another and simply waste your energy. A captain is needed to give direction. That captain is the guru. If Kierkegaard accepts Christ, then he is accepting some guidance.

Disciple: Kierkegaard felt that the directions of God are expressed through scripture and the individual conscience. In his *Journals* he wrote, "There is a God—His will is made known to me in holy scripture and in my conscience."

Śrīla Prabhupāda: That's all right, but to know God's will you need more than that. Besides following the holy scriptures and your conscience, you have to associate with saintly persons and follow the instructions of the bona fide spiritual master. *Sādhu, śāstra, guru vākya, cittete kariyā aikya:* "We can approach God by understanding a saintly person [*sādhu*], studying the Vedic scriptures [*śāstra*], and following the instructions of the bona fide spiritual master [guru]." *Sādhu, śāstra,* and guru corroborate one another. A *sādhu* is he who talks and acts in terms of the scriptures. And the guru is a *sādhu* who personally teaches his disciples according to the scriptures. A guru cannot manufacture words that are not in the scriptures. When we receive instructions from all three, we can progress perfectly in our understanding of the Supreme Personality of Godhead.

Disciple: Kierkegaard thought that because God sees "everything as equally important and equally insignificant, [He] can only be interested in one thing: obedience."

Śrīla Prabhupāda: Yes, and God *demands* that full obedience (*sarva-dharmān parityajya mām ekaṁ śaraṇaṁ vraja*). Our primary obedience should be to the Supreme Personality of Godhead, and we should obey the spiritual master because he is the representative of God. If a person carries out the orders of God, he can become a bona fide spiritual master, or guru. A guru does not manufacture anything. He simply presents what God speaks in the scriptures. It is not that we accept just anyone's proclamations about God. Statements must be corroborated by the standard scriptures.

Disciple: Kierkegaard said, "As an act of worship offered to God, we should renounce everything."

Śrīla Prabhupāda: Worship begins with the renunciation of ulterior motives. Our only business is to love God, and a first-class religious system teaches its followers to love God without ulterior motive. Such worship cannot be checked by material considerations. In any condition we can love God, and God will help us to love Him.

Chapter EIGHT

SCHOPENHAUER

The German philosopher Arthur Schopenhauer (1788–1860) took some of his ideas from the Indian Vedic literature but many more from Buddhist writings, and he ended up espousing an atheistic and pessimistic doctrine. Śrīla Prabhupāda shows how his idea of nirvāṇa, extinguishing one's will, is self-defeating and ultimately impossible to achieve.

Disciple: For Schopenhauer, happiness meant inactive satisfaction—nirvāṇa. Since he thought that the will to enjoy the material world is the irrational urge that brings about all suffering, he advocated the extinction of the will. In his main book, *The World as Will and Idea,* he wrote, "The Indian *Vedas* and *Purāṇas* have no better simile than a dream for the actual [material] world, which they call 'the web of *māyā,*' and they use none more frequently." From this Schopenhauer concluded, "Life is a long dream. . . . What is this world of perception but my idea?" He goes on to conclude that life is a projection of the will.

Śrīla Prabhupāda: Yes, material life is a projection of the material will, or material desire. And nirvāṇa means that material desires are finished. But the living entity cannot be desireless, because he is an eternal spiritual being. Thus, even when he finishes his material desires, he still has spiritual desires. In the materially conditioned state, these spiritual desires are covered by material desires, but in any case desire is the constant companion of the soul, or living entity.

The soul transmigrates in this material world from one body to another, and he creates desires according to the type of body he gets. God's supreme will affords the living entity various bodies so that he can fulfill his minute will, which is made up of material desires. In other words, the living entity wills something, and the supreme will (God, or Kṛṣṇa), understanding the finite will of the living entity, gives him facilities to fulfill his particular desire. In this way, the will of the living entities is the cause of this material existence.

However, Schopenhauer was wrong in thinking that you can become happy by extinguishing your will. Since you are a living being, you must *always* have desires. If your desires are stopped, you become like a stone. So instead of trying to put an end to all desire, you should try to cleanse the diseased form of desire (*sarvopādhi-vinirmuktam*). That cleansing process is Kṛṣṇa consciousness (*bhakti*). Presently our desires are desires of the body. When the living entity acquires the body of an American, a European, a Chinaman, or whatever, he desires like a human being. When he changes his body to that of a dog, he spends his time barking. According to his desires, he has received a particular type of body. But these desires are temporary, and thus the living entity moves from one body to another. Because he is materially covered, he considers the temporary world to be reality; but because it is constantly changing, it is not. Therefore, in one sense, this material world is all a dream.

Disciple: And trying to enjoy this dream is the source of frustration?

Śrīla Prabhupāda: Yes, because it is a fact that we cannot fulfill our material desires, which come and go like dreams. All material activities, subtle or gross, are manifestations of various dreamlike desires. Therefore, the impersonalistic Māyāvādī philosophers say *brahma satyaṁ, jagan mithyā:* "The dreamer is a fact, but the dream is false." Our Vaiṣṇava philosophy agrees that the dreamer is the factual living entity, but we say that the dream of this material world is not false but temporary. Therefore the dreamer has to come to the real, eternal spiritual platform so that his flickering material dreams can be extinguished. As explained in the *Nārada-pañcarātra:*

> *sarvopādhi-vinirmuktaṁ tat-paratvena nirmalam*
> *hṛṣīkeṇa hṛṣīkeśa-sevanaṁ bhaktir ucyate*

"*Bhakti,* or devotional service, means engaging all our senses in the service of the Lord, the Supreme Personality of Godhead, the master of all the senses. When the spirit soul renders service unto the Supreme, there are two side effects: he becomes free from all false material designations, and his senses become purified." When one abandons the dream and awakens to reality, that is Kṛṣṇa consciousness, or *bhakti.*

Disciple: Then will, or desire, can never be annihilated?

Śrīla Prabhupāda: No. The *Bhagavad-gītā* [3.5] states that we cannot live for a second without desires. Because we are living, we must will and desire at every moment.

Disciple: What about the Buddhists? They advocate a state of desirelessness.

Śrīla Prabhupāda: They believe that if you dismantle this material body, there will no longer be will, desire, or suffering. But this is not a fact. The fact is that you are an eternal spirit soul; you do not die after the destruction of the body. Consequently, thinking, feeling, and willing are actually carried from this body to another body in the process of transmigration. When the body dies, the living entity's will carries him away, and according to the quality of his will, he receives another body. That body may be the body of a demigod, a dog, a human, or whatever. In any case, will or desire is the carrier.

Disciple: Schopenhauer was greatly influenced by some of the Vedic writings. He wrote, "Every keen pleasure is an error and an illusion, for no attained wish can give lasting satisfaction. . . . All pain rests on the absence or passing away of such illusory pleasure. Thus both pain and pleasure arise from defective knowledge. The wise man, therefore, holds himself equally aloof from joy and sorrow, and no event disturbs his composure."

Śrīla Prabhupāda: In this material world people say, "This is good, and that is bad." But actually there is no question of good and bad, because everything material is on the temporary platform. Also, the *Bhagavad-gītā* states that the pains and pleasures experienced in the material world do not touch the spirit soul. When a spirit soul is under the illusion that he is his material body, he becomes concerned with the body's pains and pleasures—because he thinks that those pains and pleasures are his. But this is not a fact. Therefore Kṛṣṇa advises:

mātrā-sparśās tu kaunteya śītoṣṇa-sukha-duḥkha-dāḥ
āgamāpāyino 'nityās tāṁs titikṣasva bhārata

"O son of Kuntī, the nonpermanent appearance of happiness and distress, and their disappearance in due course, are like the appearance and disappearance of winter and summer seasons. They arise from sense perception, O scion of Bharata, and one must learn to tolerate them without being disturbed." [*Bhagavad-gītā* 2.14] Since pleasures and pains come and go in due course, they are not the reality. So why bother about them? If I feel pain, let me tolerate it and go about my business of serving Kṛṣṇa.

Disciple: Schopenhauer saw happiness in the world as at best a negative state—simply a momentary suspension of suffering.

Śrīla Prabhupāda: Yes, that is explained by Caitanya Mahāprabhu. Sometimes when a man is to be punished, he is held under water to the point of suffocation. Then he is let up, and when he can finally breathe, he thinks, "Ah! Happiness at last!" But he is then immersed in the water for another period of suffering. So the point is that real happiness means to be relieved of suffering permanently, not for just a few moments.

Disciple: Schopenhauer felt that the greatest crime of man was that he was ever born.

Śrīla Prabhupāda: That's all right, but when you understand that there is a crime, you must understand that there is someone to punish you for that crime. If you suffer because of that crime, you must understand that there is someone who has judged you to be a criminal.

Disciple: Schopenhauer would disagree. He wrote, "Human life must be some kind of mistake." And because he thought the world mad or irrational, he concluded that it could not possibly have an author. He believed that if there were a God, He would have set the world in order.

Śrīla Prabhupāda: We have certainly experienced that there are madmen in the world, but there are also hospitals where such men can be treated. The world may be mad, but God is providing hospitalization and treatment—the process of Kṛṣṇa consciousness. Unfortunately, Schopenhauer had no knowledge of the hospital or the treatment. He speaks of sinful life, but he does not accept the judge who gives the punishment for sinful life. He sees that the world is mad, but he does not know the treatment for madmen.

Disciple: In *The World as Will and Idea,* Schopenhauer wrote, "If we narrowly analyze the reality of our body and its actions . . . we find nothing in it except the will; with this the body's reality is exhausted." He goes on to state that "the genitals are the focus of the will."

Śrīla Prabhupāda: As I said before, one wills in accordance with his body. We should understand that we have nothing to do with this material world, which is the production of the material will. We are spiritual, and when we will spiritually, we are Kṛṣṇa conscious. When we will materially, we get different types of material bodies. It is true that the basis of material life is sex. *Yan maithunādi-gṛhamedhi-sukhaṁ hi tuccham:* "The basic principle of those who are addicted to the material world is the insignificant pleasure that comes from *maithuna,* sexual intercourse." The strong desire for sex will continue as long as we are in material existence, because sex is the center of all material pleasure. However, when we get a taste of spiritual pleasure—pleasure in Kṛṣṇa consciousness—we can give up sex. *Paraṁ dṛṣṭvā nivartate:* by experiencing a superior pleasure, we can give up an inferior one.

Disciple: Schopenhauer considered sex to be selfishness, whereas real love means sympathy.

Śrīla Prabhupāda: Sex is animalistic. It is not love but lust. Sex simply means the mutual satisfaction of the material senses, and that is lust. All this lust is taking place under the name of love, and out of illusion people mistake this lust for love. One who has real love—love for Kṛṣṇa and for all living entities—thinks, "People are suffering from a lack of Kṛṣṇa consciousness. Let me do something for them so that they can understand the value of life."

Disciple: Schopenhauer considered that immoral acts result from a sense of egoism.

Śrīla Prabhupāda: Yes, that is so. To be immoral means to avoid surrendering to the will of Kṛṣṇa. Immoral people think, "Why should I surrender to Kṛṣṇa? Kṛṣṇa is an ordinary person like me." Such thinking is demonic. Rascals cannot understand that by surrendering unto the supreme will and satisfying the supreme will, they can attain salvation.

Disciple: Schopenhauer felt that it is possible to crush egoism and desire by love.

Śrīla Prabhupāda: Yes—but we must direct that love toward Kṛṣṇa. If I do not love Kṛṣṇa, I cannot surrender to Him, and if I do not surrender to Kṛṣṇa, my false egoism will continue. So the more you love Kṛṣṇa, the more your surrender is perfect. But when there is a lack of love, the mentality by which you can surrender will not develop. For instance, if you have some love for me, you will carry out my orders. There is no question of forcing you to surrender. Or take the example of a child: a small child naturally surrenders to his parents because there is love for the parents. In the same way, the living entity is free to love Kṛṣṇa or to reject Him. Without freedom, there cannot be love. Therefore Kṛṣṇa consciousness means learning to love Kṛṣṇa.

Disciple: Schopenhauer looked on love as compassionate sympathy for one who is suffering. Through this compassionate love we can lose our selfish desire.

Śrīla Prabhupāda: Why should we love those who are suffering but not those who are enjoying?

Disciple: Schopenhauer saw everyone as suffering.

Śrīla Prabhupāda: We agree that everyone within the material nature is suffering. Therefore Kṛṣṇa descends and speaks the *Bhagavad-gītā* to deliver all fallen souls. Similarly, a Vaiṣṇava takes *sannyāsa,* the renounced order, out of compassion for others—because a *sannyāsī's* only duty is to preach the message of Kṛṣṇa consciousness. People in this world are suffering because of ignorance. They think, "Oh, now I have a nice car, an apartment, and a girlfriend; therefore I am happy." Actually, this is not happiness but suffering. Because the Vaiṣṇava loves Kṛṣṇa and understands that he is part and parcel of Kṛṣṇa, he realizes that the conditioned living entities are suffering for want of Kṛṣṇa consciousness. Therefore, out of compassion the Vaiṣṇava takes *sannyāsa* and goes forth to preach.

Disciple: Schopenhauer saw the pleasures of this world as ultimately frustrating.

Śrīla Prabhupāda: If he had taken his frustration seriously, it might have made him successful. I receive many letters from frustrated students who understand that frustration is hell. Eventually they come to understand that they should seek the real shelter—Kṛṣṇa consciousness. So frustration is really not so bad. If you are put into a dangerous position and you know how to save yourself from it, that very danger can become a source of pleasure for you.

Disciple: In *The World as Will and Idea,* Schopenhauer wrote, "Eternal becoming, endless flux, characterizes the inner nature of will. Finally, the same thing shows itself in human endeavors and desires, which always delude us by presenting their satisfaction as the final end of will. As soon as we attain our desired objects, they no longer appear the same; therefore, they soon grow stale or forgotten, and we throw them aside as vanished illusions."

Śrīla Prabhupāda: Yes, all this is going on, and therefore the living entity acquires one body after another.

Disciple: Schopenhauer saw everyone going through a constant transition from desire to satisfaction, and from satisfaction to a new desire. For Schopenhauer, it is this flux from desire to satisfaction that characterizes the will's activities in the phenomenal world. Outside this flux, he thought, there is only nirvāṇa, extinction of the will.

Śrīla Prabhupāda: That is not a fact. One has to understand that behind the will and its satisfaction is a *person who is willing*. Schopenhauer did not take that person into consideration; he considered only the will and its satisfaction. It is the individual soul who is willing. If the soul succeeds in stopping this flickering willing, what next? Even the stopping of the will is temporary. You may stop one kind of willing, but you will adopt another kind of willing and another kind of satisfaction. We must understand that behind the whimsical will is the spirit soul. When that spirit soul understands his real identification as the eternal servant of Kṛṣṇa, his will is purified. One should not be satisfied by simply annihilating the whimsical will. One should understand the real will of the real person. That is the beginning of spiritual life.

It will not help simply to negate the temporary material will. One has to will in reality, and that is his eternal willing—that is Kṛṣṇa consciousness. In the material world, the living entity directs his will toward sense satisfaction because he has forgotten the spiritual field of willing. When the same will is directed toward satisfying the senses of the Supreme—Kṛṣṇa—that is the eternal willing of the living entity. *Jīvera 'svarūpa' haya—kṛṣṇera 'nitya-dāsa'*: "When one comes to the platform of real knowledge, he understands that he is the eternal servant of God." When we concentrate our will on how to serve God, we attain our real position of eternality, bliss, and knowledge.

Disciple: Schopenhauer apparently believed in life after death. He wrote, "If a man fears death as his annihilation, it is just as if he were to think that the sun cries out at evening, 'Woe is me! For I go down to eternal night.'"

Śrīla Prabhupāda: Yes, because the will is eternal, death is not the stoppage of life. One simply gets another body. In the *Bhagavad-gītā* Kṛṣṇa says, *tathā dehāntara-prāptiḥ:* "When the body dies, the soul transmigrates to another body." This is proof that the life of the person is eternal. And because the person is eternal, his desire and will are also eternal. But Schopenhauer did not know what that eternal willing is. The eternal will of every living entity is to serve Kṛṣṇa always.

Disciple: Schopenhauer looked on Indian philosophy as a philosophy of the denial of the will—

Śrīla Prabhupāda: But he did not study Vedic philosophy and religion perfectly. He simply had some idea of some portions of the impersonalistic and Buddhistic philosophies. Evidently he did not know about Vaiṣṇavism. Although he touched the *Bhagavad-gītā,* he did not study it thoroughly. There Kṛṣṇa tells Arjuna that if he simply tries to attain knowledge of God—Kṛṣṇa—his will and his life will be purified, and he will return back to Godhead upon giving up his body. In the fourth chapter of the *Bhagavad-gītā* [4.9] Kṛṣṇa says,

janma karma ca me divyam evaṁ yo vetti tattvataḥ
tyaktvā dehaṁ punar janma naiti mām eti so 'rjuna

"One who knows the transcendental nature of My appearance and activities does not, upon leaving the body, take his birth again in this material world, but attains My eternal abode, O Arjuna."

Either Schopenhauer did not study the *Bhagavad-gītā* very thoroughly, or he could not understand it for want of a real spiritual master. According to the *Gītā* itself, one should go to a bona fide guru who has actually seen the truth. Schopenhauer simply speculated on the basis of his own experience, and consequently, although everything is there in the *Bhagavad-gītā,* he could not see it.

Disciple: According to Schopenhauer, the man of knowledge is imperturbable in any condition. He wrote, "Such a man would regard death as a false illusion, an impudent specter which frightens the weak but has no power over him who knows that he is himself the will of which the whole world is the objectification or copy, and that therefore he is always certain of life. . . ."

Śrīla Prabhupāda: This is contradictory. On the one side Schopenhauer has a desire for the certainty of life, and on the other he says that nirvāṇa, annihilation, is the only answer. Which does he want? He simply tried to adjust things to fit his theory. But he couldn't understand the philosophy behind purification of the will.

Disciple: Apparently he had no other solution than the suppression of the will.

Śrīla Prabhupāda: But that is not possible. In order to be happy, you must change the *quality* of your willing through purification. The purification process is *bhakti*—chanting and hearing the name, qualities, and pastimes of the Lord (*śravaṇaṁ kīrtanaṁ viṣṇoḥ*). That purifies the will. Schopenhauer missed the point. Although he accepted the fact that life is eternal, he thought that its purpose is nirvāṇa, putting an end to the will. Unfortunately, he did not know what nirvāṇa is. Nirvāṇa means putting an end to the whimsical will and coming to the platform of willing in Kṛṣṇa consciousness.

Disciple: For Schopenhauer, there were three means of salvation—aesthetic, ethical, and religious. Through aesthetic salvation—contemplation of the Platonic ideals—we rise above passion through poetry, music, and art. Through the contemplation of these higher ideals, we reach a plane of desirelessness.

Śrīla Prabhupāda: This is not a new idea; it is mentioned in the *Bhagavad-gītā: paraṁ dṛṣṭvā nivartate.* The students of this Kṛṣṇa consciousness movement have abandoned their abominable living habits because they have received a better life—with superior thoughts, philosophy, food, song, poetry, and art. When the mind is filled with Kṛṣṇa consciousness, there is no chance of its engaging in the contemplation of nonsense.

Disciple: For Schopenhauer, aesthetic salvation is a temporary experience. For instance, when one looks at a beautiful painting, he transcends the lower levels of consciousness and for a few moments becomes "will-less," or desireless.

Śrīla Prabhupāda: Yes, we agree that this may be the case, but we wish to remain in that higher consciousness continuously, not momentarily. This is possible if we practice. By practice a child learns to read and write, and thus he becomes educated. It is not a momentary thing. If we practice Kṛṣṇa consciousness daily, lower consciousness will automatically vanish. For instance, we worship the Deities in the temple—that is actual aesthetic salvation. But unless you apply the aesthetic sense with reverence and respect, you cannot derive benefit from worshiping the Deities.

Disciple: According to Schopenhauer, you achieve ethical salvation by attempting to satisfy your will. When you satisfy your will, no new desires can arise, and you experience happiness.

Śrīla Prabhupāda: Apart from the individual will, there is the supreme will. If we satisfy the supreme will, we are happy. But we cannot know the supreme will directly, and therefore we must approach a spiritual master. Our philosophy is that by satisfying the spiritual master, the representative of God, we satisfy the supreme will (*yasya prasādād bhagavat-prasādaḥ*).

Disciple: For Schopenhauer, the third and most effective type of salvation is religious salvation. He felt that by denying the will through asceticism, you can attain the state of nirvāṇa, nothingness.

Śrīla Prabhupāda: But Schopenhauer did not know that since the soul is eternal, willing is also eternal—although the will may be suppressed for some time. For instance, after death, when a living entity enters a mother's womb, he spends nine months developing his next body, and there is a temporary suspension of the will. But when he emerges from his mother's womb, he resumes the willing process. Death simply means a suspension of the will for a few months—that's all. If you fail to train your willing process properly you have to suffer, life after life. But if you train your will properly—to serve Kṛṣṇa's supreme will—you can go to Kṛṣṇa's supreme planet immediately after death.

Chapter NINE

DARWIN

The British scientist Charles Darwin (1809–1882) laid the foundation of modern evolutionary theory with his concept of the development of all forms of life through the slow-working process of natural selection. His work has exerted a major influence on the life sciences and earth sciences and on modern thought in general. Here Śrīla Prabhupāda challenges the crux of Darwin's theory by pointing out two critical omissions: the overseeing intelligence of God and the transmigration of the immortal soul from body to body.

Disciple: Darwin tried to show how the origin of living species could be fully explained by the purely mechanical, unplanned action of natural forces. By the process he called "natural selection," all the higher, complex forms of life gradually evolved from more primitive and rudimentary ones. In a given animal population, for example, some individuals will have traits that make them adapt better to their environment; these more fit individuals will survive to pass

on their favorable traits to their offspring. The unfit will gradually be weeded out naturally. Thus a cold climate will favor those who have, say, long hair or fatty tissue, and the species will then gradually evolve in that direction.
Śrīla Prabhupāda: The question is that in the development of the body, is there any plan that a particular kind of body—with, as you say, long hair or fatty tissue—should exist under certain natural conditions? Who has made these arrangements? That is the question.
Disciple: No one. Modern evolutionists ultimately base their theory on the existence of chance variations.
Śrīla Prabhupāda: That is nonsense. There is no such thing as chance. If they say "chance," then they are nonsense. Our question remains. Who has created the different circumstances for the existence of different kinds of animals?
Disciple: For example, a frog may lay thousands of eggs, but out of all of them only a few may survive to adulthood. Those who do are more fit than the others. If the environment did not favorably select the fittest, then too many frogs—
Śrīla Prabhupāda: Yes, frogs and many other animals lay eggs by the hundreds. A snake gives birth to scores of snakes at a time, and if all were allowed to exist, there would be a great disturbance. Therefore, big snakes devour the small snakes. That is nature's law. But behind nature's law is a brain. That is our proposition. Nature's law is not blind, because behind it there is a brain, and that brain is God. We learn this from the *Bhagavad-gītā* [9.10]: *mayādhyakṣeṇa prakṛtiḥ sūyate sa-carācaram.* Whatever is taking place in material nature is being directed by the Supreme Lord, who maintains everything in order. So the snake lays eggs by the score, and if many were not killed, the world would be overwhelmed by snakes. Similarly, male tigers kill the cubs. The economic theory of Malthus states that whenever there is overpopulation, there must be an outbreak of war, epidemic, famine, or the like to curb it. These natural activities do not take place by chance but are planned. Anyone who says they are a matter of chance has insufficient knowledge.

Disciple: But Darwin has a huge amount of evidence—
Śrīla Prabhupāda: Evidence? That is all right. We also have got evidence. Evidence must be there. But as soon as there is evidence, there should be no talk of "chance."
Disciple: For example, out of millions of frogs, one may happen to be better adapted to living in the water.
Śrīla Prabhupāda: But that is not by chance! That is by plan! He doesn't know that. As soon as one says "chance," it means his knowledge is imperfect. A man says "chance" when he cannot explain. It is evasive. So the conclusion is that he is without perfect knowledge and therefore unfit for giving *any* knowledge. He is cheating, that's all.
Disciple: Well, Darwin sees a "plan" or "design" in a sense, but—
Śrīla Prabhupāda: If he sees a plan or design, then whose design? As soon as you recognize a design, you must acknowledge a designer. If you see a plan, then you must accept a planner. That he does not know.
Disciple: But the "plan" is only the involuntary working of nature.
Śrīla Prabhupāda: Nonsense. There *is* a plan. The sun rises daily according to exact calculation. It does not follow *our* calculation; rather, we calculate according to the sun. Experiencing that in such-and-such season the sun rises at such-and-such time, we learn that according to the season the sun rises exactly on the minute, the second. It is not by whimsy or chance but by minute plan.
Disciple: But can't you say it's just mechanical?
Śrīla Prabhupāda: Then who made it mechanical? If something is mechanical, then there must be a mechanic, a brain, who made the machine. Here is something mechanical [*Śrīla Prabhupāda points to a Telex machine*]: Who made it? This machine has not come out by itself. It is made of iron, and the iron did not mold itself into a machine; there is a brain who made the machine possible. So everything in nature has a plan or design, and behind that plan or design is a brain, a very big brain.

Disciple: Darwin tried to make the appearance and disappearance of living forms seem so natural that God is removed from the picture. Evolutionary theory makes it appear as if combinations of material ingredients created life and then various species evolved one from another naturally.
Śrīla Prabhupāda: That is foolishness. Combination means God. God is combining. Combination does not take place automatically. Suppose I am cooking. There are many ingredients gathered for cooking, but they do not combine together by themselves. I am the cooker, and in cooking I combine together ghee, spices, rice, dhal, and so on, and in this way, nice dishes are produced. Similarly, the combination of ingredients in nature requires God. Otherwise, how does the moment arise in which the combination takes place? Do you place all the ingredients in the kitchen and in an hour come back and say, "Oh, where is my meal?" Nonsense! Who will cook your meal? You'll starve. But take help of a living being, and then we'll cook and we can eat. This is our experience. So if there is combination, then who is combining? The scientists are fools not to know how combination takes place.
Disciple: Scientists now say life arose out of four basic elements: carbon, hydrogen, nitrogen, and oxygen.
Śrīla Prabhupāda: If the basic principle is chemicals, who made the chemicals? That question should be asked.
Disciple: Isn't it possible that one day science will discover the source of these chemicals?
Śrīla Prabhupāda: There is no question of discovering: the answer is already known, although it may not be known to *you.* We know. The *Vedānta* says, *janmādy asya yataḥ:* the original source of everything is Brahman, Kṛṣṇa. Kṛṣṇa says, *ahaṁ sarvasya prabhavo mattaḥ sarvaṁ pravartate:* "I am the origin of everything." [*Bhagavad-gītā* 10.8] So we know that there is a big brain who is doing everything. We know. The scientists may not know; that is their foolishness.
Disciple: They might say the same thing about us.
Śrīla Prabhupāda: No, they cannot say the same thing about us. We accept Kṛṣṇa, but not blindly. Our predecessors, the

great *ācāryas* and learned scholars, have accepted Kṛṣṇa as the origin of everything, so we are not following blindly. We claim that Kṛṣṇa is the origin, but what claim can the scientist make? As soon as he says "chance," it means that he has no knowledge. We don't say "chance." We have an original cause; but he says chance. Therefore he has no knowledge.
Disciple: They try to trace the origin by means of excavation. And they have found that gradually through the years the animal forms are evolving toward increasingly more complex and specialized forms, from invertebrates to fish, then to amphibians, then to reptiles and insects, to mammals and birds, and finally to humans. In that process many species, like the dinosaurs, appeared, flourished, and then disappeared forever, became extinct. Eventually, primitive apelike creatures appeared, and from them man gradually developed.
Śrīla Prabhupāda: Is the theory that the human body comes from the monkeys?
Disciple: Humans and monkeys are related. They come from the same—
Śrīla Prabhupāda: Related? Everything is related; that is another thing. But if the monkey body is developing into a human body, then why, after the human body is developed, doesn't the monkey species cease to exist?
Disciple: The humans and the monkeys are branches of the same tree.
Śrīla Prabhupāda: Yes, and both are now existing. Similarly, we say that at the time the evolutionists say life began, there were human beings existing.
Disciple: They find no evidence for that.
Śrīla Prabhupāda: Why no evidence?
Disciple: In the ground. By excavation. They find no evidence in the ground.*
Śrīla Prabhupāda: Is the ground the only evidence? Is there no other evidence?

*In fact, from the time of Darwin up to the present, scientists have found abundant archeological evidence indicating that human beings lived

Disciple: The only evidence they accept is the testimony of their senses.
Śrīla Prabhupāda: But they still cannot prove that there was no human being at the time they say life originated. They cannot prove that.
Disciple: It appears that in certain layers of earth there are remains of apelike men—
Śrīla Prabhupāda: Apelike men or manlike apes are still existing now, alongside human beings. If one thing has been developed by the transformation of another thing, then that original thing should no longer be in existence. When in this way a cause has produced its effect, the cause ceases to exist. But in this case we see that the cause is still present, that there are still monkeys and apes.
Disciple: But monkeys did not cause men; both came from the same common ancestor. That is their account.
Śrīla Prabhupāda: We say that we *all* come from God, the same ancestor, the same father. The original father is Kṛṣṇa. As Kṛṣṇa says in the *Bhagavad-gītā* [14.5], *sarva-yoniṣu kaunteya:* "Of as many forms as there are . . ." *ahaṁ bīja-pradaḥ pitā:* "I am the seed-giving father." So what is your objection to this?
Disciple: Well, if I examine the layers of earth, I find in the deepest layers no evidence—
Śrīla Prabhupāda: You are packed up with layers of earth, that's all. That is the boundary of your knowledge. But that is not knowledge; there are many other evidences.
Disciple: But surely if men were living millions of years ago, they would have left evidence, tangible evidence, behind them. I could see their remains.
Śrīla Prabhupāda: So I say that in advanced human societies

---

millions of years ago, long before the Darwinian evolutionists say they did. However, because this evidence contradicts Darwinian theories, it tends to be omitted in science texts written by Darwinists. For a review of this evidence, see *Forbidden Archeology,* by Michael Cremo and Richard Thompson.

bodies are burned after death, cremated. So where does your excavator get his bones?
Disciple: Well, that's possible, but—
Śrīla Prabhupāda: According to our Vedic system, the body is burned to ashes after death. Where, therefore, would the rascal get the bones? Animals are not burned; their bones remain. But human beings are burned, and therefore they cannot find their bones.
Disciple: I'm just saying that it appears, through layer after layer of deposits in the earth, that biological forms tend to progress from simple and primitive forms to more and more complex and specialized ones, until finally civilized man appears.
Śrīla Prabhupāda: But at the present moment both simple and complex forms are existing. One did not develop into the other. For example, my childhood body has developed into my adult body, and the child's body is no longer there. So if the higher, complex species developed from the simpler, lower species, then we should see no simple species. But all species are now existing simultaneously.

When I see all 8,400,000 species of life existing, what is the question of development? Each species exists now, and it existed long ago. You might not have seen it, but you have no proper source of knowledge. You might have missed it. That is another thing.
Disciple: But all the evidence shows otherwise. Five hundred million years ago there were no land animals; there were only aquatics.
Śrīla Prabhupāda: That is nonsense. You cannot give a history of five hundred million years! Where is the history of five hundred million years? You are simply imagining. You say "historical evidence," but where is your evidence? You cannot give a history for more than three thousand years, and you are speaking about five hundred million. This is all nonsense.
Disciple: If I dig far into the ground, layer by layer—
Śrīla Prabhupāda: By dirt you are calculating five hundred

million years? It could be *ten* years. You cannot give the history of human society past three thousand years, so how can you speak of five hundred million years ago? Where were you then? Were you there, so you can say that all these species were not there? This is imagination. In this way everyone can imagine and say some nonsense.

We accept evolution, but not that the forms of the species are changing. The bodies are all already there, but the soul is evolving by changing bodies and by transmigrating from one body to another. I have evolved from my childhood body to my adult body, and now my childhood body is extinct. But there are many other children. Similarly, all the species are now existing simultaneously, and they were all there in the past.

For example, if you are traveling in a train, you find first class, second class, third class; they are all existing. If you pay a higher fare and enter the first-class carriage, you cannot say, "Now the first class is created." It was always existing. So the defect of the evolutionists is that they have no information of the soul. The soul is evolving, transmigrating, from one compartment to another compartment, simply changing place. The *Padma Purāṇa* says that there are 8,400,000 species of life, and the soul evolves through them. This evolutionary process we accept: the soul evolves from aquatics to plants, to insects, to birds, to animals, and then to the human forms. But all these forms are already there. They do not change. One does not become extinct and another survive. All of them are existing simultaneously.

Disciple: But Darwin says there are many species, like dinosaurs, that are seen to be extinct.

Śrīla Prabhupāda: What has he seen? He is not so powerful that he can see everywhere or everything. His power to see is limited, and by that limited power he cannot conclude that one species is extinct. That is not possible. No real scientist will accept that. After all, all the senses by which you gather knowledge are limited, so how can you say this is finished or that is extinct? You cannot see. You cannot search out. The

earth's circumference is twenty-five thousand miles; have you searched through all the layers of rock and soil over the whole earth? Have you excavated all those places?
Disciple: No.
Śrīla Prabhupāda: Therefore our first charge against Darwin is this: He says there were no human beings millions of years ago. That is not a fact. We now see human beings existing along with all other species, and it should be concluded that this situation always existed. Human life has always been there. Darwin cannot prove that there was no human life millions of years ago.
Disciple: We don't see any dinosaurs existing.
Śrīla Prabhupāda: *You* do not see because you have no power to see. Your senses are very limited, so what you see or don't see cannot be authoritative. So many people—the majority of people—say, "I don't see God." Shall we accept, then, that there is no God? Are we crazy for being devotees of God?
Disciple: No, but dinosaurs—
Śrīla Prabhupāda: But simply by dinosaurs being missing you cannot make your case. What about all the other species?
Disciple: Many, many others are also extinct.
Śrīla Prabhupāda: Say I accept that many are extinct—because the evolutionary process means that as an earlier species gradually changes into a later species, the earlier vanishes, becomes extinct. But we see that many monkeys are still here. Man evolved from the simians, but simians have not disappeared. Monkeys are here, and men are here.
Disciple: But still I'm not convinced. If we make geological investigations all over the world, not just here and there, but in many parts of the world, and in every case we find the same thing
Śrīla Prabhupāda: But I say you have not studied all over the world. Has Darwin studied all the continents on this planet? Has he gone down into the depths of the seas and there excavated all the layers of the earth? No. So his knowledge is imperfect. This is the relative world, and here everyone speaks with relative knowledge. Therefore we should accept

knowledge from a person who is not within this relativity.

Disciple: Actually, Darwin hit upon his theory because of what he observed on his voyage in 1835 to the Galapagos Islands, off the coast of South America. He found there species that exist nowhere else.

Śrīla Prabhupāda: That means he has not seen all the species. He has not traveled all over the universe. He has seen one island, but he has not seen the whole creation. So how can he determine what species exist and don't exist? He has studied one part of this earth, but there are many millions of planets. He has not seen all of them; he has not excavated the depths of all the planets. So how can he conclude, "This is nature"? He has not seen everything, nor is it possible for any human being to see everything.

Disciple: Let's just confine ourselves to this planet.

Śrīla Prabhupāda: No, why should we? Nature is not only on this planet.

Disciple: Because you said that on this planet there were complex forms of living beings millions and millions of years ago.

Śrīla Prabhupāda: We are not talking about this planet, but about anywhere. You are referring to nature. Nature is not limited or confined to this planet. You cannot say that. Nature, material nature, includes millions of universes, and in each and every universe there are millions of planets. If you have studied only this planet, your knowledge is insufficient.

Disciple: But you said before that millions of years ago on this planet there were horses, elephants, civilized men—

Śrīla Prabhupāda: Yes, yes.

Disciple: But from hundreds of different sources there is no evidence.

Śrīla Prabhupāda: I say they are existing now—men, horses, snakes, insects, trees. So why not millions of years ago?

Disciple: Because there is no evidence.

Śrīla Prabhupāda: That doesn't mean . . . ! You limit your study to one planet. That is not full knowledge.

Disciple: I just want to find out for the time being about—

Śrīla Prabhupāda: Why the time being? If you are not perfect in your knowledge, then why should I accept your theory? That is my point.
Disciple: Well, if you claim that millions of years ago there were complex forms of life on this planet—
Śrīla Prabhupāda: Whether on this planet or on another planet, that is not the point. The point is that all species exist and keep on existing by the arrangement of nature. We learn from the Vedic texts that there are 8,400,000 species established. They may be in your neighborhood or they may be in my neighborhood—the number and types are fixed. But if you simply study your neighborhood, it is not perfect knowledge. Evolution we admit. But your evolutionary theory is not perfect. Our theory of evolution is perfect. From the *Vedas* we know that there are 8,400,000 forms of bodies provided by nature, but the soul is the same in all, in spite of the different types of body. There is no change in the soul, and therefore the *Bhagavad-gītā* [5.18] says that one who is wise, a paṇḍita, does not see the species or the class; he sees oneness, equality. *Paṇḍitāḥ sama-darśinaḥ.* One who sees to the bottom sees the soul, and he does not find there any difference between all these species.
Disciple: So Darwin and other material scientists who have no information about the soul—
Śrīla Prabhupāda: They're missing the whole point.
Disciple: They say that all living things tend to evolve from lower to higher. In the history of the earth—
Śrīla Prabhupāda: That may be accepted. For example, in an apartment building there are different kinds of apartments: first-class apartments, second-class apartments, third-class apartments. According to your desire and qualification, as you are fit to pay the rent, you are allowed to move up to the better apartments. But the different apartments are already there. *They* are not evolving. The residents are evolving by moving to new apartments as they desire.
Disciple: As they desire.
Śrīla Prabhupāda: Yes. According to our mentality at the

time of death, we get another "apartment," another body. But the "apartment" is already there, not that I'm creating the "apartment."

And the classes of "apartments" are fixed at 8,400,000. Just like the hotel-keeper: he has experience of his customers coming and wanting different kinds of facilities. So he has made all sorts of accommodations to oblige all kinds of customers. Similarly, this is God's creation. He knows how far a living entity can think, so He has made all these different species accordingly. When God thinks, "Come on, come here," nature obliges. *Prakṛteḥ kriyamāṇāni guṇaiḥ karmāṇi sarvaśaḥ* [*Bhagavad-gītā* 3.27]: Nature is offering facility. God, Kṛṣṇa, is sitting in the heart of the living entity as Paramātmā, and He knows, "He wants this." So the Lord orders nature, "Give him this apartment," and nature obliges: "Yes, come on; here is your apartment." This is the real explanation.

Disciple: I understand and accept that. But I'm still puzzled as to why there is no geological evidence that in former times on this planet there were more complex forms.

Śrīla Prabhupāda: Why are you taking geological evidence as final? Is it final? Science is progressing. You cannot say it is final.

Disciple: But I have excavated all parts of the world, and every time—

Śrīla Prabhupāda: No. You have not excavated all parts of the world.

Disciple: Well, on seven continents.

Śrīla Prabhupāda: Seven continents is not the whole world. You say you have excavated the whole world, but we say no, not even an insignificant portion. So your knowledge is limited. Dr. Frog has examined his three-foot-wide well, and now he claims to know the ocean.

Experimental knowledge is always imperfect, because one experiments with imperfect senses. Therefore, scientific knowledge *must* be imperfect. Our source of knowledge is different. We do not depend on experimental knowledge.

Now you see no dinosaurs, nor have I seen all the 8,400,000 different forms of life. But my source of knowledge is different. You are an experimenter with imperfect senses. I have taken knowledge from the perfect person, who has seen everything, who knows everything. Therefore, my knowledge is perfect.

Say, for example, that I receive knowledge from my mother: "Here is your father." But you are trying to search out your father on your own. You don't go to your mother and ask; you just search and search. Therefore, no matter how much you search, your knowledge will always remain imperfect.

Disciple: And your knowledge says that millions of years ago there were higher forms of life on this planet.

Śrīla Prabhupāda: Oh, yes, because our Vedic information is that the first created being is the *most* intelligent person within the universe—Lord Brahmā, the cosmic engineer. So how can we accept your theory that intellect develops by evolution? We have received our Vedic knowledge from Brahmā, who is so perfect.

Dr. Frog has studied his three-foot well, his little reservoir of water. The Atlantic Ocean is also a reservoir of water, but there is a vast difference. Dr. Frog cannot inform us about the Atlantic Ocean. But we take knowledge from the one who has made the Atlantic Ocean. So our knowledge is perfect.

Disciple: But wouldn't there be evidence in the earth, some remains?

Śrīla Prabhupāda: Our evidence is intelligence, not stones and bones. Our evidence is intelligence. We get Vedic information by disciplic succession from the most intelligent. It is coming down by *śruti,* hearing. Vyāsadeva heard from Nārada, Nārada heard from Brahmā—millions and millions of years ago. Millions and billions of our years pass, and it is not even one day for Brahmā. So millions and millions of years are not very astonishing to us. But Brahmā was born of Kṛṣṇa, and intelligent philosophy has been existing in our universe from the date of Brahmā's birth. Brahmā was first educated by God, and His knowledge has been passed down to us in the Vedic literature. So we get such intelligent information in the *Vedas.*

But those so-called scientists and philosophers who do not follow this system of descending knowledge, who do not accept knowledge thus received from higher authorities—they can't have any perfect knowledge, no matter what research work they carry out with their blunt senses. So whatever they say, we take it as imperfect.

Our method is different from theirs. They are searching after dead bones, and we are searching after living brains. This point should be stressed. They are dealing with dead bones, and we are dealing with living brains. So which should be considered better?

Chapter TEN

MILL

The Briton John Stuart Mill (1806–1873) belonged to a school of philosophy called utilitarianism. An economist as well as a philosopher, Mill had a great impact on 19th-century British thought, not only in philosophy and economics but also in the areas of political science, logic, and ethics. His motto: "The greatest good for the greatest number." Here Śrīla Prabhupāda points out the glaring fallacy: Who's to say what "the greatest good" is?

Disciple: Mill claimed that the world, or nature, can be improved by man's efforts, but that perfection is not possible.
Śrīla Prabhupāda: In one sense, that is correct. This world is so made that although you make it perfect today, tomorrow it will deteriorate. Nonetheless, the world can be improved by Kṛṣṇa consciousness. You can better the world by bringing people to Kṛṣṇa consciousness and delivering the message of Kṛṣṇa to whomever you meet. That is the best social activity you can perform.
Disciple: The goal of the utilitarians was more specifically to

obtain whatever the people desire or require. Their motto is "The greatest good for the greatest number."

Śrīla Prabhupāda: The people desire happiness. The utilitarians try to give people artificial happiness, happiness separate from Kṛṣṇa, but we are trying to give direct happiness, happiness that is connected with Kṛṣṇa. If we purify our existence, we can attain eternal happiness, spiritual bliss. Everyone is working hard for happiness, but how can happiness be attained in a diseased condition? The material disease is an impediment to happiness. This disease has to be cured.

Disciple: Mill felt that virtues like courage, cleanliness, and self-control are not instinctive in man but have to be cultivated. In *Nature* he writes, "The truth is that there is hardly a single point of excellence belonging to human character which is not decidedly repugnant to the untutored feelings of human nature. . . ."

Śrīla Prabhupāda: Yes. Therefore there are educational systems in human society. Men should be educated according to the instructions given in the Vedic literatures. The *Bhagavad-gītā* is the grand summation of all Vedic literature, and therefore everyone should read it. But they should read it as it is, without interpretation.

Disciple: For Mill, there are several ways to ascertain knowledge. For instance, we can determine the cause and the effects of things by determining whether the phenomena under investigation have only one circumstance in common. If so, we can conclude that the circumstance alone is the cause of the effect.

Śrīla Prabhupāda: Certainly there is the natural law of cause and effect, but if we go further to determine the ultimate cause, we arrive at Lord Kṛṣṇa. Everything has an original cause. If you try to find out the original cause of all causes, that is called *darśana.* Therefore books of genuine philosophy are called *darśana-śāstra*. If we continue to search out the ultimate cause, we arrive at Kṛṣṇa, the original cause of everything.

Disciple: But what kind of test can we apply to phenomena to

find out the cause? How can we determine that God is the cause behind everything?
Śrīla Prabhupāda: For every phenomenon, there is a cause, and we know that God is the ultimate cause. Mill may give many methods for studying immediate causes, but we are interested in the ultimate cause of everything. The ultimate cause has full independence to do anything and everything beyond our calculation. Everything that we see is but an effect of His original push.
Disciple: If we see rain falling and want to prove that God is the cause of rain, what test can we apply?
Śrīla Prabhupāda: The *śāstras,* the Vedic literatures. We are advised to see through the *śāstras* because we cannot see directly. Since our senses are defective, direct perception has no value. Therefore we have to receive knowledge through authoritative instruction.
Disciple: In other words, when we see an apple fall from a tree, we have to see through the eyes of the *śāstras* in order to see God in that act?
Śrīla Prabhupāda: God has made His laws so perfect that one cause effects one thing, and that in turn effects another, and so on. We may see an apple grow and explain it as "nature," but this nature is working according to certain laws. An apple has a certain color and taste because it grows according to specific laws set down by Kṛṣṇa. Kṛṣṇa's energies are perfect and are working perfectly. Everything is being carried out under systematic laws, although we may not perceive how these laws are working.
Disciple: Scientists admit that nothing can come out of nothing.
Śrīla Prabhupāda: If something emerges, there must be a cause in the background. We say that the root cause of everything is the Supreme Brahman, the Absolute Truth, or the Supreme Personality of Godhead.
Disciple: Mill would certainly not agree that God is the cause of everything, because one of the things we see in this world is evil, and he considered God to be at war with it. Man's role,

he thought, is to help God end this war. He writes: "If Providence is omnipotent, Providence intends whatever happens, and the fact of its happening proves that Providence intended it. If so, everything which a human being can do is predestined by Providence and is a fulfillment of its designs. But if, as is the more religious theory, Providence intends not all which happens, but only what is good, then indeed man has it in his power, by his voluntary actions, to aid the intentions of Providence."

Śrīla Prabhupāda: Providence desires only the good. The living entity is in this material world due to the improper utilization of his will. Because the living entity wants to enjoy this material world, God is so kind that He gives him facilities and directions. When a child wants to play in a certain way, he is guided by some nurse or servant hired by the parents. Our position is something like that. We have given up the company of God to come to this material world to enjoy ourselves. So God has allowed us to come here, saying, "All right, enjoy this experience, and when you understand that this material enjoyment is ultimately frustrating, you can come back." Thus the Supreme Lord is guiding the enjoyment of all living beings, especially human beings, so that they may return home, back to Godhead. Nature is the agent acting under the instructions of God. If the living entity is overly addicted to misusing his freedom, he is punished. This punishment is a consequence of the living entity's desire. God does not want a human being to become a village hog, but when one develops such a mentality by eating anything and everything, God gives the facility by providing the body of a hog so that he can even eat stool. God is situated in everyone's heart and is noting the desires of the living entity from within. According to one's desires, God orders material nature to provide a particular body. In this way one continues transmigrating from body to body, in various species of life.

Disciple: Mill further writes: "Limited as, on this showing, the divine power must be by inscrutable but insurmountable obstacles, who knows what man could have been created without desires which never are to be, and even which never ought to be, fulfilled?" Thus Mill concludes that the existence of evil, or pain and death, excludes the existence of an omnipotent God. He sees man in a position to "aid the intentions of Providence" by surmounting his evil instincts. God is not infinite in His power, because if He were, there would be no evil.

Śrīla Prabhupāda: Evil is undoubtedly created by God, but this was necessary due to the human being's misuse of his free will. God gives man good directions, but when man is disobedient, evil is naturally there to punish him. Evil is not desired by God, yet it is created because it is necessary. The government constructs prisons not because it wants to but because they are necessary. The government prefers to construct universities so that people can attain an education and become highly enlightened. But because some people misuse their independence and violate the state laws, prisons are necessary. We suffer due to our own evil activities. Thus God, being supreme, punishes us. When we are under the protection of God, nothing is evil; everything is good. God does not desire to create evil, but man's evil activities provoke God to create an evil situation.

Disciple: In the Judeo-Christian tradition, God is at war with Satan. In the Vedic literatures, there are also wars between the demigods and the demons, as well as between Kṛṣṇa and the demons, but these wars do not seem to be taken as serious confrontations between God and His enemies. Isn't Kṛṣṇa's mood always playful?

Śrīla Prabhupāda: Since Kṛṣṇa is all-powerful, when He is fighting with demons He is actually playing. This fighting does not affect His energy. It is like a father fighting with his small child. The father may seem to be fighting seriously, but he is only playing: one slap is sufficient to subdue the child. Similarly, Kṛṣṇa sometimes plays by giving the demons a chance to fight Him, but one strong slap is sufficient to end the fight. There is no question of fighting with God on an equal level. He is omnipotent. However, when a living entity is disobedient and harasses the devotees, God kills him. When Kṛṣṇa descends on this earth, He chastises the demons and protects His devotees (*paritrāṇāya sādhūnāṁ vināśāya ca duṣkṛtām*). Whenever there is a fight between the demons and the demigods, God takes the side of the demigods.

Disciple: Mill saw it more like an actual struggle between God and Satan, or evil.

Śrīla Prabhupāda: There is a struggle because the demons are always transgressing God's rules. A demon is one who rejects God's rules, and a demigod is one who accepts them. That is the main difference, as stated in the *śāstras.*

Disciple: But Mill pictures God Himself as struggling hard in the fight to conquer the demons.

Śrīla Prabhupāda: God has no reason to struggle. According to the *Vedas,* He is so powerful that He has nothing to strive for (*na tasya kāryaṁ karaṇaṁ ca vidyate*). Just as a king may have many servants, ministers, and soldiers to carry out his desires, Kṛṣṇa has many energies that act according to His order. Kṛṣṇa Himself has nothing to do but play on His flute and enjoy Himself. That is why the *Vedas* declare, *ānanda-mayo 'bhyāsāt:* "God is always blissful."

So, God has no reason to struggle for anything because nobody is equal to or greater than Him (*na tat-samaś cābhyadikaś ca dṛśyate*). But if God is not working hard, then how are things happening? *Parāsya śaktir vividhaiva śrūyate:* Through the agency of God's multi-energies everything is going on systematically and naturally (*svābhāvikī jñāna-bala-kriyā ca*). For example, by God's order the sun rises in the morning, exactly on time. So although God is enjoying Himself, the universe is going on according to His orders. There is no question of God struggling against evil. His various agents can kill all the evil elements in the world easily enough.

Disciple: Mill believed that God is good, but that He is involved in a world not of His own making.

Śrīla Prabhupāda: Is God to be judged by Mr. Mill? God is good, but not as good as Mr. Mill thinks He ought to be? Is this his opinion of God? Is God good in all conditions? Or is God only good when Mr. Mill considers Him good? What is God's position?

Disciple: Mill says that the presence of evil indicates that if God were all-powerful, He would not be completely good.

Śrīla Prabhupāda: Therefore God has to depend on the opinion of Mr. Mill. Is it that Mr. Mill does not approve of all God's activities?

Disciple: He maintains that God is good but that He is limited in His power. If His power were absolute, everything would be good.

Śrīla Prabhupāda: How nonsensical! Everything *is* good! That is our philosophy. When God kills a demon, immediately flowers are showered from the sky. Whatever God does is good. Kṛṣṇa danced with other men's wives in the dead of night, and this activity is worshiped as the *rāsa-līlā.* However, if an ordinary man does this, he is immediately condemned as a debauchee. In all circumstances, God is good and worshipable. It is not that we subject God to our judgment, saying, "Oh yes, You are good, but not so good." Fools think, "I am better than God. I can create my own God." God creates us; we cannot create God. Unfortunately, Mill did not know what is evil and what is good. He should have known that whatever is created by God is good, even if it appears to be evil to us. We may think that such-and-such is evil, but actually it is good. If we do not know how it is good, that is our fault. God cannot be placed under our judgment. In all circumstances, God is good.

Disciple: Mill was particularly interested in the role of authority. In *Utility of Religion,* he writes, "Consider the enormous influence of authority on the human mind. . . . Authority is the evidence on which the mass of mankind believe everything which they are said to know except facts of which their own senses have taken cognizance. It is the evidence on which even the wisest receive all those truths of science, or facts in history or in life, of which they have not personally examined the proofs."

Śrīla Prabhupāda: You can neither defy nor deny real authority.

We are presenting our Kṛṣṇa consciousness movement on this principle. We should carry out the orders of the authority, and Kṛṣṇa, or God, is the supreme authority. Whatever He says must be accepted without interpretation. In this way, everyone can be happy. Those who are sane do not hesitate to accept God's authority, and they become happy abiding by His orders. Those who exactly follow the instructions of the supreme authority are also authorities. The spiritual master is the authoritative servant, and God is the authoritative master. If we follow the instructions of the authoritative servant, we in turn become authoritative servants of the spiritual master.

Disciple: Concerning morality, Mill writes: "Belief, then, in the supernatural, great as are the services which it rendered in the earlier stages of human development, cannot be considered to be any longer required either for enabling us to know what is right and wrong in social morality, or for supplying us with motives to do right and to abstain from wrong."

Śrīla Prabhupāda: Morality means abiding by the orders of God. That is real morality. Other moralities are manufactured, and they differ in different countries. Religion and real morality, however, function according to the same principle. Religion means carrying out the orders of God, and morality means following those principles whereby we can fulfill the desires of God. Before the Battle of Kurukṣetra, Arjuna considered killing to be immoral, but when he understood from the instructions of Kṛṣṇa that the fight was necessary, he decided to carry out his duty as a *kṣatriya.* So this is morality. Ultimately, morality means carrying out the desires of God.

Disciple: For Mill, there are two moral sanctions of conduct. One is internal, which is our conscience and sense of duty.

Śrīla Prabhupāda: What does he mean by conscience? A sense of duty is different from the conscience. It is our duty to receive instructions from higher personalities. If we do not, how can we know our duty?

Disciple: Mill felt that our duty is that which produces the most good for the most people.

Śrīla Prabhupāda: That is all so vague. What if everyone wants to take drugs? Is it our duty to help them? How can a rascal understand what his duty is? One has to be trained to know.

Disciple: Mill would say that there is a rational or guiding principle for action, and this is the golden rule of the Christians: "Do unto others as you would have them do unto you."

Śrīla Prabhupāda: This means that you have to approach Christ. You cannot manufacture golden rules yourself. You have to abide by the orders of Christ, and that means approaching a superior authority.

Disciple: The second sanction of moral conduct is external: the fear of displeasing other men or God. We hope to win favor through acting morally.

Śrīla Prabhupāda: This also means accepting authority. Therefore the *Vedas* tell us that if we want to be really learned, we must approach a guru. Did John Stuart Mill have a guru?

Disciple: His father, James Mill, was also a great philosopher.

Śrīla Prabhupāda: In any case, we must accept some authority, be it Christ or Kṛṣṇa. Our duty lies in following the orders of the higher authority. Of course, we accept Kṛṣṇa, the Supreme Personality of Godhead, as our authority.

Disciple: Mill himself rejected many basic Christian tenets, and he even believed that there is no intrinsic value in the belief in the immortality of the soul. He writes: "Those who believe in the immortality of the soul generally quit life with fully as much if not more reluctance as those who have no such expectation."

Śrīla Prabhupāda: We have daily experience of how the soul continues, even though the body changes. In our own family we can see that the body of an infant changes into the body of a boy, a young man, a middle-aged man, and then an old man. In any condition, the soul is the same. Why is it difficult to understand the immortality of the soul? If we cannot understand it, we are not very intelligent.

yasyātma-buddhiḥ kuṇape tri-dhātuke
sva-dhīḥ kalatrādiṣu bhauma ijya-dhīḥ
yat-tīrtha-buddhiḥ salile na karhicij
janeṣv abhijñeṣu sa eva go-kharaḥ

"A human being who identifies this body made of three elements with his self, who considers the by-products of the body to be his kinsmen, who considers the land of his birth worshipable, and who goes to a place of pilgrimage simply to take a bath rather than meet men of transcendental knowledge there, is to be considered like an ass or a cow." [*Bhāg.* 10.84.13] If a person does not understand the immortality of the soul, he is an animal. There is no question of belief. It is a fact. If a man says, "I don't believe I will grow old," he is ignorant of the facts. If he does not die when he is young, he necessarily grows old. This is a question of common sense, not of beliefs. In the *Bhagavad-gītā* [2.12] Kṛṣṇa says that there was never a time when we did not exist nor will there ever be a time when we will cease to exist. The soul is immortal; he never takes birth and he never dies. This is the beginning of knowledge. First of all, we must understand what we are. If we do not, we will surely be wrongly directed. We will take care of the body just as a foolish man might take care of a bird cage and neglect the bird within it.

Disciple: Mill was not only a utilitarian but a humanist, and he felt that a humanistic religion can have a greater beneficial effect than a supernatural religion. A humanistic religion would foster unselfish feelings and would have man at the center.

Śrīla Prabhupāda: Without God, how can it be a religion? As I have already explained, religion means carrying out the orders of God.

Disciple: Concerning immortality, Mill asserts that there is no evidence for the immortality of the soul, and none against it.

Śrīla Prabhupāda: What does he need to be convinced? There is a great deal of evidence. It is mankind's misfortune that a person like Mill cannot understand a simple truth that even a child can understand.

Disciple: Ultimately, Mill considered the whole domain of the supernatural to be removed from the region of belief into that of simple hope.
Śrīla Prabhupāda: It is neither hope nor belief, but a fact. At any rate, to those who are Kṛṣṇa conscious, it is a fact. Kṛṣṇa came and gave Arjuna instructions, and those instructions are recorded.
Disciple: Mill was such a staunch humanist that he wrote: "I will call no being good who is not what I mean when I apply that epithet to my fellow creatures, and if such a being can sentence me to hell for not so calling him, to hell I will go."
Śrīla Prabhupāda: God is always good, and if one does not know the goodness of God, he is imperfect. According to all Vedic literatures, God is always good and always great. What does Mill consider to be a good man?
Disciple: One who works for what he calls "the greatest happiness principle," that is, the greatest happiness for everyone on earth.
Śrīla Prabhupāda: Can any man do good for all?
Disciple: Christ said that no man is good, that there is only one good, and that is God.
Śrīla Prabhupāda: Yes, that is a fact. You may think that such-and-such man is good, but he is limited in his power. He may still think in terms of his nation or society. Only a pure devotee of Kṛṣṇa can be good because he abides by the order of the Supreme Good. Even if one has the desire to be a good man, it is not possible independent of God. In any case, these are all mental concoctions: good and bad. One who is not God conscious is necessarily bad, and one who is God conscious is good. This should be the only criterion.
Disciple: But what of Mill's contention that the good gives the greatest pleasure to the greatest number of people?
Śrīla Prabhupāda: And what if the people are fools and rascals? The greatest number of people may say that cigarettes are very nice, but does this mean that they are desirable?
Disciple: Mill distinguishes between the quality and the quantity of pleasure. Certain pleasures are superior to others.

Śrīla Prabhupāda: When you have quality, the quantity naturally decreases. For instance, ordinary people take pleasure in eating, sleeping, mating, drinking, smoking, and so on. The pleasure of Kṛṣṇa consciousness is a transcendental pleasure, but the people who take to it are very few. Generally, since conditioned souls are fools, the pleasure that is most popular is the one followed by the greatest number of fools. According to our Vedic philosophy, man is born a fool, but he can be made intelligent through education and culture.
Disciple: Mill advocated utilizing those principles that can give the pleasure of highest quality to the maximum people. He also wrote: "It is better to be a human being dissatisfied than a pig satisfied. It is better to be Socrates dissatisfied than a fool satisfied."
Śrīla Prabhupāda: But how often will you find a Socrates? You cannot find Socrates loitering on every street. There will only be one in millions. There is no question of the maximum number of people enjoying pleasure as Socrates did. Men of Socrates' caliber are a minimum. In the *Bhagavad-gītā* [7.3] Kṛṣṇa says,

manuṣyāṇāṁ sahasreṣu kaścid yatati siddhaye
yatatām api siddhānāṁ kaścin māṁ vetti tattvataḥ

"Out of many thousands of men, one may endeavor for perfection, and of those who have achieved perfection, hardly one knows Me in truth." This is not a question of quantity, but of quality.
Disciple: Mill felt that the highest quality of pleasure might also be enjoyed by a larger number. All men should be trained to find pleasure according to this higher standard.
Śrīla Prabhupāda: This means that the maximum pleasure should be introduced to the maximum number of people. Unfortunately, it is not accepted by the greatest number but only by a few. The Kṛṣṇa consciousness movement, for instance, cannot be understood by the masses. Only a few who are fortunate can understand. There may be millions of stars

in the sky, but there is only one moon, and that is sufficient to drive away the darkness. It is not possible to have many moons, although there may be many glowworms.
Disciple: Mill was trying to ascertain that standard of pleasure which is most desirable.
Śrīla Prabhupāda: That he does not know. That he has to learn from the devotees of Kṛṣṇa. Ordinary men take sex to be the highest pleasure, and the entire material world is existing because of sex, but how long does this sex pleasure last? Only a few minutes. A wise man wants pleasure that doesn't end in only a few minutes but that continues perpetually. As Kṛṣṇa says in the *Bhagavad-gītā* [5.21–22]:

bāhya-sparśeṣv asaktātmā vindaty ātmani yat sukham
sa brahma-yoga-yuktātmā sukham akṣayam aśnute

ye hi saṁsparśa-jā bhogā duḥkha-yonaya eva te
ādy-antavantaḥ kaunteya na teṣu ramate budhaḥ

Here the word *akṣayam* means "eternal," and *sukham* means "pleasure." Here Kṛṣṇa states that those who are intelligent are not interested in transient pleasure but in eternal pleasure. They know their constitutional position; they know they are not the body. The pleasures of the body are transient and are sought by rascals. If one identifies with the body, he naturally seeks bodily pleasure. One who knows that he is not the body but eternal spirit soul seeks eternal spiritual pleasure through *bhakti-yoga*.
Disciple: Mill believed that a small amount of a higher type of pleasure is superior to a greater amount of a lower type.
Śrīla Prabhupāda: Yes, that is our philosophy. In the *Bhagavad-gītā* [2.40] Kṛṣṇa says:

nehābhikrama-nāśo 'sti pratyavāyo na vidyate
sv-alpam apy asya dharmasya trāyate mahato bhayāt

"In *bhakti-yoga* there is no loss or diminution, and a little advancement on this path can protect one from the most dangerous type of fear." Even if one falls down from Kṛṣṇa consciousness, he still gains from what little he has experienced. On the other hand, if one works very hard but does not take to devotional service, all his labors go in vain. There are many students who come to Kṛṣṇa consciousness for a few days and then go away, but they return again because the quality is so great. Kṛṣṇa consciousness is so potent. Except for Kṛṣṇa consciousness, everything is being dissipated by time. Everything in this world is transient, but because we are eternal spirit souls, we should accept only that which has permanent value. It is foolishness to be satisfied with anything else.

Chapter ELEVEN

MARX

With his Communist Manifesto—beginning with the ominous "A specter is haunting Europe—the specter of communism" and ending with the clarion call "Workers of the world, unite!"—the German philosopher Karl Marx (1818–1883) launched the communist movement. In the following dialogue, Śrīla Prabhupāda focuses on why those who have tried to put Marx's philosophy into practice have been frustrated in their attempts to eradicate greed from human nature and society at large.

Disciple: Karl Marx contended that philosophers have only interpreted the world; the point is to change it. His philosophy is often called "dialectical materialism" because it comes from the dialectic of George Hegel—thesis, antithesis, and synthesis. When applied to society, his philosophy is known as communism. His idea is that for many generations the bourgeoisie have competed with the proletariat, and that this conflict will terminate in the communist society. In other words, the workers will overthrow the capitalistic class and establish a so-called dictatorship of the proletariat, which will finally become a classless society.

Śrīla Prabhupāda: But how is a classless society possible? Men naturally fall into different classes. Your nature is different from mine, so how can we artificially be brought to the same level?

Disciple: His idea is that human nature, or ideas, are molded by the means of production. Therefore everyone can be trained to participate in the classless society.

Śrīla Prabhupāda: Then training is required?

Disciple: Yes.

Śrīla Prabhupāda: And what will be the center of training for this classless society? What will be the motto?

Disciple: The motto is "From each according to his ability, to each according to his need." The idea is that everyone would contribute something, and everyone would get what he needed.

Śrīla Prabhupāda: But everyone's contribution is different. A scientific man contributes something, and a philosopher contributes something else. The cow contributes milk, and the dog contributes service as a watchdog. Even the trees, the birds, the beasts—everyone is contributing something. So, by nature a reciprocal arrangement is already there among social classes. How can there be a classless society?

Disciple: Well, Marx's idea is that the means of production will be owned in common. No one would have an advantage over anyone else, and thus one person could not exploit another. Marx is thinking in terms of profit.

Śrīla Prabhupāda: First we must know what profit actually is. For example, the American hippies already had "profit." They were from the best homes, their fathers were rich—they had everything. Yet they were not satisfied; they rejected it. No, this idea of a classless society based on profit-sharing is imperfect. Besides, the communists have not created a classless society. We have seen in Moscow how a poor woman will wash the streets while her boss sits comfortably in his car. So where is the classless society? As long as society is maintained, there must be some higher and lower classification. But if the central point of society is one, then whether one works in a lower or a higher position, he doesn't care. For example, our body has different parts—the head, the legs, the hands—but everything works for the stomach.

Disciple: Actually, the Russians supposedly have the same idea: they claim the common worker is just as glorious as the top scientist or manager.

Śrīla Prabhupāda: But in Moscow we have seen that not everyone is satisfied. One boy who came to us was very unhappy because in Russia young boys are not allowed to go out at night.

Disciple: The Russian authorities would say that he has an improper understanding of Marxist philosophy.

Śrīla Prabhupāda: That "improper understanding" is inevitable. They will never be able to create a classless society because, as I have already explained, everyone's mentality is different.

Disciple: Marx says that if everyone is engaged according to his abilities in a certain type of production, and everyone works for the central interest, then everyone's ideas will become uniform.

Śrīla Prabhupāda: Therefore we must find out the real central interest. In our International Society for Krishna Consciousness, everyone has a central interest in Kṛṣṇa. Therefore one person is speaking, another is typing, another is going to the press or washing dishes, and no one is grudging, because they are all convinced they are serving Kṛṣṇa.

Disciple: Marx's idea is that the center is the state.

Śrīla Prabhupāda: But the state cannot be perfect. If the Russian state is perfect, then why was Khrushchev driven from power? He was elected premier. Why was he driven from power?

Disciple: Because he was not fulfilling the aims of the people.

Śrīla Prabhupāda: Well, then, what is the guarantee the next premier will do that? There is no guarantee. The same thing will happen again and again. Because the center, Khrushchev, was imperfect, people begrudged their labor. The same thing is going on in noncommunist countries as well. The government is changed, the prime minister is deposed, the president is impeached. So what is the real difference between Russian communism and other political systems? What is happening in other countries is also happening in Russia, only they call it by a different name. When we talked with Professor Kotovsky of Moscow University, we told him he had to surrender: either he must surrender to Kṛṣṇa or to Lenin, but he must surrender. He was taken aback at this.

Disciple: From studying history, Marx concluded that the characteristics of culture, the social structure, and even the thoughts of the people are determined by the means of economic production.

Śrīla Prabhupāda: How does he account for all the social disruption in countries like America, which is so advanced in economic production?

Disciple: He says that capitalism is a decadent form of economic production because it relies on the exploitation of one class by another.

Śrīla Prabhupāda: But there is exploitation in the communist countries also. Khrushchev was driven out of power because he was exploiting his position. He was giving big government posts to his son and son-in-law.

Disciple: He was deviating from the doctrine.

Śrīla Prabhupāda: But since any leader can deviate, how will perfection come? First the person in the center must be perfect; then his dictations will be correct. Otherwise, if the leaders are all imperfect men, what is the use of changing this or that? The corruption will continue.

Disciple: Presumably the perfect leader would be the one who practiced Marx's philosophy without deviation.

Śrīla Prabhupāda: But Marx's philosophy is also imperfect! His proposal for a classless society is unworkable. There must be one class of men to administer the government and one class of men to sweep the streets. How can there be a

His Divine Grace A. C. Bhaktivedanta Swami Prabhupāda

*The Founder-*Ācārya *of the International Society for Krishna Consciousness and the greatest exponent of Kṛṣṇa consciousness in the modern world.*

PLATE ONE: Lord Caitanya (center), accompanied by His plenary expansion Nityānanda Prabhu (to Lord Caitanya's right), His incarnation Advaita Prabhu (to Nityānanda's right), His internal energy Gadādhara Paṇḍita (to Lord Caitanya's left), and His pure devotee Śrīvāsa Ṭhākura. Together they spread love of Godhead through the chanting of the Hare Kṛṣṇa mantra.

PLATE TWO: When we practice the yoga of devotion in full consciousness of Lord Kṛṣṇa, He reveals Himself in all His glory, dispelling all doubts. Here He reveals His universal form to Arjuna. (*p.* 24)

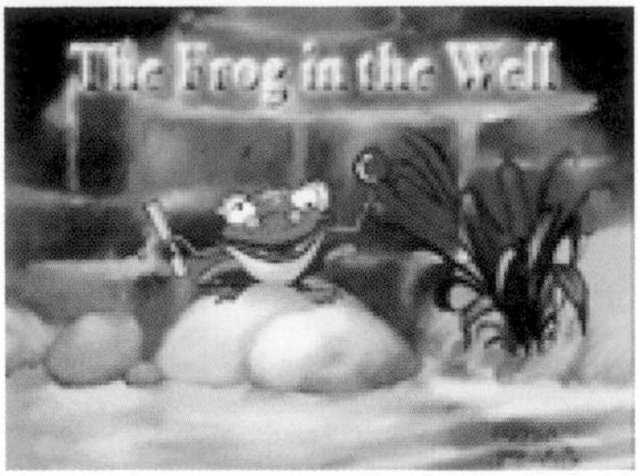
The Frog in the Well

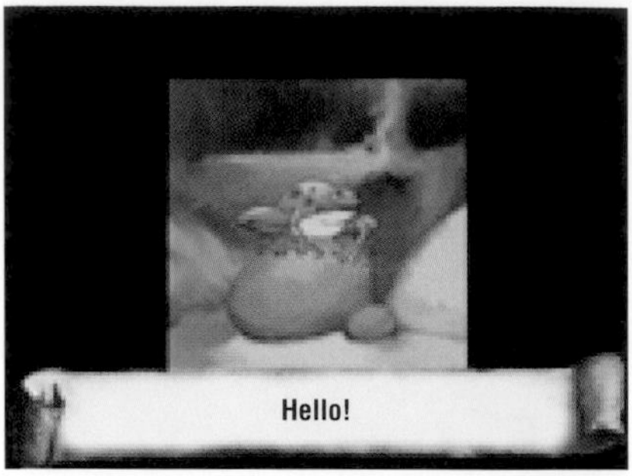
Hello!

Uhhh! Where did you come from?

I came from the ocean.

It's much bigger than your well.

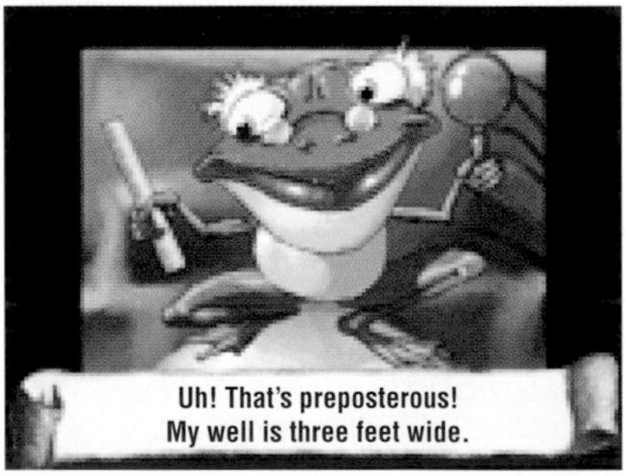
Uh! That's preposterous!
My well is three feet wide.

You don't understand.

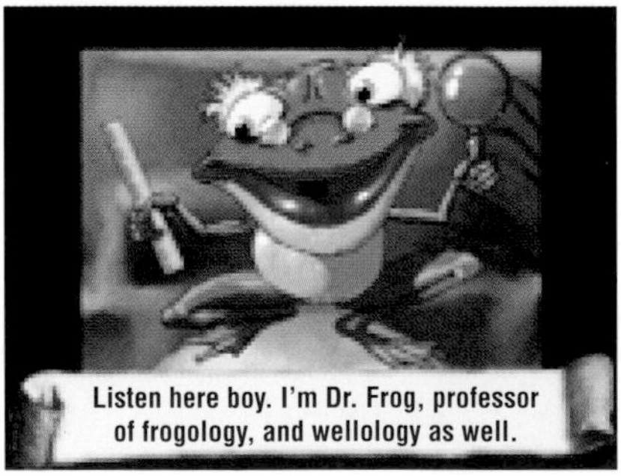
Listen here boy. I'm Dr. Frog, professor
of frogology, and wellology as well.

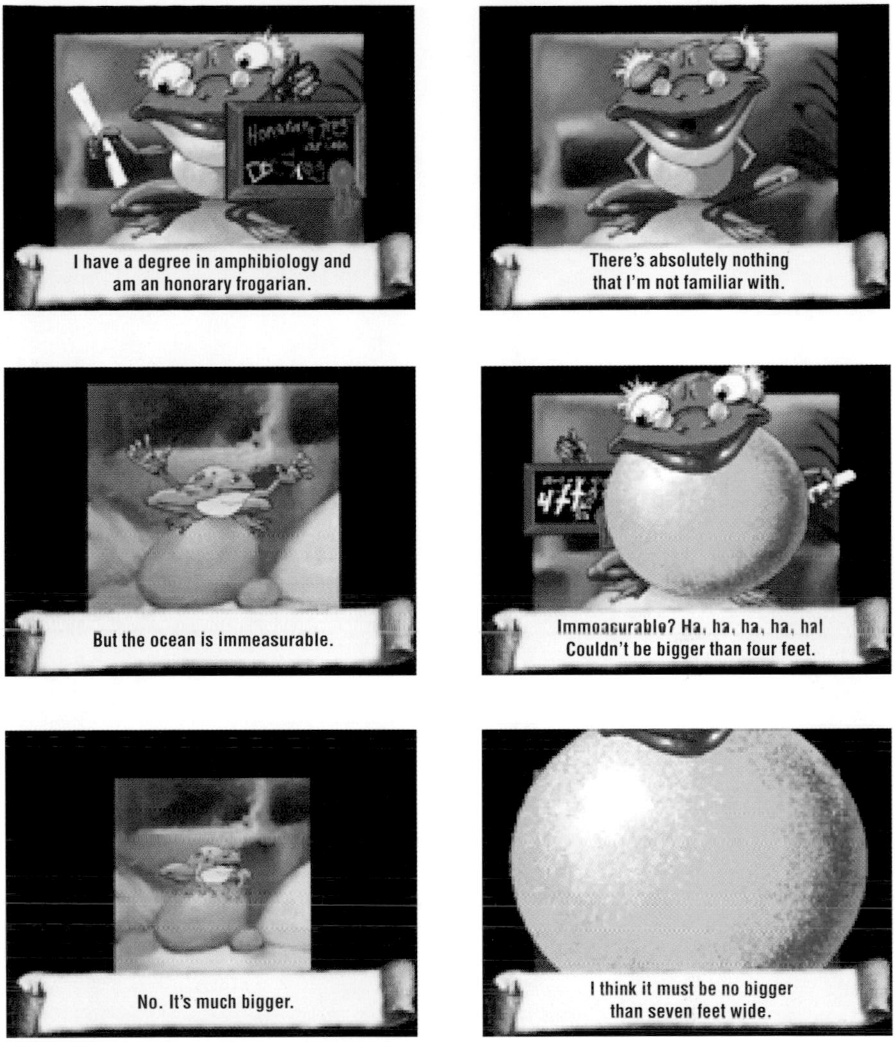

I have a degree in amphibiology and am an honorary frogarian.
There's absolutely nothing that I'm not familiar with.
But the ocean is immeasurable.
Immeasurable? Ha, ha, ha, ha, ha! Couldn't be bigger than four feet.
No. It's much bigger.
I think it must be no bigger than seven feet wide.

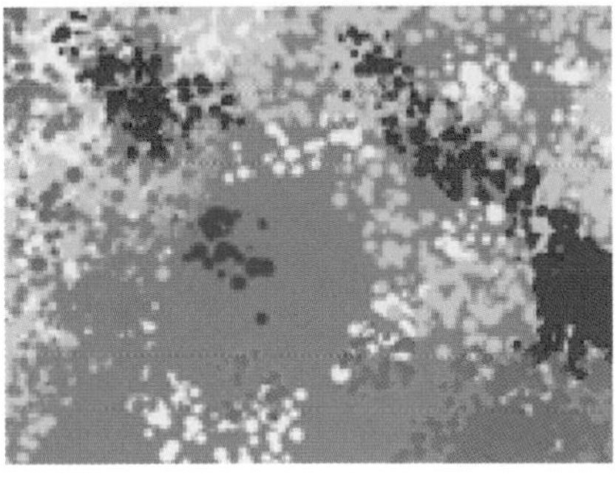

PLATE THREE: Our material senses and mind are woefully inadequate for perceiving or understanding the Supreme Lord, whose qualities are infinite in their magnitude and variety. The effort to do so is ludicrous, like the well-bound Dr. Frog's effort to comprehend the size of the ocean. (*p.* 22)

PLATE FOUR: Knowledge of the science of God, originating with Lord Kṛṣṇa, has been passed down unchanged through a chain of spiritual masters since the beginning of time. There is no need to change it or speculate about it. It is perfect knowledge. (*p.* ix)

PLATE FIVE: The barbarous practice of slaughtering and eating animals results in great suffering. The infallible law of karma decrees that whoever is responsible—the slaughterer, the consumer, the preparer, and the facilitator—must all suffer the same fate in a future life. (*p.* 15)

PLATE SIX: God is the reservoir of everything, and therefore whatever we see that is beautiful emanates from a very minute part of God's beauty. (*p.* 63)

classless society? Why should a sweeper be satisfied seeing someone else in the administrative post? He will think, "He is forcing me to work as a sweeper in the street while he sits comfortably in a chair." In our International Society, I am also holding the superior post: I am sitting in a chair, and you are offering me garlands and the best food. Why? *Because you see a perfect man whom you can follow.* That mentality must be there. Everyone in the society must be able to say, "Yes, here is a perfect man. Let him sit in a chair, and let us all bow down and work like menials." Where is that perfect man in the communist countries?

Disciple: The Russians claim that Lenin is a perfect man.

Śrīla Prabhupāda: Lenin? But no one is following Lenin. Lenin's only perfection was that he overthrew the czar's government. What other perfection did he show? The people are not happy simply reading Lenin's books. I studied the people in Moscow. They are unhappy. The government cannot force them to be happy artificially. Unless there is a perfect, ideal man in the center, there cannot possibly be a classless society.

Disciple: Perhaps they see the workers and the managers in the same way that we do—in the absolute sense. Since everyone is serving the state, the sweeper is as good as the administrator.

Śrīla Prabhupāda: But unless the state gives perfect satisfaction to the people, there will always be distinctions between higher and lower classes. In the Russian state, that sense of perfection in the center is lacking.

Disciple: Their goal is the production of material goods for the enhancement of human well-being.

Śrīla Prabhupāda: That is useless! Economic production in America has no comparison in the world, yet still people are dissatisfied. The young men are confused. It is nonsensical to think that simply by increasing production everyone will become satisfied. No one will be satisfied. Man is not meant simply for eating. He has mental necessities, intellectual necessities, spiritual necessities. In India many people sit alone silently in the jungle and practice yoga. They do not require anything. How will increased production satisfy them? If someone were to say to them, "If you give up this yoga practice, I will give you two hundred bags of rice," they would laugh at the proposal. It is animalistic to think that simply by increasing production everyone will become satisfied. Real happiness does not depend on either production or starvation, but upon peace of mind. For example, if a child is crying but the mother does not know why, the child will not stop simply by giving him some milk. Sometimes this actually happens: the mother cannot understand why her child is crying, and though she is giving him her breast, he continues to cry. Similarly, dissatisfaction in human society is not caused solely by low economic production. That is nonsense. There are many causes of dissatisfaction. The practical example is America, where there is sufficient production of everything, yet the young men are becoming hippies. They are dissatisfied, confused. No, simply by increasing economic production people will not become satisfied. Marx's knowledge is insufficient. Perhaps because he came from a country with many poor people, he had that idea.

Disciple: Yes, now we've seen that production of material goods alone will not make people happy.

Śrīla Prabhupāda: Because they do not know that real happiness comes from spiritual understanding. That understanding is given in the *Bhagavad-gītā:* God is the supreme enjoyer, and He is the proprietor of everything. We are not actually enjoyers; we are all workers. These two things must be there: an enjoyer and a worker. For example, in our body the stomach is the enjoyer and all other parts of the body are workers. So this system is natural: there must always be someone who is the enjoyer and someone who is the worker. It is present in the capitalist system also. In Russia there is always conflict between the managers and the workers. The workers say, "If this is a classless society, why is that man sitting comfortably and ordering us to work?" The Russians have not been able to avoid this dilemma, and it cannot be avoided. There *must* be one class of men who are the directors or enjoyers and another class of men who are the workers. Therefore the only way to have a truly classless society is to find that method by which both the managers and the workers will feel equal happiness. For example, if the stomach is hungry and the eyes see some food, immediately the brain will say, "O legs, please go there!" and "Hand, pick it up," and "Now please put it into the mouth." Immediately the food goes into the stomach, and as soon as the stomach is satisfied, the eyes are satisfied, the legs are satisfied, and the hand is satisfied.

Disciple: But Marx would use this as a perfect example of communism.

Śrīla Prabhupāda: But he has neglected to find out the real stomach.

Disciple: His is the material stomach.

Śrīla Prabhupāda: But the material stomach is always hungry again; it can never be satisfied. In the Kṛṣṇa consciousness movement we have the substance for feeding our brains, our minds, and our souls. *Yasya prasādād bhagavat-prasādaḥ.* If the spiritual master is satisfied, then Kṛṣṇa is satisfied, and if Kṛṣṇa is satisfied, then everyone is satisfied. Therefore you are all trying to satisfy your spiritual master. Similarly, if the communist countries can come up with a dictator who, if satisfied, automatically gives satisfaction to all the people, then we will accept such a classless society. But this is impossible. A classless society is possible only when Kṛṣṇa is in the center. For the satisfaction of Kṛṣṇa, the intellectual can work in his own way, the administrator can work in his way, the merchant can work in his way, and the laborer can work in his way—and they can all be perfectly satisfied in their own position. This is truly a classless society.

Disciple: How is this different from the communist country, where all sorts of men contribute for the same central purpose, which is the state?

Śrīla Prabhupāda: The difference is that if the state is not perfect, no one will willingly contribute to it. They may be forced to contribute, but they will not voluntarily contribute unless there is a perfect state in the center. For example, the hands,

legs, and brain are working in perfect harmony for the satisfaction of the stomach. Why? Because they know without a doubt that by satisfying the stomach they will all share the energy and also be satisfied. Therefore, unless the people have this kind of perfect faith in the leader of the country, there is no possibility of a classless society.
Disciple: The communists theorize that if the worker contributes everything to the central fund, he will get complete satisfaction in return.
Śrīla Prabhupāda: Yes, but if he sees imperfection in the center, he will not work enthusiastically because he will have no faith that he will get full satisfaction. That perfection of the state will never be there, and therefore the workers will always remain dissatisfied.
Disciple: The propagandists play upon this dissatisfaction and tell the people that foreigners are causing it.
Śrīla Prabhupāda: But if the people were truly satisfied, they could not be influenced by outsiders. If you are satisfied that your spiritual master is perfect—that he is guiding you nicely—will you be influenced by outsiders?
Disciple: No.
Śrīla Prabhupāda: Because the communist state will never be perfect, there is no possibility of a classless society.
Disciple: Marx examines history and sees that in Greek times, in Roman times, and in the Middle Ages slaves were always required for production.
Śrīla Prabhupāda: The Russians are also creating slaves—the working class. Joseph Stalin stayed in power simply by killing all his enemies. He killed so many men that he is recorded in history as the greatest criminal. He was certainly imperfect, yet he held the position of dictator, and the people were forced to obey him.
Disciple: His successors have denounced him.
Śrīla Prabhupāda: That's all well and good, but his successors should also be denounced. The point is that in any society there must be a leader, there must be directors, and there must be workers, but everyone should be so satisfied in

performing their duties that they forget the difference.
Disciple: No envy.
Śrīla Prabhupāda: Ah, no envy. But that perfection is not possible in the material world. Therefore Marx's theories are useless.
Disciple: But on the other hand, we see that the capitalists also make slaves of their workers.
Śrīla Prabhupāda: Wherever there is materialistic activity, there must be imperfection. But if they make Kṛṣṇa the center, then all problems will be resolved.
Disciple: Are you saying that any materialistic system of organizing the means of production is bound to be full of exploitation?
Śrīla Prabhupāda: Yes, certainly, certainly! The materialistic mentality *means* exploitation.
Disciple: Then what is the solution?
Śrīla Prabhupāda: Kṛṣṇa consciousness!
Disciple: How is that?
Śrīla Prabhupāda: Just make Kṛṣṇa the center and work for Him. Then everyone will be satisfied. As it is stated in the *Śrīmad-Bhāgavatam* [4.31.14]:

yathā taror mūla-niṣecanena
tṛpyanti tat-skandha-bhujopaśākhāḥ
prāṇopahārāc ca yathendriyāṇāṁ
tathaiva sarvārhaṇam acyutejyā

If you simply pour water on the root of a tree, all the branches, twigs, leaves, and flowers will be nourished. Similarly, everyone can be satisfied simply by *acyutejyā. Acyuta* means Kṛṣṇa, and *ijyā* means worship. So this is the formula for a classless society: Make Kṛṣṇa the center and do everything for Him. There are no classes in our International Society for Krishna Consciousness. Now you are writing philosophy, but if I want you to wash dishes, you will do so immediately because you know that whatever you do, you are working for Kṛṣṇa and for your spiritual master. In the material world different kinds of work have different values, but in Kṛṣṇa consciousness everything is done on the absolute platform. Whether you wash dishes or write books or worship the Deity, the value is the same because you are serving Kṛṣṇa. That is a classless society. Actually, the perfect classless society is Vṛndāvana. In Vṛndāvana, some are cowherd boys, some are cows, some are trees, some are fathers, some are mothers, but the center is Kṛṣṇa, and everyone is satisfied simply by loving Him. When all people become Kṛṣṇa conscious and understand how to love Him, then there will be a classless society. Otherwise it is not possible.

Disciple: Marx defines communism as "The common or public ownership of the means of production, and the abolition of private property." In our International Society for Krishna Consciousness, don't we have the same idea? We also say, "Nothing is mine." We have also abolished private property.

Śrīla Prabhupāda: While the communist says, "Nothing is mine," he thinks everything belongs to the state. The state, however, is simply an extended "mine." For example, if I am the head of a family, I might say, "I do not want anything for myself, but I want many things for my children." Mahatma Gandhi, who sacrificed so much to drive the English out of India, was at the same time thinking, "I am a very good man; I am doing national work." Therefore, this so-called nationalism or so-called communism is simply extended selfishness. The quality remains the same. The real change occurs when we say, "Nothing belongs to me; everything belongs to God, Kṛṣṇa, and therefore I should use everything in His service." That is factual abolition of private property.

Disciple: Marx says that the capitalists are parasites living at the cost of the workers.

Śrīla Prabhupāda: But the communists are also living at the cost of the workers: the managers are drawing big salaries, and the common workers are dissatisfied. Indeed, their godless society is becoming more and more troublesome. Unless everyone accepts God as the only enjoyer and himself simply as His servant, there will always be conflict. In the broad sense, there is no difference between the communists and the capitalists because God is not accepted as the supreme enjoyer and proprietor in either system. Actually, no property belongs to either the communists or the capitalists. Everything belongs to God.

Disciple: Marx condemns the capitalists for making a profit. He says that profit-making is exploitation and that the capitalists are unnecessary for the production of commodities.

Śrīla Prabhupāda: Profit-making may be wrong, but that exploitative tendency is always there, whether it is a communist or a capitalist system. In Bengal it is said that during the winter season the bedbugs cannot come out because of the severe cold. So they become dried up, being unable to suck any blood. But as soon as the summer season comes, the bugs get the opportunity to come out, so they immediately bite someone and suck his blood to their full satisfaction. Our mentality in this material world is the same: to exploit others and become wealthy. Whether you are a communist in the winter season or a capitalist in the summer season, your tendency is to exploit others. Unless there is a change of heart, this exploitation will go on.

I once knew a mill worker who acquired some money. Then he became the proprietor of the mill and took advantage of his good fortune to become a capitalist. Henry Ford is another example. He was an errand boy, but he got the opportunity to become a capitalist. There are many such instances. So, to a greater or lesser degree, the propensity is always there in human nature to exploit others and become wealthy. Unless this mentality is changed, there is no point in changing from a capitalist to a communist society. Material life means that everyone is seeking some profit, some adoration, and some position. By threats the state can force people to curb this tendency, but for how long? Can they change everyone's mind by force? No, it is impossible. Therefore, Marx's proposition is nonsense.

Disciple: Marx thinks the minds of people can be changed by forced conditioning.

Śrīla Prabhupāda: That is not possible. Even a child cannot be convinced by force, what to speak of a mature, educated man. We have the real process for changing people's minds: chanting the Hare Kṛṣṇa mantra. *Ceto-darpaṇa-mārjanam:* This process cleanses the heart of material desires. We have seen that people in Moscow are not happy. They are simply waiting for another revolution. We talked to one working-class boy who was very unhappy. When a pot of rice has boiled, you can take one grain and press it between your fingers, and if it is soft you can understand all the rice is cooked. Thus we can understand the position of the Russian people from the sample of that boy. We could also get further ideas by talking with Professor Kotovsky from the India Department of Moscow University. How foolish he was! He said that after death everything is finished. If this is his knowledge, and if that young boy is a sample of the citizenry, then the situation in Russia is very bleak. They may theorize about so many things, but we could not even purchase sufficient groceries in Moscow. There were no vegetables, fruits, or rice, and the milk was of poor quality. If that Madrasi gentleman had not contributed some dhal and rice, then practically speaking we would have starved. The Russians' diet seemed to consist of only meat and liquor.
Disciple: The communists play upon this universal profit motive. The worker who produces the most units at his factory is glorified by the state or receives a small bonus.
Śrīla Prabhupāda: Why should he get a bonus?
Disciple: To give him some incentive to work hard.
Śrīla Prabhupāda: Just to satisfy his tendency to lord it over others and make a profit, his superiors bribe him. This Russian communist idea is very good, provided the citizens do not want any profit. But that is impossible, because everyone wants profit. The state cannot destroy this tendency either by law or by force.
Disciple: The communists try to centralize everything—money, transport, etc.—in the hands of the state.
Śrīla Prabhupāda: But what benefit will there be in that? As

soon as all the wealth is centralized, the members of the central government will appropriate it, just as Khrushchev did. These are all useless ideas as long as the tendency for exploitation is not reformed. The Russians have organized their country according to Marx's theories, yet all their leaders have turned out to be cheaters. Where is their program for reforming this cheating propensity?

Disciple: Their program is to first change the social condition, and then, they believe, the corrupt mentality will change automatically.

Śrīla Prabhupāda: Impossible. Such repression will simply cause a reaction in the form of another revolution.

Disciple: Are you implying that the people's mentality must first be changed, and then a change in the social structure will naturally follow?

Śrīla Prabhupāda: Yes. But the leaders will never be able to train all the people to think that everything belongs to the state. This idea is simply utopian nonsense.

Disciple: Marx has another slogan: "Human nature has no reality." He says that man's nature changes through history according to material conditions.

Śrīla Prabhupāda: He does not know the real human nature. It is certainly true that everything in this cosmic creation, or *jagat,* is changing. Your body changes daily. Everything is changing, just like waves in the ocean. This is not a very advanced philosophy. Marx's theory is also being changed; it cannot last. But man does have a fundamental nature that never changes: his spiritual nature. We are teaching people to come to the standard of acting according to their spiritual nature, which will never change. Acting spiritually means serving Kṛṣṇa. If we try to serve Kṛṣṇa now, we will continue to serve Kṛṣṇa when we go to Vaikuṇṭha, the spiritual world. Therefore, loving service to Lord Kṛṣṇa is called *nitya,* or eternal. As Kṛṣṇa says in the *Bhagavad-gītā, nitya-yukta upāsate:* "My pure devotees perpetually worship Me with devotion."

The communists give up Kṛṣṇa and replace Him with the

state. Then they expect to get the people to think, "Nothing in my favor; everything in favor of the state." But people will never accept this idea. It is impossible; let the rascals try it! All they can do is simply force the people to work, as Stalin did. As soon as he found someone opposed to him, he immediately cut his throat. The same disease is still there today, so how will their program be successful?

Disciple: As I mentioned, they think human nature has no reality of its own. It's simply a product of the environment. Thus, by putting a man in the factory and making him identify with the state and something like scientific achievement, they think they can transform him into a selfless person.

Śrīla Prabhupāda: But because he has the basic disease, envy, he will remain selfish. When he sees that he is working so hard but that the profit is not coming to him, his enthusiasm will immediately slacken. In Bengal there is a proverb: "As a proprietor I can turn sand into gold, but as soon as I am no longer the proprietor, the gold becomes sand." The Russian people are in this position. They are not as rich as the Europeans or the Americans, and because of this they are unhappy.

Disciple: One of the methods the authorities in Russia use is to constantly whip the people into believing there may be a war at any moment. Then they think, "To protect our country, we must work hard."

Śrīla Prabhupāda: If the people cannot make any profit on their work, however, they will eventually lose all interest in the country. The average man will think, "Whether I work or not, I get the same result. I cannot adequately feed and clothe my family." Then he will begin to lose his incentive to work. A scientist will see that despite his high position, his wife and children are dressed just like the common laborer.

Disciple: Marx says that industrial and scientific work is the highest kind of activity.

Śrīla Prabhupāda: But unless the scientists and the industrialists receive sufficient profit, they will be reluctant to work for the state.

Disciple: The Russian goal is the production of material

goods for the enhancement of human well-being.
Śrīla Prabhupāda: Their "human well-being" actually means, "If you don't agree with me, I'll cut your throat." This is their "well-being." Stalin had his idea of "human well-being," but anyone who disagreed with his version of it was killed or imprisoned. They may say that a few must suffer for the sake of many, but we have personally seen that Russia has achieved neither general happiness nor prosperity. For example, in Moscow none of the big buildings have been recently built. They are old and ravaged, or poorly renovated. Also, at the stores the people had to stand in long lines to make purchases. These are indications that economic conditions are unsound.
Disciple: Marx considered religion an illusion that must be condemned.
Śrīla Prabhupāda: The divisions between different religious faiths may be an illusion, but Marx's philosophy is also an illusion.
Disciple: Do you mean that it's not being practiced?
Śrīla Prabhupāda: In the sixty years since the Russian Revolution, his philosophy has become distorted. On the other hand, Lord Brahmā began the Vedic religion countless years ago, and though foreigners have been trying to devastate it for the last two thousand years, it is still intact. Vedic religion is not an illusion, at least not for India.
Disciple: Here is Marx's famous statement about religion. He says, "Religion is the sigh of the oppressed creature, the heart of the heartless world, just as it is the spirit of the spiritless situation. It is the opium of the people."
Śrīla Prabhupāda: He does not know what religion is. His definition is false. The *Vedas* state that religion is the course of action given by God. God is a fact, and His law is also a fact. It is not an illusion. Kṛṣṇa gives the definition of religion in the *Bhagavad-gītā* [18.66]: *sarva-dharmān parityajya mām ekaṁ śaraṇaṁ vraja.* To surrender unto God—this is religion.
Disciple: Marx believed that everything is produced from economic struggle and that religion is a technique invented

by the capitalists to dissuade the masses from revolution by promising them a better existence after death.

Śrīla Prabhupāda: He himself has created a philosophy that is presently being enforced by coercion and killing.

Disciple: And he promised that in the future things would improve. So he's guilty of the very thing he condemns religion for.

Śrīla Prabhupāda: As we have often explained, religion, or dharma, is that part of our nature which is permanent, which we cannot give up. No one can give up his religion. And what is that religion? Service. Marx desires to serve humanity by putting forward his philosophy. Therefore that is his religion. Everyone is trying to render some service. The father is trying to serve his family, the statesman is trying to serve his country, and the philanthropist is trying to serve all humanity. Whether you are Karl Marx or Stalin or Mahatma Gandhi, a Hindu, a Muslim, or a Christian, you must serve. Because we are presently rendering service to so many people and so many things, we are becoming confused. Therefore, Kṛṣṇa advises us to give up all this service and serve Him alone:

sarva-dharmān parityajya mām ekaṁ śaraṇaṁ vraja
ahaṁ tvāṁ sarva-pāpebhyo mokṣayiṣyāmi mā śucaḥ

"Abandon all varieties of service and just surrender unto Me. I shall deliver you from all sinful reactions. Do not fear." [*Bhagavad-gītā* 18.66]

Disciple: The communists—and even to a certain extent the capitalists—believe that service for the production of goods is the only real service. Therefore they condemn us because we are not producing anything tangible.

Śrīla Prabhupāda: How can they condemn us? We are giving service to humanity by teaching the highest knowledge. A high court judge does not produce any grains in the field. He sits in a chair and gets $75,000 or $100,000 a year. Does that mean he is not rendering any service? Of course he is. The theory that unless one performs manual labor in the factory or the fields he is not doing service would simply give credit to the peasant and the worker. It is a peasant philosophy.

There is a story about a king and his prime minister. Once the king's salaried workers complained, "We are actually working, and this minister is doing nothing, yet you are paying him such a large salary. Why is that?"

The king then called his minister in and also had someone bring in an elephant. "Please take this elephant and weigh it," the king said to his workers. The workers took the elephant to all the markets, but they could not find a scale large enough to weigh the animal.

When they returned to the palace the king asked, "What happened?"

One of the workers answered, "Sir, we could not find a scale large enough to weigh the elephant."

Then the king addressed his prime minister, "Will you please weigh this elephant?"

"Yes, sir," said the prime minister, and he took the elephant away. He returned within a few minutes and said, "It weighs 10,650 pounds."

All the workers were astonished. "How did you weigh the elephant so quickly?" one of them asked.

"Did you find some very large scale?"

The minister replied, "No. It is impossible to weigh an elephant on a scale. I went to the river, took the elephant on a boat, and noted the watermark. After taking the elephant off the boat, I put weights in the boat until the same watermark was reached. Then I had the elephant's weight."

The king said to his workers, "Now do you see the difference?"

One who has intelligence has strength, not the fools and rascals. Marx and his followers are simply fools and rascals. We don't take advice from them; we take advice from Kṛṣṇa or His representative.

Disciple: So religion is not simply a police force to keep people in illusion?

Śrīla Prabhupāda: No. Religion means to serve the spirit.

That is religion. Everyone is rendering service, but no one knows where his service will be most successful. Therefore Kṛṣṇa says, "Serve Me, and you will serve the spiritual society." This is real religion. The Marxists want to build a so-called perfect society without religion, yet even up to this day, because India's foundation is religion, people all over the world adore India.

Disciple: Marx says that God does not create man; rather, man creates God.

Śrīla Prabhupāda: That is more nonsense. From what he says, I can tell he is a nonsensical rascal and a fool. One cannot understand that someone is a fool unless he talks. A fool may dress very nicely and sit like a gentleman amongst gentlemen, but we can tell the fools from the learned men by their speech.

Disciple: Marx's follower was Nikolai Lenin. He reinforced all of Marx's ideas and added a few of his own. He believed that revolution is a fundamental fact of history. He said that history moves in leaps, and that it progresses toward the communist leap. He wanted Russia to leap into the dictatorship of the proletariat, which he called the final stage of historical development.

Śrīla Prabhupāda: No. We can say with confidence—and they may note it carefully—that after the Bolshevik Revolution there will be many other revolutions, because as long as people live on the mental plane there will be only revolution. Our proposition is that one should give up all these mental concoctions and come to the spiritual platform. Then there will be no more revolution because one will be fully satisfied. As Dhruva Mahārāja said, *svāmin kṛtārtho 'smi varaṁ na yāce:* "My dear Lord, now that I am seeing You I am completely satisfied." So God consciousness is the final revolution. There will be repeated revolutions in this material world unless people come to Kṛṣṇa consciousness.

Disciple: The Hare Kṛṣṇa revolution.

Śrīla Prabhupāda: The Vedic injunction is that people are searching after knowledge, and that when one understands the Absolute Truth, he understands everything. *Yasmin vijñāte sarvam evaṁ vijñātaṁ bhavati.* People are trying to approach an objective, but they do not know that the final objective is Kṛṣṇa. They are simply trying to make adjustments with so many materialistic revolutions. They have no knowledge that they are spiritual beings and that unless they go back to the spiritual world and associate with the Supreme Spirit, God, there is no question of happiness. We are like fish out of water. Just as a fish cannot be happy unless he is in the water, we cannot be happy apart from the spiritual world. We are part and parcel of the Supreme Spirit, Kṛṣṇa, but we have left His association and fallen from the spiritual world because of our desire to enjoy this material world. So unless we reawaken the understanding of our spiritual position and go back home to the spiritual world, we can never be happy. We can go on theorizing for many lifetimes, but we will only see one revolution after another. The old order changes, yielding its place to the new. Or in other words, history repeats itself.

Disciple: Marx says that there are always two conflicting properties in material nature, and that the inner pulsation of opposite forces causes history to take leaps from one revolution to another. He claims that the communist revolution is the final revolution because it is the perfect resolution of all social and political contradictions.

Śrīla Prabhupāda: If the communist idea is spiritualized, then it will become perfect. As long as the communist idea remains materialistic, it cannot be the final revolution. They believe that the state is the owner of everything. But the state is not the owner; the real owner is God. When they come to this conclusion, then the communist idea will be perfect. We also have a communistic philosophy. They say that everything must be done for the state, but in our International Society for Krishna Consciousness we are actually practicing perfect communism by doing everything for Kṛṣṇa. We know Kṛṣṇa is the supreme enjoyer of the result of all work (*bhoktāraṁ yajña-tapasām*). The communist philosophy as it is now practiced is vague, but it can become perfect if they accept the conclusion of the *Bhagavad-gītā*—that Kṛṣṇa is the supreme proprietor, the supreme enjoyer, and the supreme friend of everyone. Then people will be happy. Now they mistrust the state, but if the people accept Kṛṣṇa as their friend, they will have perfect confidence in Him, just as Arjuna was perfectly confident in Kṛṣṇa on the Battlefield of Kurukṣetra. The great victory of Arjuna and his associates on the Battlefield of Kurukṣetra showed that his confidence in Kṛṣṇa was justified:

yatra yogeśvaraḥ kṛṣṇo yatra pārtho dhanur-dharaḥ
tatra śrīr vijayo bhūtir dhruvā nītir matir mama

"Wherever there is Kṛṣṇa, the master of all mystics, and wherever there is Arjuna, the supreme archer, there will also certainly be opulence, victory, extraordinary power, and morality. That is my opinion." [*Bhagavad-gītā* 18.78] So if Kṛṣṇa is at the center of society, then the people will be perfectly secure and prosperous. The communist idea is welcome, provided they are prepared to replace the so-called state with God. That is religion.

Chapter TWELVE

NIETZSCHE

Friedrich Nietzsche (1844–1900) was a German philosopher and poet whose work has greatly influenced modern thinkers. Perceiving that traditional Christian values had lost their influence in society, he coined the phrase "God is dead." His concept of the Übermensch, or "superman," was misinterpreted by the Nazis to try to justify their aggression. Here Śrīla Prabhupāda explains who the Übermensch really is.

Disciple: Schopenhauer spoke of the "blind will" of the individual as being the basic propelling force that keeps the soul tied to material existence, to transmigration from body to body. Nietzsche, on the other hand, spoke of *der Wille zur Macht,* the "will to power," which is a different kind of will. This will is not used for subjugating others but for mastering one's lower self. It is characterized by self-control and an interest in art and philosophy. Most people are envious of others, but it is the duty of the noble man, the philosopher, to transcend this envy by sheer willpower. In Nietzsche's own words, the philosopher "shakes off with one shrug much vermin that would have buried itself deep in others." When the philosopher has rid himself of resentment and envy, he can even embrace his enemies with a kind of Christian love.

Śrīla Prabhupāda: This is called spiritual power. Envy is a symptom of conditioned life. In the *Śrīmad-Bhāgavatam* it is stated that the neophyte who wants to understand the Vedic literatures should not be envious. In this material world, everyone is envious. People are even envious of God and His instructions. Consequently people do not like to accept Kṛṣṇa's instructions. Although Kṛṣṇa is the Supreme Personality of Godhead and is accepted as such by all the *ācāryas,* there are nonetheless foolish men called *mūḍhas* who either reject Kṛṣṇa's instructions or try to screw out some contrary meaning from them. This envy is symptomatic of conditioned souls. Unless we are liberated from conditioned life, we will remain confused under the influence of the external, material energy. Until we come to the spiritual platform, there is no possibility of escaping from envy and pride by so-called willpower. A person in the transcendental (*brahma-bhūta*) stage is described in the *Bhagavad-gītā* [18.54] as *samaḥ sarveṣu bhūteṣu:* He can look at everyone with the same spiritual understanding.

Disciple: Nietzsche calls the man who possesses spiritual power the *Übermensch,* a word meaning literally "above-man" and often translated as "superman." The *Übermensch* is totally self-controlled, unafraid of death, simple, aware, and self-reliant. He is so powerful that he can change the lives of others simply on contact. Nietzsche never referred to any historical person as the *Übermensch,* nor did he consider himself such.

Śrīla Prabhupāda: We accept the guru as the genuine superman because he is worshiped like God and can put one in touch with God and His grace. *Yasya prasādād bhagavat-prasādaḥ:* "By the mercy of the guru one receives the mercy of the Supreme Personality of Godhead." Caitanya Mahāprabhu also accepts this: *guru-kṛṣṇa-prasāde pāya* *bhakti-latā-bīja:* "By the mercy of Kṛṣṇa and the guru one receives information about spiritual life so that he can return home, back to Godhead." Śrī Caitanya Mahāprabhu requested everyone to become a guru, or superman. The superman distributes transcendental knowledge strictly according to the authorized version he has received from his superior. This is called *paramparā,* the disciplic succession. One superman delivers this supreme knowledge to another superman, and this knowledge was originally delivered by God Himself.

Disciple: In *Thus Spake Zarathustra,* Nietzsche concludes that all men want power. At the top of this hierarchy in the quest for power is the *Übermensch.* Thus the *Übermensch* would be one who has conquered his passions and attained all good qualifications. His actions are creative, and he does not envy others. He is constantly aware that death is always present, and he is so superior to others that he is almost like God in the world.

Śrīla Prabhupāda: In Sanskrit the real *Übermensch* or superman is called a *svāmī* or *gosvāmī,* who is described by Rūpa Gosvāmī as one who can control his words, mind, anger, tongue, belly, and genitals. These are the six forces that drive men to commit sinful activities. A *gosvāmī* can control these forces, especially the genitals, belly, and tongue, which are very hard to control. Bhaktivinoda Ṭhākura says, *tā'ra madhye jihvā ati-lobhamaya sudurmati:* The force of the tongue is very great, and for its gratification we create many artificial edibles. Nonsensical habits like smoking, drinking, and meat-eating have entered society simply due to the urges of the tongue. Actually, there is no need for these things. A person does not die simply because he cannot smoke, eat meat, or drink liquor. Rather, *without* these indulgences he can elevate himself to the highest platform. It is therefore said that one who can control the tongue can control the urges of the other senses also. One who can control all the senses—beginning with the tongue—is called a *gosvāmī,* or, as Nietzsche would say, the *Übermensch.* But this is impossible for an ordinary man.

Disciple: Nietzsche believed that everyone has a "will to power," but that the weak seek power vainly. For instance, in his will to power, Hitler sought to subjugate as much of the world as possible, but he was ultimately unsuccessful, and he brought disaster upon himself and Germany. Instead of trying to conquer himself, he attempted to conquer others, and this is the will to power misdirected or misinterpreted.
Śrīla Prabhupāda: Men like Hitler are not able to control the force of anger. A king or national leader has to use anger properly. Narottama Dāsa Ṭhākura says that we should control our powers and apply them in the proper cases. We may become angry, but our anger must be controlled. For example, although Caitanya Mahāprabhu taught that we should be very submissive—humbler than the grass and more tolerant than a tree—He became very angry upon seeing His dear devotee Nityānanda Prabhu hurt by Jāgai and Mādhāi. Everything can be properly utilized in the service of Kṛṣṇa, but not for personal aggrandizement. In the material world, everyone is certainly after power, but the real superman is not after power for himself. He himself is a mendicant, a *sannyāsī,* but he acquires power for the service of the Lord. For instance, I came to America not to acquire material power but to distribute Kṛṣṇa consciousness. By the grace of Kṛṣṇa, all facilities have been afforded, and now, from the material point of view, I have become somewhat powerful. But this is not for my personal sense gratification; it is all for spreading Kṛṣṇa consciousness. The conclusion is that power for Kṛṣṇa's service is very valuable, but power for our own sense gratification is condemned.
Disciple: Hitler twisted Nietzsche's philosophy, claiming that he was the *Übermensch,* although Nietzsche clearly says that the *Übermensch* is not intent on subjugating others but on subjugating his own passions. Such a superman is beyond good and evil and is not subject to mundane dualities.
Śrīla Prabhupāda: Yes, because the superman acts on behalf of God, he is transcendental. At the beginning of the *Bhagavad-gītā,* Arjuna was thinking like an ordinary person

in his reluctance to fight. From the material point of view, nonviolence is a good qualification. Arjuna was excusing his enemies, although they had insulted him and his wife and usurped his kingdom. He pleaded before Kṛṣṇa that it would be better to let them enjoy his kingdom—"I am not going to fight." Materially this appeared very laudable, but spiritually it was not, because Kṛṣṇa wanted him to fight. Finally Arjuna carried out Kṛṣṇa's order and fought. Clearly, this kind of fighting was not for personal aggrandizement but for the service of Kṛṣṇa. So by using his power for the service of the Lord, Arjuna became a superman.

Disciple: In his writings on religion, Nietzsche expressed a dislike for the nihilism of the Buddhists and the caste system of the Hindus, especially the Hindu treatment of the untouchables.

Śrīla Prabhupāda: That is a later concoction by the caste Hindus. The true Vedic religion does not speak of untouchables. Caitanya Mahāprabhu Himself demonstrated His system by accepting so-called untouchables like Haridāsa Ṭhākura, who was born in a Muslim family. Although Haridāsa Ṭhākura was not accepted by Hindu society, Caitanya Mahāprabhu personally indicated that he was most exalted. Haridāsa Ṭhākura would not enter the temple of Lord Jagannātha because he did not want to create a commotion, but Caitanya Mahāprabhu Himself came to see Haridāsa every day. It is a basic principle of the Vedic religion that one should not be envious of anyone. Kṛṣṇa Himself says in the *Bhagavad-gītā* [9.32]:

> *māṁ hi pārtha vyapāśritya ye 'pi syuḥ pāpa-yonayaḥ*
> *striyo vaiśyās tathā śūdrās te 'pi yānti paraṁ gatim*

"O son of Pṛthā, those who take shelter of Me—though they be lowborn, women, *vaiśyas,* or *śūdras*—can achieve the supreme destination." So despite birth in a lower family, if one is a devotee he is eligible to return home, back to Godhead. The *śāstras* do not speak of untouchables.

Everyone is eligible to practice Kṛṣṇa consciousness and return to Godhead, provided the necessary spiritual qualifications are there.

Disciple: Nietzsche believed that by stressing the value of going to the transcendental world, a person would come to resent this world. He therefore personally rejected all formal religions.

Śrīla Prabhupāda: This material world is described as a place of suffering (*duḥkhālayam aśāśvatam*). We do not know whether Nietzsche realized this or not, but if one actually understands the soul, he can realize that this material world is a place of suffering. Being part and parcel of God, the soul has the same qualities possessed by God. God is *sac-cid-ānanda-vigraha,* eternal, full of knowledge and bliss, and the living entities in the spiritual world have the same nature. But in material life their eternality, knowledge, and bliss are absent. It is therefore better that we learn to detest material existence and try to give it up (*paraṁ dṛṣṭvā nivartate*). The *Vedas* enjoin that we understand the spiritual world and try to return there (*tamasi mā jyotir gama*). The spiritual world is the kingdom of light, and this material world is the kingdom of darkness. The sooner we learn to avoid the world of darkness and return to the kingdom of light, the better it will be for us.

Disciple: Nietzsche was greatly influenced by the Greeks, and he was astounded that out of so few men, so many great individuals emerged. He attributed this to their struggling with their evil instincts, and he thought that even today, with the help of favorable measures, great individuals might be reared who would surpass all others. Thus Nietzsche believed that mankind ought to be constantly striving to produce great men—this and nothing else is man's duty.

Śrīla Prabhupāda: Everyone is trying to be a great man, but one's greatness is genuine when he becomes God realized. The word *veda* means "knowledge," and a person is great when he is conversant with the lessons of the *Vedas.* The object of knowledge, as described by the *Bhagavad-gītā,* is God or the self. There are different methods for self-realization.

However, since every individual is part and parcel of God, if one realizes God, he automatically realizes himself. God is compared to the sun. If the sun is out, we can see everything very clearly. Similarly, in the *Vedas* it is said, *yasmin vijñāte sarvam evaṁ vijñātaṁ bhavati:* "By understanding God, we understand all other things." Then we automatically become jolly (*brahma-bhūtaḥ prasannātmā*). The word *prasannātmā* means "jolly." At that time we can see that everyone is exactly like ourselves (*samaḥ sarveṣu-bhūteṣu*) because everyone is part and parcel of the Supreme Lord. At this point, real service to the Lord begins, and we attain the platform of knowledge, bliss, and eternity.

Disciple: Nietzsche was emphatic in stating that there has never yet been a superman. He writes, "All too similar are men to each other. Verily even the greatest I found all too human." Nor does the superman evolve in the Darwinian sense. Nietzsche thought the *Übermensch* a possibility at present if man uses all his spiritual and physical energies. He wrote, "Dead are all the gods; now do we desire the superman to live." But how is the *Übermensch* possible without an object for his spiritual energies?

Śrīla Prabhupāda: We become supermen if we engage in the service of the Supreme Person. The Supreme Being is a person, and the superman is also a person. *Nityo nityānāṁ cetanaś cetanānām:* "God is the chief among all personalities." The superman has no other business than carrying out the orders of the Supreme Being. Kṛṣṇa, or God, wants to make everyone a superman. He therefore orders, *sarva-dharmān parityajya mām ekaṁ śaraṇaṁ vraja:* "Give up everything and simply surrender to Me." [*Bhagavad-gītā* 18.66] If we can understand and follow this instruction, we are supermen. The ordinary man thinks, "I have my independence and can do something myself. Why should I surrender?" However, as soon as he realizes that his only duty is to surrender to Kṛṣṇa, that he has no other duty in this material world, he becomes the superman. This consciousness is attained after many, many births (*bahūnāṁ janmanām ante*).

After many lifetimes, when one actually attains full knowledge of Kṛṣṇa, he surrenders unto Him. As soon as he surrenders, he becomes the superman.

Disciple: Nietzsche would reject dependence on anything exterior to the superman himself. In other words, he would reject "props." But isn't it impossible for a man to elevate himself to that platform without depending on the Supreme Lord?

Śrīla Prabhupāda: Of course, and therefore Kṛṣṇa says, "Depend upon Me." You have to be dependent, and if you do not depend on Kṛṣṇa, you have to depend on the dictations of *māyā,* illusion. There are many philosophers and politicians who depend on others or on their own whimsical ideas, but we should depend on the perfect instructions of God. The fact is that every living being is dependent; he cannot be independent. If he voluntarily depends on the instructions of God, he becomes the genuine superman.

Disciple: Nietzsche's superman appears to resemble the *haṭha-yogī,* who elevates himself by his own efforts seemingly independent of God.

Śrīla Prabhupāda: Yes, *seemingly.* As soon as a *haṭha-yogī* gets some extraordinary mystic powers, he thinks that he has become God. This is another mistake, since no one can become God. A yogī may attain some mystical powers by practice or by the favor of the Lord, but these powers are not sufficient to enable him to *become* God. There are many who think that through meditation or *haṭha-yoga* it is possible to become equal to God, but this is another illusion, another dictation of *māyā. Māyā* is always saying, "Why depend on God? You can become God yourself."

Disciple: Independence seems to be central to Nietzsche's philosophy. In a sense, his superman is somewhat like Hiraṇyakaśipu, who performed so many penances to gain immortality and who made the demigods tremble to see his austerities.

Śrīla Prabhupāda: Yes, and ultimately he was outwitted by the Supreme Himself. Actually, it is not good to struggle for material power and control over others. If one becomes a devout servant of God, he becomes the superman automatically and acquires many sincere followers. One does not have to undergo severe austerities; everything can be mastered in one stroke.

Disciple: And what of sense control?

Śrīla Prabhupāda: If one becomes a devotee of the Supreme Lord, he controls his senses automatically, but he never thinks that he has become God, or the supreme controller.

Disciple: One last point on Nietzsche. He believed in what is called eternal recurrence—that is, after this universe has been destroyed, it will be repeated again after many eons.

Śrīla Prabhupāda: In the *Bhagavad-gītā* it is stated, *bhūtvā bhūtvā pralīyate:* "This material world is created at a certain point, maintained for a certain period, and then destroyed." [*Bhagavad-gītā* 8.19] This material world is created for the conditioned soul, who is put here in order to learn his position as the eternal servant of God. Lord Brahmā, the first created being in the universe, is given the Vedic instructions, and he distributes them through the disciplic succession, which descends from Brahmā to Nārada, from Nārada to Vyāsadeva, from Vyāsadeva to Śukadeva Gosvāmī, and so on. These instructions enjoin the conditioned soul to return home, back to Godhead. If the conditioned soul rejects these instructions, he remains in the material world until it is annihilated. At that time he remains in an unconscious state, just like a child within the womb of his mother. In due course of time his consciousness revives, and he again takes birth. The point is that anyone can take advantage of the Vedic instructions, become a superman or *Übermensch,* and go back to Godhead. Unfortunately, the conditioned living entities are so attached to the material world that they repeatedly want to take up material bodies. In this way history repeats itself, and there is again creation, maintenance, and destruction.

Chapter THIRTEEN

FREUD

The founder of psychoanalysis, Sigmund Freud (1856–1939) spent most of his life in Vienna investigating the intricacies of the human mind and formulating ideas that have largely guided the treatment of mental illness in the West up to the present day. Here Śrīla Prabhupāda points out that because Freud ignores the real craziness of materialistic life—the misidentification of the self with the body—all his analyses and treatments are ultimately futile.

Disciple: Sigmund Freud's idea was that many psychological problems originate with traumatic experiences in childhood or infancy. His method of cure was to have the patient try to recall these painful events and analyze them.

Śrīla Prabhupāda: But he did not know that one must again become an infant. After this life, one will be put into another womb, and the same traumatic experiences will happen again. Therefore it is the duty of the spiritual master and the parents to save the child from taking another birth. The opportunity of this human form of life is that we can understand the horrible experiences of birth, death, old age, and disease and act so that we shall not be forced to go through the same things again. Otherwise, after death we shall have to take birth in a womb and suffer repeated miseries.

Disciple: Freud treated many people suffering from neuroses. For instance, suppose a man is sexually impotent. By recalling his childhood, he may remember some harmful experience with his father or mother that caused him to be repelled by women. In this way he can resolve the conflict and lead a normal sex life.

Śrīla Prabhupāda: However, even in the so-called normal condition, the pleasure derived from sexual intercourse is simply frustrating and insignificant. For ordinary men attached to the materialistic way of life, their only pleasure is sexual intercourse. But the *śāstras* say, *yan maithunādi-gṛhamedhi-sukhaṁ hi tuccham:* the pleasure derived from sexual intercourse is tenth class at best. Because they have no idea of the pleasure of Kṛṣṇa consciousness, the materialists regard sex as the highest pleasure. And how is it actually experienced? We have an itch, and when we scratch it, we feel some pleasure. But the aftereffects of sexual pleasure are abominable. The mother has to undergo labor pains, and the father has to take responsibility for raising the children nicely and giving them an education. Of course, if one is irresponsible like cats and dogs, that is another thing. But for those who are actually gentlemen, is it not painful to bear and raise children? Certainly. Therefore everyone is avoiding children by contraceptive methods. But much better is to follow the injunction of the *śāstras:* Simply try to tolerate the itching sensation and avoid so much pain. This is real psychology. That itching sensation can be tolerated if one practices Kṛṣṇa consciousness. Then one will not be very attracted by sex life.

Disciple: Freud's philosophy is that people have neuroses or disorders of their total personality—various conflicts and anxieties—and that all these originate with the sexual impulse.

Śrīla Prabhupāda: That we admit. An embodied living being must have hunger, and he must have the sex impulse. We find that even in the animals these impulses are there.
Disciple: Freud believed that the ego tries to restrain these primitive drives, and that all anxieties arise from this conflict.
Śrīla Prabhupāda: Our explanation is as follows: Materialistic life is no doubt very painful. As soon as one acquires a material body, he must always suffer three kinds of miseries: miseries caused by other living beings, miseries caused by the elements, and miseries caused by his own body and mind. So the whole problem is how to stop these miseries and attain permanent happiness. Unless one stops his materialistic way of life, with its threefold miseries and repeated birth and death, there is no question of happiness. The whole Vedic civilization is based on how one can cure this materialistic disease. If we can cure this disease, its symptoms will automatically vanish. Freud is simply dealing with the symptoms of the basic disease. When you have a disease, sometimes you have headaches, sometimes your leg aches, sometimes you have a pain in your stomach, and so on. But if your disease is cured, then all your symptoms disappear. That is our program.
Disciple: In his theory of psychoanalysis, Freud states that by remembering and reevaluating emotional shocks from our childhood, we can release the tension we are feeling now.
Śrīla Prabhupāda: But what is the guarantee that one will not get shocked again? He may cure the results of one shock, but there is no guarantee that the patient will not receive another shock. Therefore Freud's treatment is useless. Our program is total cure—no more shocks of any kind. If one is situated in real Kṛṣṇa consciousness, he can face the most severe type of adversity and remain completely undisturbed. In our Kṛṣṇa consciousness movement, we are giving people this ability. Freud tries to cure the reactions of one kind of shock, but other shocks will come, one after another. This is how material nature works. If you solve one problem, another problem arises immediately. And if you solve that one, another

one comes. As long as you are under the control of material nature, these repeated shocks will come. But if you become Kṛṣṇa conscious, there are no more shocks.

Disciple: Freud's idea is that the basic instinct in the human personality is the sexual drive, or libido, and that if the expressions of a child's sexuality are inhibited, then his personality becomes disordered.

Śrīla Prabhupāda: Everyone has the sex appetite: this tendency is innate. But our *brahmacarya* system restricts a child's sex life from the earliest stages of his development and diverts his attention to Kṛṣṇa consciousness. As a result there is very little chance that he will suffer such personality disorders. In the Vedic age the leaders of society knew that if a person engaged in unrestricted sex indulgence, then the duration of his materialistic life would increase. He would have to accept a material body birth after birth. Therefore the *śāstras* enjoin that one may have sexual intercourse only if married and only for procreation. Otherwise it is illicit. In our Kṛṣṇa consciousness society, we prohibit illicit sex, but not legal sex. In the *Bhagavad-gītā* [7.11] Kṛṣṇa says, *dharmāviruddho bhūteṣu kāmo 'smi bharatarṣabha:* "I am sexual intercourse that is not against religious principles." This means that sex must be regulated. Everyone has a tendency to have sex unrestrictedly—and in Western countries they are actually doing this—but according to the Vedic system, there must be restrictions. And not only must sex be restricted, but meat-eating, gambling, and drinking as well. So in our Society we have eliminated all these things, and our Western students are becoming pure devotees of Kṛṣṇa. The people at large, however, must at least restrict these sinful activities, as explained in the Vedic *śāstras.*

The Vedic system of *varṇāśrama-dharma* is so scientific that everything is automatically adjusted. Life becomes very peaceful and happy, and everyone can make progress in Kṛṣṇa consciousness. If the Vedic system is followed by human society, there will be no more of these mental disturbances.

Disciple: Freud says that sexual energy is not only expressed in sexual intercourse, but is associated with a wide variety of pleasurable bodily sensations such as pleasures of the mouth, like eating and sucking.

Śrīla Prabhupāda: That is confirmed in the *śāstras: yan maithunādi-gṛhamedhi-sukham.* The only pleasure in this material world is sex. The word *ādi* indicates that the basic principle is *maithuna,* sexual intercourse. The whole system of materialistic life revolves around this sexual pleasure. But this pleasure is like one drop of water in the desert. The desert requires an ocean of water. If you find one drop of water in a desert, you can certainly say, "Here is some water." But what is its value? Similarly, there is certainly some pleasure in sex life, but what is the value of that pleasure? Compared to the unlimited pleasure of Kṛṣṇa consciousness, it is like one drop of water in the desert. Everyone is seeking unlimited pleasure, but no one is becoming satisfied. They are having sex in so many different ways, and the young girls walking on the street are almost naked. The whole society has become degraded. Every woman and girl is trying to attract a man, and the men take advantage of the situation. There is a saying in Bengal: "When milk is available in the marketplace, what is the use of keeping a cow?" So men are declining to keep a wife because sex is so cheap. They are deserting their families.

Disciple: Freud says that as the child grows up, he begins to learn that by giving up immediate sensual satisfaction, he can gain a greater benefit later on.

Śrīla Prabhupāda: But even this so-called greater benefit is illusory, because it is still based on the principle of material pleasure. The only way to entirely give up these lower pleasures is to take to Kṛṣṇa consciousness. As Kṛṣṇa states in the *Bhagavad-gītā* [2.59], *paraṁ dṛṣṭvā nivartate:* "By experiencing a higher taste, he is fixed in consciousness." And as Yāmunācārya said, "Since I have been engaged in the transcendental loving service of Kṛṣṇa, realizing ever-new pleasure in Him, whenever I think of sex pleasure I spit at the thought, and my lips curl in distaste." That is Kṛṣṇa consciousness. Our prescription is that in the beginning of life the child should be taught self-restraint (*brahmacarya*) and when he is past twenty he can marry. In the beginning he should learn how to restrain his senses. If a child is taught to become saintly, his semen rises to his brain, and he is able to understand spiritual values. Wasting semen decreases intelligence. So from the beginning, if he is a *brahmacārī* and does not misuse his semen, then he will become intelligent and strong and fully grown.

For want of this education, everyone's brain and bodily growth are being stunted. After the boy has been trained as a *brahmacārī,* if he still wants to enjoy sex he may get married. And because he has been trained from childhood to renounce materialistic enjoyment, when he is fifty years old he can retire from household life. At that time naturally his first-born son will be twenty-five years old, and he can take responsibility for maintaining the household. Household life is simply a license for sex life—that's all. Sex is not required, but one who cannot restrain himself is given a license to get married and have sex. The Vedic system of education is the real program that will save society. By speculating on some shock that may or may not have occurred in childhood, one will never discover the root disease. The sex impulse, as well as the impulse to become intoxicated and to eat meat, is present from the very beginning of life. Therefore one must restrain himself. Otherwise he will be implicated.

Disciple: So the Western system of bringing up children seems artificial because the parents either repress the child too severely or don't restrict him at all.

Śrīla Prabhupāda: That is not good. The Vedic system is to give the child direction for becoming Kṛṣṇa conscious. There must be some repression, but our use of repression is different. We say the child must rise early in the morning, worship the Deity in the temple, and chant Hare Kṛṣṇa. In the beginning, force may be necessary. Otherwise the child will not become habituated. But the idea is to divert his attention to

Kṛṣṇa conscious activities. Then, when he realizes he is not his body, all difficulties will disappear. As one increases his Kṛṣṇa consciousness, he becomes indifferent to all these material things. So Kṛṣṇa consciousness is the prime remedy—the panacea for all diseases.

Disciple: Freud divided the personality into three departments: the ego, the superego, and the id. The id is the irrational instinct for enjoyment. The ego is one's image of his own body, and is the instinct for self-preservation. The superego represents the moral restrictions of parents and other authorities.

Śrīla Prabhupāda: It is certainly true that everyone has some false egoism, or *ahaṅkāra.* For example, Freud thought he was Austrian. That is false ego, or identifying oneself with one's place of birth. We are giving everyone the information that this identification with a material body is ignorance. It is due to ignorance only that I think I am Indian, American, Hindu, or Muslim. This is egoism of the inferior quality. The superior egoism is, "I am Brahman. I am an eternal servant of Kṛṣṇa." If a child is taught this superior egoism from the beginning, then automatically his false egoism is stopped.

Disciple: Freud says that the ego tries to preserve the individual by organizing and controlling the irrational demands of the id. In other words, if the id sees something, like food, it automatically demands to eat it, and the ego controls that desire in order to preserve the individual. The superego reinforces this control. So these three systems are always conflicting in the personality.

Śrīla Prabhupāda: But the basic principle is false, since Freud has no conception of the soul existing beyond the body. He is considering the body only. Therefore he is a great fool. According to *bhāgavata* philosophy, anyone in the bodily concept of life—anyone who identifies this body, composed of mucus, bile, and air, as his self—is no better than an ass.

Disciple: Then these interactions of the id, the ego, and the superego are all bodily interactions?

Śrīla Prabhupāda: Yes, they are all subtle bodily interactions.

The mind is the first element of the subtle body. The gross senses are controlled by the mind, which in turn is controlled by the intelligence. And the intelligence is controlled by the ego. So if the ego is false, then everything is false. If I falsely identify with this body because of false ego, then anything based on this false idea is also false. This is called *māyā,* or illusion. The whole of Vedic education aims at getting off this false platform and coming to the real platform of spiritual knowledge, called *brahma-jñāna.* When one comes to the knowledge that he is spirit soul, he immediately becomes happy. All his troubles are due to the false ego, and as soon as the individual realizes his true ego, the blazing fire of material existence is immediately extinguished. These philosophers are simply describing the blazing fire, but we are trying to get him out of the burning prison house of the material world altogether. They may attempt to make him happy within the fire, but how can they be successful? He must be saved from the fire. Then he will be happy. That is the message of Caitanya Mahāprabhu, and that is Lord Kṛṣṇa's message in the *Bhagavad-gītā.* Freud identifies the body with the soul. He does not know the basic principle of spiritual understanding, which is that we are not this body. We are different from this body and are transmigrating from one body to another. Without this knowledge, all his theories are based on a misunderstanding.

Not only Freud, but everyone in this material world is under illusion. In Bengal, a psychiatrist in the civil service was once called to give evidence in a case where the murderer was pleading insanity. The civil servant examined him to discover whether he was actually insane or not. In the courtroom he said, "I have tested many persons, and I have concluded that everyone is insane to some degree. In the present case, if the defendant is pleading insanity, then you may acquit him if you like, but as far as I know, everyone is more or less insane." And that is our conclusion as well. Anyone who identifies with his material body must be crazy, because his life is based on a misconception.

Disciple: Freud also investigated the problem of anxiety, which he concluded was produced when the impulses of the id threaten to overpower the rational ego and the moral superego.
Śrīla Prabhupāda: Anxiety will continue as long as one is in the material condition. No one can be free from anxiety in conditioned life.
Disciple: Is it because our desires are always frustrated?
Śrīla Prabhupāda: Yes. Your desires must be frustrated because you desire something that is not permanent. Suppose I wish to live forever, but since I have accepted a material body, there is no question of living forever. Therefore I am always anxious that death will come. I am afraid of death, when the body will be destroyed. This is the cause of all anxiety: acceptance of something impermanent as permanent.
Disciple: Freud says that anxiety develops when the superego represses the primitive desires of the id to protect the ego. Is such repression of basic instincts very healthy?
Śrīla Prabhupāda: Yes. For us repression means restraining oneself from doing something which, in the long run, is against one's welfare. For example, suppose you are suffering from diabetes and the doctor says, "Don't eat any sweet food." If you desire to eat sweets, you must repress that desire. Similarly, in our system of *brahmacarya* there is also repression. A *brahmacārī* should not sit down with a young woman, or even look at one lustfully. He may desire to do so, but he must repress the desire. This is called *tapasya,* or voluntary repression.
Disciple: But aren't these desires given outlet in other ways? For instance, instead of looking at a beautiful woman, we look at the beautiful form of Kṛṣṇa.
Śrīla Prabhupāda: Yes, that is our process: *paraṁ dṛṣṭvā nivartate.* If you have a better engagement, you can give up an inferior engagement. When you are captivated by seeing the beautiful form of Kṛṣṇa, naturally you have no more desire to look at the so-called beautiful form of a young woman.
Disciple: What are the effects of childhood experiences

on a person's later development?
Śrīla Prabhupāda: Children imitate whoever they associate with. You all know the movie *Tarzan.* Tarzan was brought up by apes, and he took on the habits of apes. If you keep children in good association, their psychological development will be very good—they will become like demigods. But if you keep them in bad association, they will turn out to be demons. Children are a blank slate. You can mold them as you like, and they are eager to learn.
Disciple: So a child's personality doesn't develop according to a fixed pattern?
Śrīla Prabhupāda: No. You can mold them in any way, like soft dough. However you put them into the mold, they will come out—like *bharats, capātīs,* or *kacaurīs*. Therefore if you give children good association, they will develop nicely, and if you put them in bad association, they will develop poorly. They have no independent psychology.
Disciple: Actually, Freud had a rather pessimistic view of human nature: he believed that we are all beset with irrational and chaotic impulses that cannot be eliminated.
Śrīla Prabhupāda: This is not only pessimism, but evidence of his poor fund of knowledge. He did not have perfect knowledge, nor was he trained by a perfect man. Therefore his theories are all nonsense.
Disciple: He concluded that it was impossible to be happy in this material world, but that one can alleviate some of the conflicts through psychoanalysis. He thought one can try to make the path as smooth as possible, but it will always be troublesome.
Śrīla Prabhupāda: It is true that one cannot be happy in this material world. But if one becomes spiritually elevated—if his consciousness is changed to Kṛṣṇa consciousness—then he will be happy.

Chapter FOURTEEN

SARTRE

The Frenchman John-Paul Sartre (1905–1980) was the most prominent exponent of existentialism. His philosophy is explicitly atheistic and pessimistic; he declared that human beings require a rational basis for their lives but are unable to achieve one and thus human life is a "futile passion." Here Śrīla Prabhupāda challenges his claim that God does not exist and that the question of His existence is not important to man.

Disciple: Descartes and Leibnitz believed that before the creation the concept of man existed in essence in the mind of God, just as a machine exists in the mind of its manufacturer before it is constructed. Sartre takes exception to this. In *The Humanism of Existentialism,* he writes: "Atheistic existentialism, which I represent, is more coherent. It states that if God does not exist, there is at least one being in whom existence precedes essence, a being who exists before he can be defined by any concept, and that this being is man, or, as Heidegger says, human reality."

Śrīla Prabhupāda: But where does human reality come from? There are also other realities. Why is he stressing human reality?
Disciple: As for man's origin, Sartre would say that man is "thrown into the world."
Śrīla Prabhupāda: Thrown by whom? The word "throw" implies a thrower.
Disciple: Sartre isn't really interested in a thrower. "Existentialism isn't so atheistic that it wears itself out showing God doesn't exist," he writes. "Rather, it declares that even if God did exist, that would change nothing. There you've got our point of view. Not that we believe that God exists, but that we think that the problem of His existence is not the issue."
Śrīla Prabhupāda: But if you and others exist, why doesn't God exist? Why deny God and His existence? Let them all exist.
Disciple: Since Sartre sees man as having been thrown into the world and abandoned, for him, God is dead.
Śrīla Prabhupāda: Abandoned by God does not mean that God is dead. You have to admit that you are condemned to the material world, but just because you are condemned, you should not think that God is also condemned. God is always in Vaikuṇṭha. He is not dead.
Disciple: Sartre believes that because we have been abandoned, we must rely on ourselves alone.
Śrīla Prabhupāda: But God has not abandoned us. God is not partial. He does not accept one person and abandon another. If you feel abandoned, it is because you have done something that has brought this condition about. If you rectify your position, you will be accepted again.
Disciple: But Sartre would deny God's existence, particularly that of a personal God.
Śrīla Prabhupāda: But his denial should be based on some logic or reason. Why mention the word "God" if God does not exist? God is there, but Sartre denies God's existence. This is inconsistent. If God does not exist, why even mention the word? His proposal is that he does not want God to exist.

Disciple: He wants to set the whole question aside in order to place emphasis on man, on human reality.
Śrīla Prabhupāda: If you believe in your existence, why not believe in the existence of another? There are 8,400,000 different species existing in multifarious forms. Why shouldn't God exist? According to the Vedic understanding, God is also a living being, but He is different in that He is the chief, supreme living being. According to the *Bhagavad-gītā, mattaḥ parataraṁ nānyat.* [*Bhagavad-gītā* 7.7] There is no living being superior to God. We all experience the fact that there are beings more intelligent than we are. God is the ultimate intelligence. Why can't a person who exceeds all others in intelligence exist? There is no question of "if God exists." God *must* exist. In the *śāstras* He is described as the superlative personality, as the superpowerful, superintelligent being. We can see in this world that everyone is not on an equal level, that there are varying degrees of perfection. This indicates that there is a superlative, and if we go on searching—either for wealth, intelligence, power, beauty, or whatever—we will find that God possesses all qualities to the superlative degree, and that every other living entity possesses His qualities partially. How, then, can we rationally deny His existence?
Disciple: According to Sartre, the first principle of existentialism is that "man is nothing else but what he makes of himself." This can be true only if there is no God to conceive of human nature.
Śrīla Prabhupāda: If man is what he makes of himself, why doesn't man exist as a superman? If his capacities are completely independent of anyone else, why is he in his present situation?
Disciple: That is also Sartre's question. He therefore emphasizes man's responsibility. "But if existence really does precede essence," he writes, "man is responsible for what he is. Thus existentialism's first move is to make every man aware of what he is and to make the full responsibility of his existence rest on him."
Śrīla Prabhupāda: If man is responsible, who gave him this

responsibility? What does he mean by responsibility? You feel responsible to someone when someone gives you duties to discharge. If there is no duty, or overseer, where is your responsibility?

Disciple: Sartre sees man as being overwhelmed by his very responsibility. He is in anguish and anxiety because he has the freedom to change himself and the world.

Śrīla Prabhupāda: This means that man is in an awkward position. He wants peace, but he does not know how to attain it. But this does not mean that peace is not possible. Peace is not possible for a man in ignorance.

Disciple: Anxiety arises from responsibility. Man thinks that he has to choose properly in order to enjoy something. If he chooses wrongly, he must suffer.

Śrīla Prabhupāda: Yes, responsibility is there, but why not take it to transfer yourself to a safe place where there is no anxiety? It may be that you do not know of a safe place, but if there is such a place, why not ask someone who knows? Why constantly remain disappointed and anxious? The safe place where there is no anxiety is called Vaikuṇṭha. The word Vaikuṇṭha means "no anxiety."

Disciple: Sartre believes that the task of existentialism is "to make every man aware of what he is and to make the full responsibility of his existence rest on him. . . . And when we say that a man is responsible for himself, we do not only mean that he is responsible for his own individuality, but that he is responsible for all men."

Śrīla Prabhupāda: Suppose I want to benefit you, and you are free. Your freedom means that you can accept or reject my good intentions. How can I be responsible for you if you don't obey? How can you be responsible for me? Sartre claims that you are responsible for others, but if others do not follow your instructions, how can you be considered responsible? This is all contradictory. Unless there is some standard, there must be contradiction. According to the Vedic version, God is the Supreme Person, and we should all be His obedient servants. God gives us some duty, and we are responsible to carry that duty out. Our real responsibility is to God. If we reject God, society becomes chaotic. Religion means avoiding chaos and meeting our responsibility to God by fulfilling our duty. Responsibility rests on us, and it is given by God. If we make spiritual progress by fulfilling our duty, we can finally live with God personally.

Disciple: Sartre claims that the existentialist does not actually want to deny God's existence. Rather, "the existentialist thinks it very distressing that God does not exist because all possibility of finding values in a heaven of ideas disappears along with Him. . . . If God didn't exist, everything would be possible. That is the very starting point of existentialism. Indeed, everything is permissible if God does not exist. . . ."

Śrīla Prabhupāda: This means that he does not know the meaning of God. As we have many times said, God is the Supreme Being, the Supreme Father who impregnates material nature with countless living entities. As soon as we accept material nature as the mother, we must accept some father. Therefore there is a conception of God the Father in all human societies. It is the father's duty to maintain his children, and therefore God is maintaining all the living entities within the universe. There is no question of rationally denying this.

Disciple: Well, Sartre at least makes the attempt. He writes: "Since we have discarded God the Father, there has to be someone to invent values. You've got to take things as they are. Moreover, to say that we invent values means nothing else but this: Life has no meaning a priori. Before you become alive, life is nothing; it's up to you to give it a meaning, and value is nothing else but the meaning that you choose."

Śrīla Prabhupāda: Therefore everyone invents his own meaning? If this is the case, how will people ever live peacefully in society? Since everyone has his own idea of life, there can be no harmony. What kind of government would exist?

Disciple: Recently, Sartre has turned to Marxism.

Śrīla Prabhupāda: But in Communist countries, there are very strong governments. It is not possible for a people to avoid government or leadership.

Disciple: Regardless of the form of government, Sartre believes that man is basically free. In fact, Sartre maintains that man is *condemned* to be free, that this is a fate from which man cannot escape.

Śrīla Prabhupāda: If man is condemned, who has condemned him?

Disciple: He's condemned by accident, thrown into the world.

Śrīla Prabhupāda: Is it simply by accident that one person is condemned and another blessed? Is it an accident that one man is in jail and another is not? What kind of philosophy is this? Such so-called philosophy simply misleads people. Nothing is accidental. We agree that the living entity is condemned to this material world, but when we speak of condemnation, we also speak of blessedness. So what is that blessedness?

Disciple: Sartre argues that man is condemned in the sense that he cannot escape this freedom. Since man is free, he is responsible for is activities.

Śrīla Prabhupāda: If you are responsible, then your freedom is not accidental. How is it you are accidentally responsible? If there is responsibility, there must be someone you are responsible to. There must be someone who is condemning you or blessing you. These things cannot happen accidentally. His philosophy is contradictory.

Disciple: Man's nature is an indefinite state of freedom. Man has no definite nature. He is continually creating it.

Śrīla Prabhupāda: This means that he is eternal. But the living entity does not change accidentally. His changes take place under certain regulations, and he attains specific bodies according to his karma, not by accident.

Disciple: But we have no fixed nature in the sense that today I may be happy and tomorrow unhappy.

Śrīla Prabhupāda: That is true to some extent. When you are placed into the sea, you have no control. You move according to the waves. This means that there is a power that is controlling you. However, if you put yourself into better circumstances, you will be able to control. Because you have placed yourself under the control of material nature, you act according to the modes of material nature.

prakṛteḥ kriyamāṇāni guṇaiḥ karmāṇi sarvaśaḥ
ahaṅkāra-vimūḍhātmā kartāham iti manyate

"The spirit soul bewildered by the influence of false ego thinks himself the doer of activities that are in actuality carried out by the three modes of material nature." [Bg 3.27] Because you are conditioned, your freedom is checked. When you are thrown into the ocean of material existence, you essentially lose your freedom. Therefore it is your duty to get yourself liberated.

Disciple: Because we are one thing today and something else tomorrow, Sartre concludes that our essential nature is "no-thingness."

Śrīla Prabhupāda: You are nothing in the sense that you are under the full control of a superior power, being carried away by the waves of *māyā*. In the ocean of *māyā,* you may say, "I am nothing," but actually you are something. Your somethingness will be very much exhibited to you when you are put on land. Out of despair, you conclude that your nature is that of nothingness. Sartre's philosophy is a philosophy of despair, and we say that it is unintelligent because despair is not the result of intelligence.

Disciple: Although the basis of our nature is nothingness, Sartre maintains that man chooses or creates his own nature.

Śrīla Prabhupāda: That is a fact. Therefore you should create your nature as something, not nothing. In order to do that, however, you have to take lessons from a higher personality. Before philosophizing, Sartre should have taken lessons form a knowledgeable person. That is the Vedic injunction:

tad-vijñānārthaṁ sa gurum evābhigacchet
samit-pāṇiḥ śrotriyaṁ brahma-niṣṭham

"In order to learn the transcendental science, one must

humbly approach a spiritual master who is learned in the *Vedas* and firmly devoted to the Absolute Truth." [*Muṇḍaka Upaniṣad* 1.2.12]

Disciple: Sartre sees our nature as always in the making, as continually becoming.

Śrīla Prabhupāda: It is not in the making. It is changing. But man can make his nature in the sense that he can decide not to change. He can understand that changes are taking place despite the fact that he does not want them. Man can mold his nature by deciding to serve Kṛṣṇa, not by dismissing the whole matter and, out of confusion and disappointment, claiming to be nothing. The attempt to make life zero is due to a poor fund of knowledge.

Disciple: Sartre sees that we are constantly choosing or making our life, but that everything ends at death. That is, man is always in the process of becoming until death. At death, everything is finished.

Śrīla Prabhupāda: Death means changing bodies. The active principle on which the body stands does not die. Death is like changing apartments. A sane man can understand this.

Disciple: Although man has no determined nature other than nothingness, Sartre sees man as a being striving to be God. He writes: "To be man means to reach toward being God. Or if you prefer, man fundamentally is the desire to be God."

Śrīla Prabhupāda: On the one hand, he denies the existence of God, and on the other, he tries to be God. If there is no God, there is no question of desiring to be God. How can one desire to be something that does not exist?

Disciple: He is simply stating that man wants to be God. As far as God's existence is concerned, he prefers to set this question aside.

Śrīla Prabhupāda: But that is the main question of philosophy! God has created everything: your mind, intelligence, body, existence, and the circumstances surrounding you. How can you deny His existence? Or set it aside as not relevant? In the *Vedas,* it is stated that in the beginning God existed, and the Bible also states that in the beginning there was God. In this material universe, existence and annihilation are both temporary. According to the laws of material nature, the body is created on a certain day, it exists for some time, and then it is eventually finished. The entire cosmic manifestation has a beginning, middle, and end. But before the creation, who was there? If God were not there, how could the creation logically be possible?

Disciple: As far as we've seen, most philosophers are concerned with resolving this question.

Śrīla Prabhupāda: Not all philosophers are denying God's existence, but most are denying His personal existence. We can understand, however, that God is the origin of everything, and that this cosmic manifestation emanates from Him. God is there, nature is there, and we are also there, like one big family.

Disciple: Sartre would not admit the existence of an originator, in whom things exist in their essence prior to creation. He would say that man simply exists, that he just appears.

Śrīla Prabhupāda: A person appears due to his father and mother. How can this be denied? Does he mean to say, "I suddenly just dropped from the sky"? Only a fool would say that he appeared without parents. From our experience we can understand that all species of life are manifest from some mother. Taken as a whole, we say that the mother is material nature. As soon as a mother is accepted, the father must also be accepted. It is most important to know where you came from. How can you put this question aside?

Disciple: Sartre believes that man's fundamental desire is the "desire to be." That is, man seeks existence rather than mere nothingness.

Śrīla Prabhupāda: That is so. Because man is eternal, he has the desire to exist eternally. Unfortunately, he puts himself under certain conditions that are not eternal. That is, he tries to maintain a position that will not endure eternally. Through Kṛṣṇa consciousness, we attain and retain our eternal position.

Disciple: Sartre feels that man wants solidity. He is not

satisfied with being a mere being-for-itself. He also desires to be being-in-itself.
Śrīla Prabhupāda: Nothing in the material world exists eternally. A tree may exist for ten thousand years, but eventually it will perish. What Sartre is seeking is actual spiritual life. In the *Bhagavad-gītā,* Kṛṣṇa speaks of another nature, a nature that is permanent, *sanātana.*

paras tasmāt tu bhāvo 'nyo 'vyakto 'vyaktāt sanātanaḥ
yaḥ sa sarveṣu bhūteṣu naśyatsu na vinaśyati

"Yet there is another unmanifest nature, which is eternal and is transcendental to this manifested and unmanifested matter. It is supreme and is never annihilated. When all in this world is annihilated, that part remains as it is." [*Bhagavad-gītā* 8.20] After the annihilation of this material universe, that eternal nature will abide.
Disciple: This desire to be being-in-itself is the desire to be God, which Sartre maintains is man's fundamental desire.
Śrīla Prabhupāda: This is more or less Māyāvāda philosophy. The Māyāvādīs believe that when they attain complete knowledge, they become God. Because man is part and parcel of God, he wants to be united with God. The conditioned soul is like a man who has been away from home for a long time. Naturally he wants to go home again.
Disciple: Sartre believes that this desire to be God is bound to fail.
Śrīla Prabhupāda: Certainly, it must fail. If man is God, how has he become something else? His very desire to be God means that he is not God at the present moment. A man cannot become God, but he can become god*ly*. Existing in darkness, we desire light. We may come into the sunshine, but this does not mean that we become the sun. When we come to the platform of perfect knowledge, we become godly, but we do not become God. If we were God, there would be no question of our becoming something other than God. There would be no question of being ignorant. Another name for Kṛṣṇa is

Acyuta, which means, "He who never falls down." This means that He never becomes not-God. He is God always. You cannot become God through some mystic practice. This desire to become God is useless because it is doomed to frustration.

Disciple: Therefore Sartre calls man a "useless passion."

Śrīla Prabhupāda: A man is not useless if he attempts to be Kṛṣṇa conscious. The attempt to be Kṛṣṇa conscious and the attempt to be Kṛṣṇa are totally different. One is godly, the other demoniac.

Disciple: Sartre then reasons that because it is impossible to become God, everything else is useless.

Śrīla Prabhupāda: That is foolishness. You are not God, but God's servant. You have chosen to attempt to become God, but you have found this to be impossible. Therefore you should give up this notion and decide to become a good servant of God instead of a servant of *māyā,* illusion. That is the proper decision.

Disciple: Sartre concludes that since things have no reason to exist, life has no essential purpose.

Śrīla Prabhupāda: Nothing can exist without a purpose, which is given by the supreme being, the cause of all causes. The defect in such philosophers is that they do not have sufficient brain substance to go further than what they superficially see. They are not capable of understanding the cause of all causes. Many modern scientists also maintain that nature, *prakṛti,* is the sole cause of everything in existence, but we do not subscribe to such a theory. We understand that God is behind nature and that nature is not acting independently. Nature is phenomena, but behind nature is the numen, God, Kṛṣṇa.

In the *Bhagavad-gītā,* philosophy like Sartre's is called demoniac. Demons do not believe in a superior cause. They consider that everything is accidental. They say that a man and a woman unite accidentally, and that their child is the result of sex and nothing more. Therefore they claim that there is no purpose to existence.

asatyam apratiṣṭhaṁ te jagad āhur anīśvaram
aparaspara-sambhūtaṁ kim anyat kāma-haitukam

"The demons say that this world is unreal, with no foundation, no God in control. They say it is produced of sex desire and has no cause other than lust." [*Bhagavad-gītā* 16.8] This type of philosophy is called demoniac because it is of the nature of darkness, ignorance.

Disciple: For Sartre, being-for-itself refers to human consciousness, which is subjective, individual, incomplete, and indeterminate. It is nothingness in the sense that it has no density or mass.

Śrīla Prabhupāda: Because he is so materialistic, his senses cannot perceive anything that is not concrete. According to Vedic philosophy, the senses and their objects are created simultaneously. Unless there is an aroma, the sense of smell has no value. Unless there is beauty, the eyes have no value. Unless there is music, the ears have no value. Unless there is something soft, the sense of touch has no value. There is no question of nothingness. There must be interaction.

Disciple: Since man's essential nature is an undetermined nothingness, Sartre believes that man is free to choose to be either a coward or a hero. Our situation is in our own hands.

Śrīla Prabhupāda: If you are tossed into the world by some superior power, what can you do? How can you become a hero? If you try to become a hero, you will be kicked all the more because you are placed here by a superior power. If a culprit under police custody attempts to become a hero, he will be beaten and punished. Actually, you are neither a coward nor a hero. You are an instrument. You are completely under the control of a superior power.

Disciple: Well, if someone is attacking you, you have the power to choose to be a hero and defend yourself, or to run.

Śrīla Prabhupāda: It is not heroic to defend oneself. That is natural. If that were the case, even a dog would be a hero when he is attacked. Even an ant can be a hero. Heroism and cowardice are simply mental concoctions. After all, you are under the control of a power that can do what He likes with you. Therefore there is no question of your becoming a hero or a coward.

Disciple: Suppose someone is in danger, and you rescue him. Isn't that being heroic?

Śrīla Prabhupāda: All you rescue is the exterior dress. Saving that dress is not heroism. It is not even protection. One can be a real hero only when he is fully empowered or fully protected. Such a person can only be a devotee, because only Kṛṣṇa can fully protect or empower.

Disciple: Being free, man is subject to what Sartre calls "bad faith," a kind of self-deception. Through bad faith, man loses his freedom and responsibility.

Śrīla Prabhupāda: You certainly have limited freedom to choose, but if you choose improperly, you have to suffer. Responsibility and freedom go hand in hand. At the same time, there must be discrimination. Without it, our freedom is blind. We cannot understand right from wrong.

Disciple: A man in bad faith drifts along from day to day without being involved, avoiding responsible decisions.

Śrīla Prabhupāda: This means that he has decided to drift. His drifting is in itself a decision.

Disciple: Sartre believes that bad faith must be replaced by a solid choosing, and by faith in that choice.

Śrīla Prabhupāda: But if he makes the wrong decision, what is the value of his action? Moths fly very valiantly and courageously into the fire. Is that a very good decision?

Disciple: Due to bad faith, people treat others as objects instead of persons. Sartre advocates rectifying this situation.

Śrīla Prabhupāda: He speaks of bad faith, but what about good faith?

Disciple: If bad faith is the avoidance of decisions, good faith would mean making decisions courageously and following them out, regardless of what these decisions are.

Śrīla Prabhupāda: But what if your decision is wrong?

Disciple: For Sartre, it is not a question of right or wrong.

Śrīla Prabhupāda: Then whatever decision I make is final and absolute? This means that the moth's decision to enter the fire is a proper decision. This is the philosophy of insects. If man can do as he pleases, where is his responsibility?

Disciple: Sartre believes that the fate of the world depends on man's decisions. Obviously, if man decides properly, the world would be a better place.

Śrīla Prabhupāda: Therefore we are trying to introduce this Kṛṣṇa consciousness in order to make the world into Vaikuṇṭha, into a place where there is no anxiety. But this is not a blind decision. It is the decision of a higher authority; therefore it is perfect.

Disciple: Many people call Sartre's philosophy pessimistic because he maintains that man is a "useless passion" vainly striving in a universe without a purpose.

Śrīla Prabhupāda: Sartre may be a useless passion, but we are not. No sane man is useless. A sane man will follow a superior authority. That is Vedic civilization. If one approaches a bona fide spiritual master, he will not be bewildered. Sartre believes that the universe is without a purpose because he is blind. He has no power to see that there is a plan. Therefore, as I have already mentioned, the *Bhagavad-gītā* calls his philosophy demoniac. Everything in the universe functions according to some plan. The sun and moon rise, and the seasons change according to plan.

Disciple: For Sartre, man stands alone in the world, yet he is not alone if he is a being-for-others. Man needs others for his own self-realization.

Śrīla Prabhupāda: This means that man requires a guru.

Disciple: Sartre does not speak of a guru but of interaction with others for self-understanding.

Śrīla Prabhupāda: Then why not interact with the best man? If we require others to understand ourselves, why should we not seek the best man for our own understanding? We should receive help from the man who knows. If you take the advice of one who can give you the right direction, your end will be glorious. That is the Vedic injunction. *Tad-vijñānārthaṁ sa gurum evābhigacchet.* [*Muṇḍaka Upaniṣad* 1.2.12]

Disciple: Sartre feels that in the presence of others, man is ashamed.

Śrīla Prabhupāda: Man is ashamed if he is not guided by a superior. If you are guided by a superior, you will be glorious, not ashamed. Your superior is that person who can lead you to the glory of Kṛṣṇa consciousness.

Chapter FIFTEEN

JUNG

Carl Jung (1865–1961) was a Swiss student of Freud's who broke with his teacher and began his own school of psychiatry. He is best known for his work in exploring the unconscious and for championing the importance of philosophy, religion, and mysticism in understanding the human mind. Here Śrīla Prabhupāda makes clear that although many of Jung's conclusions concerning the soul, God, and consciousness were correct, his lack of a self-realized guide ultimately left Jung frustrated in his spiritual search.

Disciple: Jung criticized Freud in this way: "Sexuality evidently meant more to Freud than to other people. For him it was something to be religiously observed. . . . One thing was clear: Freud, who had always made much of his irreligiosity, had now constructed a dogma. Or rather, in the place of a jealous God whom he had lost, he had substituted another compelling image, that of sexuality."
Śrīla Prabhupāda: Yes, that is a fact. He has taken sexuality

to be God. It is our natural tendency to accept a leader, and Freud simply abandoned the leadership of God and took up the leadership of sex. On the other hand, if we accept the leadership of Kṛṣṇa, our life becomes perfect. All other leadership is the leadership of *māyā*. There is no doubt that we have to accept a leader. Although Freud would not admit it, he accepted sex as his leader, and consequently he was constantly speaking about sex. Those who have taken God as their leader will speak only of God, nothing else. *Jīvera 'svarūpa' haya—kṛṣṇera 'nitya-dāsa'*. According to Caitanya Mahāprabhu's philosophy, we are all eternal servants of God, but as soon as we give up God's service, we have to accept the service of *māyā*.

Disciple: Jung sees the mind as being composed of a balance of the conscious and the unconscious, or subconscious. It is the function of the personality to integrate these. For instance, if one has a strong sex drive, he can sublimate or channel it into art or religious activity.

Śrīla Prabhupāda: That is our process. The sex impulse is natural for everyone in the material world. But if we think of Kṛṣṇa embracing Rādhārāṇī or dancing with the *gopīs,* our sex impulse is sublimated and weakened. If one hears about the pastimes of Kṛṣṇa and the *gopīs* from the right source, lusty desire within the heart will be suppressed, and one will be able to develop devotional service.

Disciple: This would be an example of what Jung would call integration or individuation, whereby the energies of the subconscious sex impulse are channeled into conscious, creative activity directed toward God realization.

Śrīla Prabhupāda: What we must understand is that Kṛṣṇa is the only *puruṣa,* the only enjoyer. If we help Him in His enjoyment, we also receive enjoyment. We are predominated, and He is the predominator. On the material platform, if a husband wants to enjoy the wife, the wife must voluntarily help him in that enjoyment. By helping him, the wife also becomes an enjoyer. Similarly, the supreme predominator, the supreme enjoyer, is Kṛṣṇa. And the predominated, the enjoyed, are the living entities. When the living entities agree to help Kṛṣṇa's sex desire, they become enjoyers.

Disciple: What is meant by Kṛṣṇa's sex desire?

Śrīla Prabhupāda: You might say "sense enjoyment." Kṛṣṇa is the supreme proprietor of the senses, and when we help Kṛṣṇa in His sense enjoyment, we also naturally partake of that enjoyment. The sweet *rasagullā* is meant to be enjoyed, and therefore the hand puts it into the mouth so that it can be tasted and go to the stomach. The hand cannot enjoy the *rasagullā* directly. Kṛṣṇa is the only direct enjoyer; all others are indirect enjoyers. By satisfying Kṛṣṇa, others will be satisfied. Upon seeing the predominator happy, the predominated become happy.

Disciple: Psychologists say that quite often the subconscious is acting through the conscious, but that we do not know it.

Śrīla Prabhupāda: Yes. The subconscious is there, but it is not always manifest. Sometimes a thought suddenly becomes manifest, just as a bubble will suddenly emerge in a pond. You may not be able to understand why it emerges, but we may assume that it was in the subconscious state and suddenly became manifest. That subconscious thought which is manifest does not necessarily have any connection with one's present consciousness. It is like a stored impression, a shadow or a photograph. The mind takes many snapshots, and they are stored.

Disciple: Jung could see that the soul is always longing for light, and he wrote of the urge within the soul to rise out of darkness. He noted the pent-up feeling in the eyes of primitive people and a certain sadness in the eyes of animals. He wrote, "There is a sadness in animals' eyes, and we never know whether that sadness is bound up with the soul of the animal or is a poignant message which speaks to us out of that existence."

Śrīla Prabhupāda: Yes. Every living entity, including man, is constitutionally a servant. Therefore everyone is seeking some master, and that is our natural propensity. You can often see a puppy attempt to take shelter of some boy or man, and that is his natural tendency. He is saying, "Give me shelter. Keep me as your friend." A child or a man also wants some shelter in order to be happy. That is our constitutional position. When we attain the human form, when our consciousness is developed, we should take Kṛṣṇa as our shelter and our leader. In the *Bhagavad-gītā* Kṛṣṇa tells us that if we want shelter and guidance, we should take His: *sarva-dharmān parityajya mām ekaṁ śaraṇaṁ vraja.* This is the ultimate instruction of the *Bhagavad-gītā.*

Disciple: Jung would say that our understanding of Kṛṣṇa as the supreme father and the cause of all causes is an archetypal understanding shared by all humans. All people have the tendency to understand someone to be their supreme father and primal cause, and they will represent Him in different ways. The archetype, however, is the same.

Śrīla Prabhupāda: Yes, it is exactly the same. Kṛṣṇa, or God, is the supreme father. A father has many sons, and all men are sons of God, born of their father. This is an experience common to everyone at all times.

Disciple: Jung believed that because there are so many subconscious factors governing our personality, we must awaken to them. Unless we do so, we are more or less slaves to our subconscious life. The point of psychoanalysis is to reveal as many aspects of our subconscious life as possible and enable us to face them.

Śrīla Prabhupāda: That is what we are teaching. We say that presently the soul is in a sleeping state, and we are telling the soul, "Please wake up! Please wake up! You are not the body! You are not the body!" It is possible to awaken the human being, but other living entities cannot be awakened. A tree, for instance, has consciousness, but he is so packed in matter that you cannot raise him to Kṛṣṇa consciousness. A human being, on the other hand, has developed consciousness, which is manifest in different stages. Lower life forms are more or less in a dream state.

Disciple: Whereas Freud was sexually oriented, Jung was more or less spiritually oriented. In his autobiography—

Memories, Dreams, Reflections—Jung writes, "I find that all my thoughts circle around God like the planets around the sun, and are as irresistibly attracted by Him. I would feel it to be the grossest sin if I were to put up any resistance to this force." Jung sees all creatures as parts of God and at the same time unique in themselves. He writes, "Man cannot compare himself with any other creature; he is not a monkey, not a cow, not a tree. I am a man. But what is it to be that? Like every other being, I am a splinter of the infinite Deity. . . ."

Śrīla Prabhupāda: It is also our philosophy that we are part and parcel of God, just as sparks are part of a fire.

Disciple: Jung further writes in his autobiography, "It was obedience which brought me grace. . . . One must be utterly abandoned to God; nothing matters but fulfilling His will. Otherwise, all is folly and meaningless."

Śrīla Prabhupāda: Very good. Surrender unto God is real spiritual life. *Sarva-dharmān parityajya.* Surrender to God means accepting that which is favorable to God and rejecting that which is unfavorable. The devotee is always convinced that God will give him all protection. He remains humble and meek and thinks of himself as a member of God's family. This is real spiritual communism. Communists think, "I am a member of a certain community," but it is a man's duty to think, "I am a member of God's family." God is the supreme father, material nature is the mother, and living entities are all sons of God. There are living entities everywhere—on land and in the air and water. There is no doubt that material nature is the mother, and according to our experience we can understand that a mother cannot produce a child without a father. It is absurd to think that a child can be born without a father. A father must be there, and the supreme father is God. In Kṛṣṇa consciousness, a person understands that the creation is a spiritual family headed by one supreme father.

Disciple: Concerning God's personality, Jung writes this: "According to the Bible, God has a personality and is the ego of the universe, just as I myself am the ego of my psychic and physical being."

Śrīla Prabhupāda: Yes. The individual is conscious of his own body, but not of the bodies of others. Besides the individual soul or consciousness in the body, there is the Paramātmā, the Supersoul, the superconsciousness present in everyone's heart. This is discussed in the *Bhagavad-gītā* [13.3], where Kṛṣṇa says,

kṣetra-jñaṁ cāpi māṁ viddhi sarva-kṣetreṣu bhārata
kṣetra-kṣetrajñayor jñānaṁ yat taj jñānaṁ mataṁ mama

"You should understand that I am also the knower in all bodies, and to understand this body and its knower is called knowledge. That is My opinion."

Disciple: Recalling his difficulties in understanding God's personality, Jung writes, "Here I encountered a formidable obstacle. Personality, after all, surely signifies character. Now, character is one thing and not another; that is to say, it involves certain specific attributes. But if God is everything, how can He still possess a distinguishable character? . . . What kind of character or what kind of personality does He have?"

Śrīla Prabhupāda: God's character is transcendental, not material, but He has attributes. For instance, He is very kind to His devotee, and this kindness may be considered one of His characteristics or attributes. Whatever qualities or characteristics we have are but minute manifestations of God's. God is the origin of all attributes and characteristics. As indicated in the *śāstra,* He also has mind, senses, feelings, sense perception, sense gratification, and everything else. Everything is there unlimitedly, and since we are part and parcel of God, we possess His qualities in minute quantities. The original qualities are in God and are manifest minutely in ourselves.

According to the *Vedas* God is a person just like us, but His personality is unlimited. Just as my consciousness is limited to this body and His consciousness is the superconsciousness within every body, so I am a person confined to this particular body and He is the superperson living within all. As Kṛṣṇa tells Arjuna in the *Bhagavad-gītā* [2.12], the personality of God and the personalities of the individual souls are eternally existing. Kṛṣṇa tells Arjuna on the battlefield, "Never was there a time when I did not exist, nor you, nor all these kings, nor in the future shall any of us cease to be." Both God and the living entity are eternally persons, but God's personality is unlimited and the individual's personality is limited. God has unlimited power, wealth, fame, knowledge, beauty, and renunciation. We have limited, finite power, knowledge, fame, and so on. That is the difference between the two personalities.

Disciple: Jung found that philosophies and theologies could not give him a clear picture of God's personality. He writes this: "'What is wrong with these philosophers?' I wondered—evidently, they know of God only by hearsay."

Śrīla Prabhupāda: Yes, that is also our complaint. The philosophers we have studied have failed to give any clear idea of God. Because they are speculating, they cannot give concrete, clear information. As far as we are concerned, our understanding of God is clear because we simply receive the information given to the world by God Himself. Kṛṣṇa is accepted as the Supreme Person by Vedic authorities; therefore we should have no reason not to accept Him as such. Nārāyaṇa, Lord Śiva, and Lord Brahmā possess different percentages of God's attributes, but Kṛṣṇa possesses all the attributes cent percent, in totality. Rūpa Gosvāmī has analyzed this in his *Bhakti-rasāmṛta-sindhu,* which we have translated as *The Nectar of Devotion.*

In any case, God is a person, and if we study man's attributes, we can also know something of God's. Just as we enjoy ourselves with friends, parents, and others, God also enjoys Himself in various relationships. There are five primary and seven secondary relationships that the living entities can have with God. Since the living entities take pleasure in these relationships, God is described as *akhila-rasāmṛta-sindhu,* the reservoir of all pleasure. There is no need to speculate about God or try to imagine Him. The process for understanding is described by Lord Kṛṣṇa in the *Bhagavad-gītā* [7.1]:

mayy āsakta-manāḥ pārtha yogaṁ yuñjan mad-āśrayaḥ
asaṁśayaṁ samagraṁ māṁ yathā jñāsyasi tac chṛṇu

"Now hear, O Arjuna, how by practicing yoga in full consciousness of Me, with mind attached to Me, you can know Me in full, free from doubt." You can learn about God by always keeping yourself under His protection, or under the protection of His representative. Then without a doubt you can perfectly understand God; otherwise there is no question of understanding Him.

Disciple: Jung goes on to point out the difference between theologians and philosophers. He writes, "At least they [the theologians] are sure that God exists, even though they make contradictory statements about Him. . . . God's existence does not depend on our proofs. . . . I understand that God was, for me at least, one of the most certain and immediate of experiences."

Śrīla Prabhupāda: Yes, that is a transcendental conviction. One may not know God, but it is very easy to understand that God is there. One has to learn about God's nature, but there is no doubt about the fact that God is there. Any sane man can understand that he is being controlled. So who is that controller? The supreme controller is God. This is the conclusion of a sane man. Jung is right when he says that God's existence does not depend on our proof.

Disciple: Jung continues to recall his early spiritual quests in this way: "In my darkness . . . I could have wished for nothing better than a real, live guru, someone possessing superior knowledge and ability, who would have disentangled from me the involuntary creations of my imagination."

Śrīla Prabhupāda: Yes. According to the Vedic instructions, in order to acquire perfect knowledge, one must have a guru (*tad vijñānārthaṁ sa gurum evābhigacchet*). The guru must factually be a representative of God. He must have seen and experienced God in fact, not simply in theory. We have to approach such a guru, and by service, surrender, and sincere inquiry we can come to understand God. The *Vedas* inform us that a person can understand God when he has received a little mercy from His Lordship; otherwise, one may speculate for millions and millions of years. As Kṛṣṇa states in the *Bhagavad-gītā* [18.55], *bhaktyā mām abhijānāti:* "One can understand Me as I am, as the Supreme Personality of Godhead, only by devotional service." This process of *bhakti* includes *śravaṇaṁ kīrtanaṁ viṣṇoḥ*—hearing and chanting about Lord Viṣṇu [Kṛṣṇa] and always remembering Him. *Satataṁ kīrtayanto māṁ:* the devotee is always glorifying the Lord. As Prahlāda Mahārāja says in *Śrīmad-Bhāgavatam* [7.9.43]:

naivodvije para duratyaya-vaitaraṇyās
tvad-vīrya-gāyana-mahāmṛta-magna-cittaḥ

"O best of the great personalities, I am not at all afraid of material existence, since wherever I stay I am fully absorbed in thoughts of Your glories and activities." The devotee's consciousness is always drowned in the ocean of the unlimited pastimes and qualities of the Supreme Lord. That is transcendental bliss. The spiritual master teaches his disciple how to always remain in the ocean of God consciousness. One who works under the directions of the *ācārya*, the spiritual master, knows everything about God.

Disciple: In 1938 Jung was invited by the British government to participate in celebrations at the University of Calcutta. Of this Jung writes, "By that time, I had read a great deal about Indian philosophy and religious history and was deeply convinced of the value of Oriental wisdom." On this visit, Jung spoke with a celebrated guru, yet he avoided so-called holy men. He writes, "I did so because I had to make do with my own truth, not to accept from others what I could not attain on my own. I would have felt it as a theft had I attempted

to learn from the holy men to accept their truth for myself."
Śrīla Prabhupāda: On the one hand, he says he wants a guru, and then on the other, he doesn't want to accept one. Doubtlessly there were many so-called gurus in Calcutta, and Jung might have seen some bogus gurus he did not like. In any case, the principle of accepting a guru cannot be avoided. It is absolutely necessary.
Disciple: Concerning consciousness after death, Jung feels that after death the individual must pick up at the level of consciousness which he left.
Śrīla Prabhupāda: Yes, and therefore, according to that consciousness, one has to accept a body. That is the process of the soul's transmigration. An ordinary person can see only the gross material body, but accompanying this body are the mind, intelligence, and ego. When the body is finished, these remain, although they cannot be seen. A foolish man thinks that everything is finished at death. But the soul carries with it the mind, intelligence, and ego—that is, the subtle body—into another gross body. This is confirmed by the *Bhagavad-gītā,* which clearly explains that although the gross body is destroyed the consciousness continues. According to one's consciousness, one acquires another body, and again, in that body, the consciousness begins to mold its future lives. If a person was a devotee in his past life, he will again become a devotee after his death. Once the material body is destroyed, the same consciousness begins to work in another body. Consequently we find that some people quickly accept Kṛṣṇa consciousness whereas others take a longer time. This indicates that the consciousness is continuing, although the body is changing. Bharata Mahārāja, for instance, changed many bodies, but his consciousness continued, and he remained fully Kṛṣṇa conscious.

We may see a person daily, but we cannot visualize his intelligence. We can understand that a person is intelligent, but we cannot see intelligence itself. When one talks, we can understand that there is intelligence at work. But why should we conclude that when the gross body is dead and no longer capable of talking, the intelligence is finished? The instrument for speech is the gross body, but we should not conclude that when the gross body is finished, intelligence is also finished. *Na hanyate hanyamāne śarīre:* after the destruction of the gross body, the mind and intelligence continue. Because they require a body to function, they develop a body, and that is the process of the soul's transmigration.

Disciple: Jung felt that the individual's level of consciousness could not supersede whatever knowledge is available on this planet.

Śrīla Prabhupāda: No. One can supersede it, provided one can acquire knowledge from the proper authority. You may not have seen India, but a person who *has* seen India can describe it to you. We may not be able to see Kṛṣṇa, but we can learn of Him from an authority who knows. In the *Bhagavad-gītā* [8.20] Kṛṣṇa tells Arjuna that there is an eternal nature. On this earth we encounter temporary nature. Here things take birth, remain for some time, change, grow old, and are finally destroyed. There is dissolution in this material world, but there is another world, in which there is no dissolution. We have no personal experience of that world, but we can understand that it exists when we receive information from the proper authority. It is not necessary to know it by personal experience. There are different stages of knowledge, and not all knowledge can be acquired by direct perception. That is not possible.

Disciple: Jung sees earthly life to be of great significance, and what a man carries with him at the time of his death to be very important. He writes, "Only here, in life on earth, can the general level of consciousness be raised. That seems to be man's metaphysical task." Since consciousness survives death, it is important that a man's consciousness be elevated while he is on this earth.

Śrīla Prabhupāda: Yes, one's consciousness should be developed. As stated in the *Bhagavad-gītā,* if one's yoga practice is incomplete or if one dies prematurely, his consciousness accompanies him, and in the next life he begins at the point where he left off. His intelligence is revived. *Tatra taṁ buddhi-saṁyogaṁ labhate paurva-dehikam.* [*Bhagavad-gītā* 6.43] In an ordinary class we can see that some students learn very quickly while others cannot understand. This is evidence for the continuation of consciousness. If one is extraordinarily intelligent, the consciousness he developed in a previous life is being revived.

Disciple: Jung points out that there is a paradox surrounding death. From the viewpoint of the ego, death is a horrible catastrophe—"a fearful piece of brutality." Yet from the viewpoint of the psyche—the soul—death is "a joyful event. In the light of eternity, it is a wedding."

Śrīla Prabhupāda: Yes, death is horrible for one who is going to accept a lower form of life, and it is a pleasure for the devotee, because he is returning home, back to Godhead.

Disciple: So death is not always joyful for the soul?

Śrīla Prabhupāda: No. How can it be? If one has not developed his spiritual consciousness—Kṛṣṇa consciousness—death is very horrible. The tendency in this life is to become very proud, and often people think, "I don't care for God. I am independent." Crazy people talk in this way, but after death they have to accept a body according to the dictations of nature. Nature says, "My dear sir, since you have worked like a dog, you can become a dog," or, "Since you have been surfing in the sea, you can now become a fish." These bodies are awarded according to a superior order (*karmaṇā daiva-netreṇa*). In whatever way we interact with the modes of material nature, in that way we are creating our next body. How can we stop this process? This is nature's way.

If we are infected by some disease, we will necessarily get that disease. There are three modes of material nature—*tamo-guṇa, rajo-guṇa,* and *sattva-guṇa,* the modes of ignorance, passion, and goodness—and our bodies are acquired according to our association with them. In general, the human form affords us a chance to make progress in Kṛṣṇa consciousness, especially when we are born in an aristocratic family, a *brāhmaṇa* family, or a Vaiṣṇava family.

Disciple: Despite his many interesting points, Jung seems to have had a limited understanding of Indian philosophy. He doesn't understand that the cycle of birth and death has a goal, although it appears to be endless. Nor does he seem to know of Kṛṣṇa's promise in the *Bhagavad-gītā* that man can overcome earthly existence by surrendering unto Him.
Śrīla Prabhupāda: Overcoming earthly existence means entering into the spiritual world. The spirit soul is eternal, and it can enter from this atmosphere into another. Kṛṣṇa clearly explains this in the *Bhagavad-gītā* [4.9]:

janma karma ca me divyam evaṁ yo vetti tattvataḥ
tyaktvā dehaṁ punar janma naiti mām eti so 'rjuna

"One who knows the transcendental nature of My appearance and activities does not, upon leaving the body, take his birth again in this material world, but attains My eternal abode, O Arjuna." Those who continue to revolve in the cycle of birth and death acquire one material body after another, but those who are Kṛṣṇa conscious go to Kṛṣṇa. They do not acquire another material body.
Disciple: Lord Kṛṣṇa says this repeatedly throughout the *Bhagavad-gītā.*
Śrīla Prabhupāda: Yes, and those who are not envious of Kṛṣṇa accept His instructions, surrender unto Him, and understand Him. For them, this is the last material birth. For those who are envious, however, transmigration continues.
Disciple: Concerning karma, Jung writes this: "The crucial question is whether a man's karma is personal or not. If it is, then the preordained destiny with which a man enters life presents an achievement of previous lives, and a personal continuity therefore exists. If, however, this is not so, and an impersonal karma is seized upon in the act of birth, then that karma is incarnated again without there being any personal continuity."
Śrīla Prabhupāda: Karma is always personal.
Disciple: Jung goes on to point out that Buddha was twice

asked by his disciples whether man's karma is personal or not, and each time he fended off the question and did not discuss the matter. To know this, the Buddha said, "would not contribute to liberating oneself from the illusion of existence."

Śrīla Prabhupāda: Buddha refused to answer because he did not teach about the soul or accept the personal soul. As soon as you deny the personal aspect of the soul, there is no question of a personal karma. Buddha wanted to avoid this question. He did not want his whole philosophy dismantled.

Disciple: Jung gives his own conclusion in this way: "Have I lived before in the past as a specific personality, and did I progress so far in that life that I am now able to seek a solution?"

Śrīla Prabhupāda: As we have mentioned earlier, that is explained in the *Bhagavad-gītā* [6.43]: *tatra taṁ buddhi-saṁyogaṁ labhate paurva-dehikam:* "On taking rebirth, one revives the consciousness of his previous life and tries to make further progress."

Disciple: Jung continues, "I imagine that I have lived in former centuries and there encountered questions I was not yet able to answer, that I had to be born again to fulfill the task that was given to me."

Śrīla Prabhupāda: That is a fact.

Disciple: "When I die, my deeds will follow along with me—that is how I imagine it."

Śrīla Prabhupāda: That is personal karma.

Disciple: Jung continues, "I will bring with me what I have done. In the meantime it is important to insure that I do not stand at the end with empty hands."

Śrīla Prabhupāda: If you are making regular progress in Kṛṣṇa consciousness, your hands will not be empty at the end. Completeness means returning home, back to Godhead. This return is not empty. A Vaiṣṇava does not want emptiness—eternal life with Kṛṣṇa is our aspiration. Materialists think that at the end of life everything will be empty; therefore they conclude that they should enjoy themselves as much as possible in this life. That is why sense enjoyment is at the core of material life.

Disciple: Jung believed that one is reborn due to karma, or selfish action. He wrote, "If karma still remains to be disposed of, then the soul relapses again into desires and returns to live once more, perhaps even doing so out of the realization that something remains to be completed. In my case, it must have been primarily a passionate urge toward understanding which brought about my birth, for that was the strongest element in my nature."

Śrīla Prabhupāda: That understanding for which Jung is longing is understanding of Kṛṣṇa. This Kṛṣṇa explains in the *Bhagavad-gītā* [7.19]:

> *bahūnāṁ janmanām ante jñānavān māṁ prapadyate*
> *vāsudevaḥ sarvam iti sa mahātmā su-durlabhaḥ*

One's understanding is complete when one comes to the point of understanding that Kṛṣṇa is everything. Then one's material journey comes to an end: *tyaktvā dehaṁ punar janma naiti.* [*Bhagavad-gītā* 4.9] When one's understanding of Kṛṣṇa is incomplete, Kṛṣṇa gives instructions by which one can understand Him completely. In the Seventh Chapter of the *Bhagavad-gītā* Kṛṣṇa says, *asaṁsayaṁ samagraṁ māṁ yathā jñāsyasi tac chṛnu:* "Now hear from Me how you can understand Me completely and without any doubt." [*Bhagavad-gītā* 7.1] If we can understand Kṛṣṇa completely, we will take our next birth in the spiritual world.

Disciple: Jung conceived of a persona, which seems identical with what we call the false ego. He wrote, "The persona . . . is the individual's system of adaptation to, or the manner he assumes in dealing with, the world. A professor, for example, has his own characteristic persona. But the danger is that people become identical with their personas—the professor with his textbook, the tenor with his voice. One can say, with a little exaggeration, that the persona is that which in reality one is not, but which oneself as well as others think one is."

Śrīla Prabhupāda: One's real persona is that one is the eternal servant of God. This is the spiritual conception of life, and when one realizes this, his persona becomes his salvation and perfection. But as long as one is in the material conception of life, one's persona is that one is the servant of one's family, community, body, nation, ideal, and so on. In either case the persona is there and must continue, but proper understanding is realizing that one is the eternal servant of Kṛṣṇa. As long as one is in the material conception, one labors under the delusion of the false ego, thinking, "I am an American," "I am a Hindu," "I am a Christian," "I am a Muslim," and so on. This is the false ego at work. In reality we are all servants of God. When we speak of a "false ego," we imply a real ego, a purified ego. One whose ego is purified understands that he is the servant of Kṛṣṇa.

Disciple: For Jung, the purpose of psychoanalysis is to come to grips with our subconscious, shadow personality. Then we can know completely who we are.

Śrīla Prabhupāda: That means attaining real knowledge. When Sanātana Gosvāmī approached Śrī Caitanya Mahāprabhu, Sanātana said, "Please reveal to me who and what I am." In order to understand our real identity, we require the assistance of a guru.

Disciple: Jung says that in the shadow personality of all males there is a bit of the female, and in all females there is a bit of the male. Because we repress these aspects of the shadow personality, we do not understand our actions.

Śrīla Prabhupāda: We say that every living entity is by nature a female, *prakṛti. Prakṛti* means "female," and *puruṣa* means "male." Although we are *prakṛti,* in this material world we are posing ourselves as *puruṣa.* Because the *jīvātmā,* the individual soul, has the propensity to enjoy as a male, he is sometimes described as *puruṣa.* But actually the *jīvātmā* is not *puruṣa.* He is *prakṛti. Prakṛti* means the predominated, and *puruṣa* means the predominator. The only predominator is Kṛṣṇa; therefore originally we are all female by constitution. But under illusion we attempt to become males, enjoyers.

This is called *māyā,* or illusion. Although a female by constitution, the living entity is trying to imitate the supreme male, Kṛṣṇa. When one comes to his original consciousness, one understands that he is not the predominator but the predominated.

Disciple: Jung wrote of the soul in this way: "If the human soul is anything, it must be of unimaginable complexity and diversity, so that it cannot possibly be approached through a mere psychology of instinct."

Śrīla Prabhupāda: According to Caitanya Mahāprabhu, we can understand the soul through training. We should understand that we are not *brāhmaṇas, kṣatriyas, sannyāsīs, brahmacārīs,* or whatever. By negation we can understand, "I am not this, I am not that." Then what *is* our identity? Caitanya Mahāprabhu says, *gopī-bhartuḥ pada-kamalayor dāsa-dāsānudāsaḥ:* "I am the servant of the servant of the servant of Kṛṣṇa, the maintainer of the *gopīs*." That is our real identity. As long as we do not identify ourselves as eternal servants of Kṛṣṇa, we will be subject to various false identifications. *Bhakti,* devotional service, is the means by which we can be purified of false identifications.

Disciple: Concerning the soul, Jung further wrote, "I can only gaze with wonder and awe at the depths and heights of our psychic nature. Its nonspatial universe conceals an untold abundance of images which have accumulated over millions of years. . . ."

Śrīla Prabhupāda: Since we are constantly changing our bodies, constantly undergoing transmigration, we are accumulating various experiences. However, if we remain fixed in Kṛṣṇa consciousness, we do not change. There is none of this fluctuation once we understand our real identity, which is, "I am the servant of Kṛṣṇa; my duty is to serve Him." Arjuna realized this after hearing the *Bhagavad-gītā,* and he told Śrī Kṛṣṇa,

> *naṣṭo mohaḥ smṛtir labdhā tvat-prasādān mayācyuta*
> *sthito 'smi gata-sandehaḥ kariṣye vacanaṁ tava*

"My dear Kṛṣṇa, O infallible one, my illusion is now gone. I have regained my memory by Your mercy, and I am now firm and free from doubt and am prepared to act according to Your instructions." [*Bhagavad-gītā* 18.73]

So after hearing the *Bhagavad-gītā* Arjuna comes to this conclusion, and his illusion is dispelled by Kṛṣṇa's mercy. Arjuna is then fixed in his original position. And what is this? *Kariṣye vacanaṁ tava:* "Whatever You say, I shall do." At the beginning of the *Bhagavad-gītā* Kṛṣṇa told Arjuna to fight, and Arjuna refused. At the conclusion of the *Bhagavad-gītā* Arjuna's illusion is dispelled, and he is situated in his original constitutional position. Thus our perfection lies in executing the orders of Kṛṣṇa.

Disciple: Jung noted that the world's religions speak of five different types of rebirth. One is metempsychosis, the transmigration of souls, and, according to this view, "one's life is prolonged in time by passing through different bodily existences; or, from another point of view, it is a life-sequence interrupted by different reincarnations. . . . It is by no means certain whether continuity of personality is guaranteed or not: there may be only a continuity of karma."

Śrīla Prabhupāda: A personality is always there, and bodily changes do not affect it. However, one identifies himself according to his body. For instance, when the soul is within the body of a dog, he thinks according to that particular bodily construction. He thinks, "I am a dog, and I have my particular activities." In human society the same conception is there. For instance, when one is born in America he thinks, "I am an American, and I have my duty." According to the body, the personality is manifest—but in all cases personality is there.

Disciple: But is this personality continuous?

Śrīla Prabhupāda: Certainly the personality is continuous. At death the soul passes into another gross body along with its mental and intellectual identifications. The individual acquires different types of bodies, but the person is the same.

Disciple: This would correspond to the second type of rebirth, which is reincarnation. Jung wrote, "This concept of rebirth necessarily implies the continuity of personality. Here the human personality is regarded as continuous and accessible to memory, so that when one is incarnated or born, one is able, at least potentially, to remember that one has lived through previous existences and that these existences were one's own—that is, that they had the same ego-form as the present life. As a rule, reincarnation means rebirth into a human body."

Śrīla Prabhupāda: Not necessarily into a human body. From *Śrīmad-Bhāgavatam* we learn that Bharata Mahārāja became a deer in his next life. The soul is changing bodies just as a man changes his clothes. The man is the same, although his clothes may be different:

vāsāṁsi jīrṇāni yathā vihāya
navāni gṛhṇāti naro 'parāṇi
tathā śarīrāṇi vihāya jīrṇāny
anyāni saṁyāti navāni dehī

"As a person puts on new garments, giving up old ones, the soul similarly accepts new material bodies, giving up the old and useless ones." [*Bhagavad gītā* 2.22] When a coat is old and cannot be used anymore, one has to purchase another. The man is the same, but his clothes are supplied according to the price he can pay. Similarly, you "purchase" a new body with the "money" (karma) you have accumulated throughout your lifetime. According to your karma, you receive a certain type of body.

Disciple: The third type of rebirth is called resurrection, and Jung notes that there are two types. "It may be a carnal body, as in the Christian assumption that this body will be resurrected." According to the Christian doctrine, at the end of the world the gross bodies will reassemble themselves and ascend into heaven or descend into hell.

Śrīla Prabhupāda: This is simply foolishness. The gross material body can never be resurrected. At the time of death the living entity leaves this material body, and the material

body disintegrates. How can the material elements reassemble themselves?
Disciple: Jung further wrote that on a higher level resurrection is no longer understood in a gross material sense: "It is assumed that the resurrection of the dead is the raising up of the *corpus gloriaficationis,* the subtle body, in the state of incorruptibility."
Śrīla Prabhupāda: This type of "resurrection" is applicable only to God and His representatives, not to others. In this case, it is not a material body that is "raised up," but a spiritual one. When God appears, He appears in a spiritual body, and this body does not change. In the *Bhagavad-gītā* Kṛṣṇa says that he spoke to the sun-god millions of years ago, and Arjuna questions how this could be possible. Kṛṣṇa replies that although Arjuna had been present he could not remember. It is possible for one to remember only if one does not change bodies—changing bodies means forgetting. But the Lord's body is purely spiritual, and a spiritual body never changes. According to the Māyāvādī conception, the Absolute Truth is impersonal, and when it appears as a person it accepts a material body. But those who are advanced in spiritual knowledge, who accept the *Bhagavad-gītā,* understand that this is not the case. Kṛṣṇa specifically says, *avajānanti māṁ mūḍhā mānuṣīṁ tanum āśritam:* "Because I appear as a human being, the unintelligent think that I am nothing but a human being." [*Bhagavad-gītā* 9.11] This is not the case. Impersonalists have no knowledge of the spiritual body.
Disciple: The fourth form of rebirth is called renovation, and this applies to "the transformation of a mortal into an immortal being, of a corporeal into a spiritual being, and of a human into a divine being. Well-known prototypes of this change are the transfiguration and ascension of Christ, and the bodily assumption of the mother of God into heaven after her death."
Śrīla Prabhupāda: We say that the spiritual body never dies but that the material body is subject to destruction. *Na hanyate hanyamāne śarīre:* the material body is subject to destruction, but after its destruction the spiritual body is still

there. The spiritual body is neither generated nor killed.

Disciple: But aren't there several examples in the *Śrīmad-Bhāgavatam* of a kind of ascension into heaven? Didn't Arjuna ascend?

Śrīla Prabhupāda: Yes, and Yudhiṣṭhira. There are many instances—especially Kṛṣṇa Himself and His associates. But we should never consider their bodies material. They didn't go through death of any sort, although their bodies traveled to the higher universe. But it is also a fact that everyone possesses a spiritual body.

Disciple: The fifth type of rebirth is indirect and is called "participation in the process of transformation." Examples of this type may be the initiation ceremony or the twice-born ceremony of the *brāhmaṇa*. "In other words," Jung wrote, "one has to witness, or take part in, some rite of transformation. This rite may be a ceremony. . . . Through his presence at the rite, the individual participates in divine grace."

Śrīla Prabhupāda: Yes, one's first birth is by one's father and mother, and the next birth is by the spiritual master and Vedic knowledge. When one takes his second birth, he comes to understand that he is not the material body. This is spiritual education. That birth of knowledge, or birth *into* knowledge, is called *dvija,* "second birth."

Disciple: Thus far we have discussed only Jung's autobiography. In one of Jung's last books, *The Undiscovered Self,* he discussed the meaning of religion and its utility in the modern world. He wrote, "The meaning and purpose of religion lie in the relationship of the individual to God (Christianity, Judaism, Islam) or to the path of salvation and liberation (Buddhism). From this basic fact all ethics is derived, which without the individual's responsibility before God can be called nothing more than conventional morality."

Śrīla Prabhupāda: First of all, we understand from the *Bhagavad-gītā* that no one can approach God without being purified of all sinful reactions. Only one who is standing on the platform of pure goodness can understand God and engage in His service. From Arjuna we understand that God is *paraṁ brahma paraṁ dhāma pavitraṁ paramaṁ bhavān:* He is "the Supreme Brahman, the ultimate, the supreme abode and purifier." [*Bhagavad-gītā* 10.12] *Paraṁ brahma* indicates the Supreme Brahman. Every living being is Brahman, or spirit, but Kṛṣṇa is the *paraṁ brahma,* the Supreme Brahman. He is also *paraṁ dhāma,* the ultimate abode of everything. He is also *pavitraṁ paramam,* the purest of the pure. In order to approach the purest of the pure, one must become completely pure, and to this end morality and ethics are necessary. Therefore, in our Kṛṣṇa consciousness movement we prohibit illicit sex, meat-eating, intoxication, and gambling—the four pillars of sinful life. If we can avoid these sinful activities, we can remain on the platform of purity. Kṛṣṇa consciousness is based on this morality, and one who cannot follow these principles falls down from the spiritual platform. Thus, purity is the basic principle of God consciousness and is essential for the re-establishment of our eternal relationship with God.

Disciple: Jung saw atheistic communism as the greatest threat in the world today. He wrote, "The communistic revolution has debased man far lower than democratic collective psychology has done, because it robs him of his freedom not only in the social but in the moral and spiritual sense. . . . The state has taken the place of God; that is why, seen from this angle, the socialist dictatorships are religious, and state slavery is a form of worship."

Śrīla Prabhupāda: Yes, I agree with him. Atheistic communism has contributed to the degradation of human civilization. But the basic principle of communist philosophy—that everyone should contribute what he can to the state and everyone has an equal right to his proper share from the state—that basic principle of real communism we accept. According to our understanding, God is the father, material nature is the mother, and the living entities are the sons. The sons have a right to live at the cost of the father. The entire universe is the property of the Supreme Personality of Godhead, and the living entities are being supported by the supreme father. However, one should be satisfied with the supplies allotted to him. According to the *Īśopaniṣad, tena tyaktena bhuñjīthāḥ:* we should be satisfied with our allotment and not envy one another or encroach upon one another's property. We should not envy the capitalists or the wealthy, because everyone is given his allotment by the Supreme Personality of Godhead. Consequently, everyone should be satisfied with what he receives.

On the other hand, one should not exploit others. One may be born in a wealthy family, but one should not interfere with the rights of others. Whether one is rich or poor, one should be God conscious, accept God's arrangement, and serve God to his fullest. This is the philosophy of *Śrīmad-Bhāgavatam,* and it is confirmed by Lord Caitanya. We should be content with our allocations from God and concern ourselves with advancing in Kṛṣṇa consciousness. If we become envious of the rich, we will be tempted to encroach upon their allotment, and in this way we are diverted from our service to the Lord. The main point is that everyone, rich or poor, should engage in God's service. If everyone does so, there will be real peace in the world.

Disciple: Concerning the socialist state, Jung further wrote, "The goals of religion—deliverance from evil, reconciliation with God, rewards in the hereafter, and so on—turn into worldly promises about freedom from care for one's daily bread, the just distribution of material goods, universal prosperity in the future, and shorter working hours." In other words, the communists place emphasis on material rewards.

Śrīla Prabhupāda: This is because they have no understanding of spiritual life, nor can they understand that the person within the body is eternal and spiritual. Therefore they recommend sense gratification.

Disciple: Jung believed, however, that socialism or Marxism cannot possibly replace religion in the proper, traditional sense. "A natural function which has existed from the beginning—like the religious function—cannot be disposed of with rationalistic and so-called enlightened criticism."

Śrīla Prabhupāda: The communists are concerned with adjusting material things, which can actually never be adjusted. They imagine that they can solve problems, but ultimately their plans will fail. The communists do not understand what religion actually is. It is not possible to avoid religion. Everything has a particular characteristic. Salt is salty, sugar is sweet, and chili is hot or pungent. These are intrinsic characteristics. Similarly, the living entity has an intrinsic characteristic, which is to render service—be he a communist, a theist, a capitalist, or whatever. In all countries people are working and rendering service to their respective governments—be they capitalists or communists—and the people are not getting any lasting benefit. Therefore we say that if people follow in the footsteps of Śrī Caitanya Mahāprabhu by serving Kṛṣṇa, they will actually be happy. Both communists and capitalists are saying, "Render service to me," but Kṛṣṇa says, *sarva-dharmān parityajya mām ekaṁ śaraṇaṁ vraja/ ahaṁ tvāṁ sarva-pāpebhyo mokṣayiṣyāmi:* "Just give up all other service and render service unto Me, and I will free you from all sinful reactions." [*Bhagavad-gītā* 18.66]

Disciple: Jung feels that materialistic Western capitalism cannot possibly defeat a pseudo religion like Marxism. He believes that the only way the individual can combat atheistic communism is to adopt a nonmaterialistic religion. He wrote, "It has been correctly realized in many quarters that the alexipharmic, the antidote, should in this case be an equally potent faith of a different and nonmaterialistic kind. . . ." So Jung sees modern man in desperate need of a religion that has immediate meaning. He feels that Christianity is no longer effective because it no longer expresses what modern man needs most.

Śrīla Prabhupāda: That nonmaterialistic religion which is above everything—Marxism or capitalism—is this Kṛṣṇa consciousness movement. Kṛṣṇa has nothing to do with any materialistic "ism," and this movement is directly connected with Kṛṣṇa, the Supreme Personality of Godhead. God demands complete surrender, and we are teaching, "You are servants, but your service is being wrongly placed. Therefore you are not happy. Just render service to Kṛṣṇa, and you will find happiness." We support neither communism nor capitalism, nor do we advocate the adoption of pseudo religions. We are only for Kṛṣṇa.

Disciple: Concerning the social situation, Jung wrote, "It is unfortunately only too clear that if the individual is not truly regenerated in spirit, society cannot be either, for society is the sum total of individuals in need of redemption."

Śrīla Prabhupāda: The basis of change is the individual. Now there are a few individuals initiated into Kṛṣṇa consciousness, and if a large percentage can thus become invigorated, the face of the world will change. There is no doubt of this.

Disciple: For Jung, the salvation of the world consists in the salvation of the individual soul. The only thing that saves man from submersion into the masses is his relationship to God. Jung wrote, "His individual relation to God would be an effective shield against these pernicious influences."

Śrīla Prabhupāda: Yes, those who take Kṛṣṇa consciousness seriously are never troubled by Marxism, this-ism, or that-ism. A Marxist may take to Kṛṣṇa consciousness, but a Kṛṣṇa conscious devotee would never become a Marxist. That is not possible. It is explained in the *Bhagavad-gītā* that one who knows the highest perfection of life cannot be misled by a third- or fourth-class philosophy.

Disciple: Jung also felt that materialistic progress could be detrimental to the individual. He wrote, "A [materially] favorable environment merely strengthens the dangerous tendency to expect everything to originate from outside—even that metamorphosis which external reality cannot provide, namely, a deep-seated change of the inner man."

Śrīla Prabhupāda: Yes, everything originates from inside, from the soul. It is confirmed by Bhaktivinoda Ṭhākura and others that material progress is essentially an expansion of the external energy—*māyā,* illusion. We are all living in illusion, and so-called scientists and philosophers can never understand God and their relationship to Him, despite their material advancement. Material advancement and knowledge are actually a hindrance to the progressive march of Kṛṣṇa consciousness. We therefore minimize our necessities to live a saintly life. We are not after luxurious living. We feel that life is meant for spiritual progress and Kṛṣṇa consciousness, not for material advancement.

Disciple: To inspire this deep-seated change in the inner man, Jung feels that a proper teacher is needed, someone to explain religion to man.

Śrīla Prabhupāda: Yes. According to the Vedic injunction, it is essential to seek out a guru—a person who is a representative of God (*sākṣād-dharitvena samasta-śāstraiḥ*). The representative of God is worshiped as God, but he never says, "I am God." Although he is worshiped as God, he is the servant of God—God Himself is always the master. Caitanya Mahāprabhu requested everyone to become a guru: "Wherever you are, simply become a guru and deliver all these people who are in ignorance." One may say, "I am not very learned. How can I become a guru?" But Caitanya Mahāprabhu said that it is not necessary to be a learned scholar, since there are many so-called learned scholars who are fools. It is only necessary to impart Kṛṣṇa's instructions, which are already there in the *Bhagavad-gītā*. Whoever explains the *Bhagavad-gītā* as it is—he is a guru. If one is fortunate enough to approach such a guru, his life becomes successful.

Disciple: Jung also laments the fact that "our philosophy is no longer a way of life, as it was in antiquity; it has turned into an exclusively intellectual and academic affair."

Śrīla Prabhupāda: That is also our opinion: mental speculation has no value in itself. One must be directly in touch with the Supreme Personality of Godhead, and using all reason, one must assimilate the instructions given by Him. One can then follow these instructions in one's daily life and do good to others by teaching the *Bhagavad-gītā*.

Disciple: On one hand, Jung sees an exclusively intellectual philosophy; on the other, denominational religions with "archaic rites and conceptions" that "express a view of the world which caused no great difficulties in the Middle Ages, but which has become strange and unintelligible to the man of today."

Śrīla Prabhupāda: That is because preachers of religion are simply dogmatic. They have no clear idea of God; they only make official proclamations. When one does not understand, he cannot make others understand. But there is no such vanity in Kṛṣṇa consciousness. Kṛṣṇa consciousness is clear in every respect. This is the expected movement Mr. Jung wanted. Every sane man should cooperate with this movement and liberate human society from the gross darkness of ignorance.

APPENDIXES

His Divine Grace
A. C. Bhaktivedanta Swami Prabhupāda

The Author

His Divine Grace A. C. Bhaktivedanta Swami Prabhupāda appeared in this world in 1896 in Calcutta, India. He first met his spiritual master, Śrīla Bhaktisiddhānta Sarasvatī Gosvāmī, in Calcutta in 1922. Bhaktisiddhānta Sarasvatī, a prominent religious scholar and the founder of sixty-four Gauḍīya Maṭhas (Vedic institutes), liked this educated young man and convinced him to dedicate his life to teaching Kṛṣṇa consciousness. Śrīla Prabhupāda became his student and, in 1932, his formally initiated disciple.

At their first meeting, in 1922, Bhaktisiddhānta Sarasvatī asked Śrīla Prabhupāda to broadcast Kṛṣṇa consciousness in English. In the years that followed, Śrīla Prabhupāda wrote a commentary on the *Bhagavad-gītā,* assisted the Gauḍīya Maṭha in its work, and, in 1944, started *Back to Godhead,* an English fortnightly magazine. Single-handedly, Śrīla Prabhupāda edited it, typed the manuscripts, checked the galley proofs, and even distributed the individual copies. The magazine is now being continued by his disciples in the West.

In 1950 Śrīla Prabhupāda retired from married life, adopting the *vānaprastha* (retired) order to devote more time to his studies and writing. He traveled to the holy city of Vṛndāvana, where he lived in humble circumstances in the historic temple of Rādhā-Dāmodara. There he engaged for several years in deep study and writing. He accepted the renounced order of life (*sannyāsa*) in 1959. At Rādhā-Dāmodara, Śrīla Prabhupāda began work on his life's masterpiece: a multivolume commentated translation of the 18,000-verse *Śrīmad-Bhāgavatam* (*Bhāgavata Purāṇa*). He also wrote *Easy Journey to Other Planets.*

After publishing three volumes of *Śrīmad-Bhāgavatam,* Śrīla Prabhupāda came to the United States, in September 1965, to fulfill the mission of his spiritual master. Subsequently, His Divine Grace wrote more than fifty volumes of authoritative commentated translations and summary studies of the philosophical and religious classics of India.

When he first arrived in New York City, Śrīla Prabhupāda was nearly penniless. Only after a year of great difficulty did he establish the International Society for Krishna Consciousness, in July of 1966. Before he passed away on November 14, 1977, he had guided the Society and seen it grow to a worldwide confederation of more than one hundred *āśramas,* schools, temples, institutes, and farm communities.

In 1972 His Divine Grace introduced the Vedic system of primary and secondary education in the West by founding the *gurukula* school in Dallas, Texas. Since then his disciples have established similar schools throughout the United States and the rest of the world.

Śrīla Prabhupāda also inspired the construction of several large international cultural centers in India. The center at Śrīdhāma Māyāpur is the site for a planned spiritual city, an ambitious project for which construction will extend over many years to come. In Vṛndāvana are the magnificent Kṛṣṇa-Balarāma Temple and International Guesthouse, *gurukula* school, and Śrīla Prabhupāda Memorial and Museum. There are also major cultural and educational centers in Mumbai, New Delhi, Baroda, and Ahmedabad. Other centers are either underway or planned in a dozen important locations on the Indian subcontinent.

Śrīla Prabhupāda's most significant contribution, however, is his books. Highly respected by scholars for their authority, depth, and clarity, they are used as textbooks in numerous college courses. His writings have been translated into over fifty languages. The Bhaktivedanta Book Trust, established in 1972 to publish the works of His Divine Grace, has thus become the world's largest publisher of books in the field of Indian religion and philosophy.

In just twelve years, in spite of his advanced age, Śrīla Prabhupāda circled the globe fourteen times on lecture tours that took him to six continents. In spite of such a vigorous schedule, Śrīla Prabhupāda continued to write prolifically. His writings constitute a veritable library of Vedic philosophy, religion, literature, and culture.

An Introduction to ISKCON And the Hare Kṛṣṇa Way of Life

What Is ISKCON?

The International Society for Krishna Consciousness (ISKCON), popularly known as the Hare Kṛṣṇa movement, is a worldwide association of devotees of Kṛṣṇa, the Supreme Personality of Godhead. God is known by many names, according to His different qualities and activities. In the Bible he is known as Jehovah ("the almighty one"), in the Koran as Allah ("the great one"), and in the *Bhagavad-gītā* as Kṛṣṇa, a Sanskrit name meaning "the all-attractive one."

The movement's main purpose is to promote the well-being of human society by teaching the science of God consciousness (Kṛṣṇa consciousness) according to the timeless Vedic scriptures of India.

Many leading figures in the international religious and academic community have affirmed the movement's authenticity. Diana L. Eck, professor of comparative religion and Indian studies at Harvard University, describes the movement as "a tradition that commands a respected place in the religious life of humankind."

In 1965, His Divine Grace A. C. Bhaktivedanta Swami, known to his followers as Śrīla Prabhupāda, brought Kṛṣṇa consciousness to America. On the day he landed in Boston, on his way to New York City, he penned these words in his diary: "My dear Lord Kṛṣṇa, I am sure that when this transcendental message penetrates [the hearts of the Westerners], they will certainly feel gladdened and thus become liberated from all unhappy conditions of life." He was sixty-nine years old, alone and with few resources, but the wealth of spiritual knowledge and devotion he possessed was an unwavering source of strength and inspiration.

"At a very advanced age, when most people would be resting on their laurels," writes Harvey Cox, Harvard University theologian and author, "Śrīla Prabhupāda harkened to the mandate of his own spiritual teacher and set out on the difficult and demanding voyage to America. Śrīla Prabhupāda is, of course, only one of thousands of teachers. But in another sense, he is one in a thousand, maybe one in a million."

In 1966, Śrīla Prabhupāda founded the International Society for Krishna Consciousness, which became the formal name for the Hare Kṛṣṇa movement.

Astonishing Growth

In the years that followed, Śrīla Prabhupāda gradually attracted tens of thousands of followers, started more than a hundred temples and ashrams, and published scores of books. His achievement is remarkable in that he transplanted India's ancient spiritual culture to the twentieth-century Western world.

New devotees of Kṛṣṇa soon became highly visible in all the major cities around the world by their public chanting and their distribution of Śrīla Prabhupāda's books of Vedic knowledge. They began staging joyous cultural festivals throughout the year and serving millions of plates of delicious vegetarian food offered to Kṛṣṇa (known as *prasādam*). As a result, ISKCON has significantly influenced the lives of millions of people. In the early 1980's A. L. Basham, one of the world's leading authorities on Indian history and culture, wrote, "The Hare Kṛṣṇa movement arose out of next to nothing in less than twenty years and has become known all over the West. This is an important fact in the history of the Western world."

Five Thousand Years of Spiritual Wisdom

Scholars worldwide have acclaimed Śrīla Prabhupāda's translations of Vedic literature. Garry Gelade, a professor at Oxford University's Department of Philosophy, wrote of them:

"These texts are to be treasured. No one of whatever faith or philosophical persuasion who reads these books with an open mind can fail to be moved and impressed." And Dr. Larry Shinn, Dean of the College of Arts and Sciences at Bucknell University, wrote, "Prabhupāda's personal piety gave him real authority. He exhibited complete command of the scriptures, an unusual depth of realization, and an outstanding personal example, because he actually lived what he taught."

The best known of the Vedic texts, the *Bhagavad-gītā* ("Song of God"), is the philosophical basis for the Hare Kṛṣṇa movement. Dating back five thousand years, it is sacred to nearly a billion people today. This exalted work has been praised by scholars and leaders the world over. Mahatma Gandhi said, "When doubts haunt me, when disappointments stare me in the face and I see not one ray of hope, I turn to the *Bhagavad-gītā* and find a verse to comfort me." Ralph Waldo Emerson wrote, "It was the first of books; it was as if an empire spoke to us, nothing small or unworthy, but large, serene, consistent, the voice of an old intelligence which in another age and climate had pondered and thus disposed of the same questions which exercise us." It is not surprising to anyone familiar with the *Gītā* that Henry David Thoreau said, "In the morning I bathe my intellect in the stupendous and cosmogonal philosophy of the *Bhagavad-gītā*."

As Dr. Shinn pointed out, Śrīla Prabhupāda's *Bhagavad-gītā* (titled *Bhagavad-gītā As It Is*) possesses unique authority not only because of his erudition but because he lived what he taught. Thus unlike the many other English translations of the *Gītā* that preceded his, which is replete with extensive commentary, Śrīla Prabhupāda's has sparked a spiritual revolution throughout the world.

Lord Kṛṣṇa teaches in the *Bhagavad-gītā* that we are not these temporary material bodies but spirit souls, or conscious entities, and that we can find genuine peace and happiness only in spiritual devotion to Him, the Supreme Personality of Godhead.

An Appearance of Kṛṣṇa in the Sixteenth Century

In the sixteenth century Kṛṣṇa appeared in Bengal as Lord Śrī Caitanya Mahāprabhu and popularized the chanting of God's names all over India. He constantly sang these names of God, as prescribed in the Vedic literatures: Hare Kṛṣṇa, Hare Kṛṣṇa, Kṛṣṇa Kṛṣṇa, Hare Hare/ Hare Rāma, Hare Rāma, Rāma Rāma, Hare Hare. This Hare Kṛṣṇa chant, or mantra, is a transcendental sound vibration. It purifies the mind and awakens the dormant love of God that resides in the hearts of all living beings. Lord Caitanya requested His followers to spread the chanting to every town and village of the world.

Anyone can take part in the chanting of the Hare Kṛṣṇa mantra and learn the science of spiritual devotion by studying the *Bhagavad-gītā As It Is*. This easy and practical process of self-realization will awaken our natural state of peace and happiness.

Kṛṣṇa Consciousness at Home

by Mahātmā dāsa

In *Beyond Illusion and Doubt* Śrīla Prabhupāda makes it clear how important it is for everyone to practice Kṛṣṇa consciousness, devotional service to Lord Kṛṣṇa. Of course, living in the association of Kṛṣṇa's devotees in a temple or ashram makes it easier to practice devotional service. But if you're determined, you can follow at home the teachings of Kṛṣṇa consciousness and thus convert your home into a temple.

Spiritual life, like material life, means practical activity. The difference is that whereas we perform material activities for the benefit of ourselves or those we consider ours, we perform spiritual activities for the benefit of Lord Kṛṣṇa, under the guidance of the scriptures and the spiritual master. The key is to accept the guidance of the scripture and the guru. Kṛṣṇa declares in the *Bhagavad-gītā* that a person can achieve neither happiness nor the supreme destination of life—going back to Godhead, back to Lord Kṛṣṇa—if he or she does not follow the injunctions of the scriptures. And *how* to follow the scriptural rules by engaging in practical service to the Lord—that is explained by a bona fide spiritual master. Without following the instructions of a spiritual master who is in an authorized chain of disciplic succession coming from Kṛṣṇa Himself, we cannot make spiritual progress. The practices outlined here are the timeless practices of *bhakti-yoga* as given by the foremost spiritual master and exponent of Kṛṣṇa consciousness in our time, His Divine Grace A. C. Bhaktivedanta Swami Prabhupāda, founder-*ācārya* of the International Society for Krishna Consciousness (ISKCON).

The purpose of spiritual knowledge is to bring us closer to God, or Kṛṣṇa. Kṛṣṇa says in the *Bhagavad-gītā* (18.55), *bhaktyā māṁ abhijānāti:* "I can be known only by devotional service." Knowledge guides us in proper action. Spiritual knowledge directs us to satisfy the desires of Kṛṣṇa through practical engagements in His loving service. Without practical application, theoretical knowledge is of little value.

Spiritual knowledge is meant to direct us in all aspects of life. We should endeavor, therefore, to organize our lives in such a way as to follow Kṛṣṇa's teachings as far as possible. We should try to do our best, to do more than is simply convenient. Then it will be possible for us to rise to the transcendental plane of Kṛṣṇa consciousness, even while living far from a temple.

Chanting the Hare Kṛṣṇa Mantra

The first principle in devotional service is to chant the Hare Kṛṣṇa *mahā-mantra* (*mahā* means "great"; *mantra* means "sound that liberates the mind from ignorance"):

Hare Kṛṣṇa, Hare Kṛṣṇa, Kṛṣṇa Kṛṣṇa, Hare Hare
Hare Rāma, Hare Rāma, Rāma Rāma, Hare Hare

You should chant these holy names of the Lord as much

as possible—anywhere and at any time—but it is also very helpful to set a specific time of the day to regularly chant. Early morning hours are ideal.

The chanting can be done in two ways: singing the mantra, called *kīrtana* (usually done in a group), and saying the mantra to oneself, called *japa* (which literally means "to speak softly"). Concentrate on hearing the sound of the holy names. As you chant, pronounce the names clearly and distinctly, addressing Kṛṣṇa in a prayerful mood. When your mind wanders, bring it back to the sound of the Lord's names. Chanting is a prayer to Kṛṣṇa that means "O energy of the Lord [Hare], O all-attractive Lord [Kṛṣṇa], O Supreme Enjoyer [Rāma], please engage me in Your service." The more attentively and sincerely you chant these names of God, the more spiritual progress you will make.

Since God is all-powerful and all-merciful, He has kindly made it very easy for us to chant His names, and He has also invested all His powers in them. Therefore the names of God and God Himself are identical. This means that when we chant the holy names of Kṛṣṇa and Rāma we are directly associating with God and being purified. Therefore we should always try to chant with devotion and reverence. The Vedic literature states that Lord Kṛṣṇa is personally dancing on your tongue when you chant His holy name.

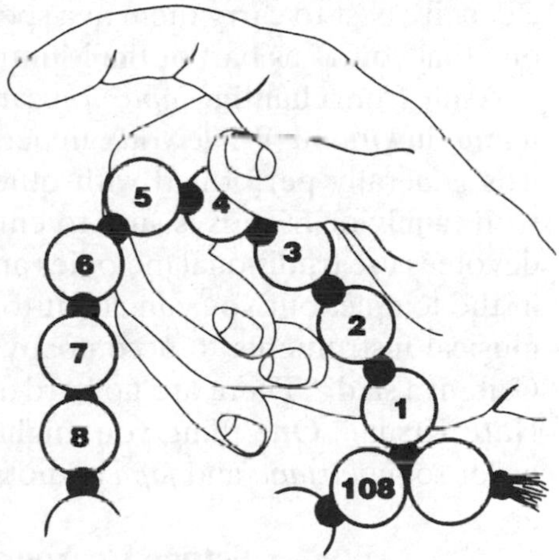

When you chant alone, it is best to chant on *japa* beads (provided in the Mantra Meditation Kit, which is available in the advertisement section at the end of this book). This not only helps you fix your attention on the holy name, but it also helps you count the number of times you chant the mantra daily. Each strand of *japa* beads contains 108 small beads and one large bead, the head bead. Begin on a bead next to the head bead and gently roll it between the thumb and middle finger of your right hand as you chant the full Hare Kṛṣṇa mantra. Then move to the next bead and repeat the process. In this way, chant on each of the 108 beads until you reach the head bead again. This is one round of *japa*. Then, without chanting on the head bead, reverse the beads and start your second round on the last bead you chanted on.

Initiated devotees vow before the spiritual master to chant at least sixteen rounds of the Hare Kṛṣṇa mantra daily. But even if you can chant only one round a day, the principle is that once you commit yourself to chanting that round, you should try to complete it every day without fail. When you feel you can chant more, then increase the minimum number of rounds you chant each day—but don't fall below that number. You can chant more than your fixed number, but you should maintain a set minimum each day. (Please note that the beads are sacred and therefore should never touch the ground or be put in an unclean place. To keep your beads clean, it's best to carry them in a special bead bag, such as the one that comes as part of the Mantra Meditation Kit.)

Aside from chanting *japa,* you can also sing the Lord's holy names in *kīrtana*. While you can perform *kīrtana* individually, it is generally performed with others. A melodious *kīrtana* with family or friends is sure to enliven everyone. ISKCON devotees use traditional melodies and instruments, especially in the temple, but you can chant to any melody and use any musical instruments to accompany your chanting. As Lord Caitanya said, "There are no hard and fast rules for chanting Hare Kṛṣṇa." One thing you might want to do, however, is order some *kīrtana* and *japa* audiotapes (see ads).

Setting Up Your Altar

You will likely find that your *japa* and *kīrtana* are especially effective when done before an altar. Lord Kṛṣṇa and His pure devotees are so kind that they allow us to worship them even through their pictures. It is something like mailing a letter: You cannot mail a letter by placing it in just any box; you must use the mailbox authorized by the government. Similarly, we cannot imagine a picture of God and worship that, but we can worship the authorized picture of God, and Kṛṣṇa accepts our worship through that picture.

Setting up an altar at home means receiving the Lord and His pure devotees as your most honored guests. Where should you set up the altar? Well, how would you seat a guest? An ideal place would be clean, well lit, and free from drafts and household disturbances. Your guest, of course, would need a comfortable chair, but for the picture of Kṛṣṇa's form a wall shelf, a mantelpiece, a corner table, or the top shelf of a bookcase will do. You wouldn't seat a guest in your home and then ignore him; you'd provide a place for yourself to sit, too, where you could comfortably face him and enjoy his company. So don't make your altar inaccessible.

What do you need for an altar? Here are the essentials:

1. A picture of Śrīla Prabhupāda.
2. A picture of Lord Caitanya and His associates.
3. A picture of Śrī Śrī Rādhā-Kṛṣṇa.

In addition, you may want an altar cloth, water cups (one for each picture), candles with holders, a special plate for offering food, a small bell, incense, an incense holder, and fresh

flowers, which you may offer in vases or simply place before each picture. If you're interested in more elaborate Deity worship, ask any of the ISKCON devotees or get in touch with the BBT (see the resources section at the back of this book).

The first person we worship on the altar is the spiritual master. The spiritual master is not God. Only God is God. But because the spiritual master is His dearmost servant, God has empowered him, and therefore he deserves the same respect as that given to God. He links the disciple with God and teaches him the process of *bhakti-yoga.* He is God's ambassador to the material world. When a president sends an ambassador to a foreign country, the ambassador receives the same respect as that accorded the president, and the ambassador's words are as authoritative as the president's. Similarly, we should respect the spiritual master as we would God, and revere his words as we would His.

There are two main kinds of gurus: the instructing guru and the initiating guru. Everyone who takes up the process of *bhakti-yoga* as a result of coming in contact with ISKCON owes an immense debt of gratitude to Śrīla Prabhupāda. Before Śrīla Prabhupāda left India in 1965 to spread Kṛṣṇa consciousness abroad, almost no one outside India knew anything about the practice of pure devotional service to Lord Kṛṣṇa. Therefore, everyone who has learned of the process through his books, his *Back to Godhead* magazine, his tapes, or contact with his followers should offer respect to Śrīla Prabhupāda. As the founder and spiritual guide of the International Society for Krishna Consciousness, he is the instructing guru of us all.

As you progress in *bhakti-yoga,* you may eventually want to accept initiation. Before he left this world in 1977, Śrīla Prabhupāda encouraged his qualified disciples to carry on his work by initiating disciples of their own in accordance with his instructions. At present there are many spiritual masters in ISKCON. To learn how you can get spiritual guidance from them, ask a devotee at your nearby temple, or write to one of the ISKCON centers listed at the end of this book.

The second picture on your altar should be one of the *pañca-tattva,* Lord Caitanya and His four leading associates. Lord Caitanya is the incarnation of God for this age. He is Kṛṣṇa Himself, descended in the form of His own devotee to teach us how to surrender to Him, specifically by chanting His holy names and performing other activities of *bhakti-yoga.* Lord Caitanya is the most merciful incarnation, for He makes it easy for anyone to attain love of God through the chanting of the Hare Kṛṣṇa *mantra*.

And of course your altar should have a picture of the Supreme Personality of Godhead, Lord Śrī Kṛṣṇa, with His eternal consort, Śrīmatī Rādhārāṇī. Śrīmatī Rādhārāṇī is Kṛṣṇa's spiritual potency. She is devotional service personified, and devotees always take shelter of Her to learn how to serve Kṛṣṇa.

You can arrange the pictures in a triangle, with the picture of Śrīla Prabhupāda on the left, the picture of Lord Caitanya and His associates on the right, and the picture of Rādhā and Kṛṣṇa, which, if possible, should be slightly larger than the others, on a small raised platform behind and in the center. Or you can hang the picture of Rādhā and Kṛṣṇa on the wall above.

Carefully clean the altar each morning. Cleanliness is essential in Deity worship. Remember, you wouldn't neglect to clean the room of an important guest, and when you establish an altar you invite Kṛṣṇa and His pure devotees to reside as the most exalted guests in your home. If you have water cups, rinse them out and fill them with fresh water daily. Then place them conveniently close to the pictures. You should remove flowers in vases as soon as they're slightly wilted, or daily if you've offered them at the base of the pictures. You should offer fresh incense at least once a day, and, if possible, light candles and place them near the pictures when you're chanting before the altar.

Please try the things we've suggested so far. It's very simple, really: If you try to love God, you'll gradually realize how much He loves you. That's the essence of *bhakti-yoga.*

Prasādam: How to Eat Spiritually

By His immense transcendental energies, Kṛṣṇa can actually convert matter into spirit. If we place an iron rod in a fire, before long the rod becomes red hot and acts just like fire. In the same way, food prepared for and offered to Kṛṣṇa with love and devotion becomes completely spiritualized. Such food is called Kṛṣṇa *prasādam,* which means "the mercy of Lord Kṛṣṇa."

Eating *prasādam* is a fundamental practice of *bhakti-yoga.* In other forms of yoga one must artificially repress the senses, but the *bhakti-yogī* can engage his or her senses in a variety of pleasing spiritual activities, such as tasting delicious food offered to Lord Kṛṣṇa. In this way the senses gradually become spiritualized and bring the devotee more and more transcendental pleasure by being engaged in devotional service. Such spiritual pleasure far surpasses any material experience.

Lord Caitanya said of *prasādam,* "Everyone has tasted these foods before. However, now that they have been prepared for Kṛṣṇa and offered to Him with devotion, these foods have acquired extraordinary tastes and uncommon fragrances. Just taste them and see the difference in the experience! Apart from the taste, even the fragrance pleases the mind and makes one forget any other fragrance. Therefore, it should be understood that the spiritual nectar of Kṛṣṇa's lips must have touched these ordinary foods and imparted to them all their transcendental qualities."

Eating only food offered to Kṛṣṇa is the perfection of vegetarianism. In itself, being a vegetarian is not enough; after all, even pigeons and monkeys are vegetarians. But when we go beyond vegetarianism to a diet of *prasādam,* our eating becomes helpful in achieving the goal of human life—reawakening the soul's original relationship with God. In the *Bhagavad-gītā* Lord Kṛṣṇa says that unless one eats only food that has been offered to him in sacrifice, one will suffer the reactions of karma.

How to Prepare and Offer Prasādam

As you walk down the supermarket aisles selecting the foods you will offer to Kṛṣṇa, you need to know what is offerable and what is not. In the *Bhagavad-gītā,* Lord Kṛṣṇa states, "If one offers Me with love and devotion a leaf, a flower, a fruit, or water, I will accept it." From this verse it is understood that we can offer Kṛṣṇa foods prepared from milk products, vegetables, fruits, nuts, and grains. (See the ads for some of the many Hare Kṛṣṇa cookbooks.) Meat, fish, and eggs are not offerable. And a few vegetarian items are also forbidden—garlic and onions, for example, which are in the mode of darkness. (Hing, or asafetida, is a tasty substitute for them in cooking and is available at most Indian groceries and ISKCON temple stores.) Nor can you offer to Kṛṣṇa coffee or tea that contain caffeine. If you like these beverages, purchase caffeine-free coffee and herbal teas.

While shopping, be aware that you may find meat, fish, and egg products mixed with other foods; so be sure to read labels carefully. For instance, some brands of yogurt and sour cream contain gelatin, a substance made from the horns, hooves, and bones of slaughtered animals. Also, make sure the cheese you buy contains no animal rennet, an enzyme from the stomach tissues of slaughtered calves. Most hard cheese sold in America contains this rennet, so be careful about any cheese you can't verify as being free from animal rennet.

Also avoid foods cooked by nondevotees. According to the subtle laws of nature, the cook acts upon the food not only physically but mentally as well. Food thus becomes an agent for subtle influences on your consciousness. The principle is the same as that at work with a painting: a painting is not simply a collection of strokes on a canvas but an expression of the artist's state of mind, which affects the viewer. So if you eat food cooked by nondevotees—employees working in a factory, for example—then you're sure to absorb a dose of materialism and karma. So as far as possible use only fresh, natural ingredients.

In preparing food, cleanliness is the most important principle. Nothing impure should be offered to God; so keep your kitchen very clean. Always wash your hands thoroughly before entering the kitchen. While preparing food, do not taste it, for you are cooking the meal not for yourself but for the pleasure of Kṛṣṇa. Arrange portions of the food on dinnerware kept especially for this purpose; no one but the Lord should eat from these dishes. The easiest way to offer food is simply to pray, "My dear Lord Kṛṣṇa, please accept this food," and to chant each of the following prayers three times while ringing a bell (see the Sanskrit Pronunciation Guide on page 233):

1. Prayer to Śrīla Prabhupāda:

nama oṁ viṣṇu-pādāya kṛṣṇa-preṣṭhāya bhū-tale
śrīmate bhaktivedānta-svāminn iti nāmine

namas te sārasvate deve gaura-vāṇī-pracāriṇe
nirviśeṣa-śūnyavādi-pāścātya-deśa-tāriṇe

"I offer my respectful obeisances unto His Divine Grace A. C. Bhaktivedanta Swami Prabhupāda, who is very dear to Lord Kṛṣṇa on this earth, having taken shelter at His lotus feet. Our respectful obeisances are unto you, O spiritual master, servant of Bhaktisiddhānta Sarasvatī Gosvāmī. You are kindly preaching the message of Lord Caitanyadeva and delivering the Western countries, which are filled with impersonalism and voidism."

2. Prayer to Lord Caitanya:

namo mahā-vadānyāya kṛṣṇa-prema-pradāya te
kṛṣṇāya kṛṣṇa-caitanya-nāmne gaura-tviṣe namaḥ

"O most munificent incarnation! You are Kṛṣṇa Himself appearing as Śrī Kṛṣṇa Caitanya Mahāprabhu. You have assumed the golden color of Śrīmatī Rādhārāṇī, and You are widely distributing pure love of Kṛṣṇa. We offer our respectful obeisances unto You."

3. Prayer to Lord Kṛṣṇa:

namo brahmaṇya-devāya go-brāhmaṇa-hitāya ca
jagad-dhitāya kṛṣṇāya govindāya namo namaḥ

"I offer my respectful obeisances unto Lord Kṛṣṇa, who is the worshipable Deity for all *brāhmaṇas,* the well-wisher of the cows and the *brāhmaṇas,* and the benefactor of the whole world. I offer my repeated obeisances to the Personality of Godhead, known as Kṛṣṇa and Govinda."

Remember that the real purpose of preparing and offering food to the Lord is to show your devotion and gratitude to Him. Kṛṣṇa accepts your devotion, not the physical offering itself. God is complete in Himself—He doesn't need anything—but out of His immense kindness He allows us to offer food to Him so that we can develop our love for Him.

After offering the food to the Lord, wait at least five minutes for Him to partake of the preparations. Then you should transfer the food from the special dinnerware and wash the dishes and utensils you used for the offering. Now you and any guests may eat the *prasādam*. While you eat, try to appreciate the spiritual value of the food. Remember that because Kṛṣṇa has accepted it, it is nondifferent from Him, and therefore by eating it you will become purified.

Everything you offer on your altar becomes *prasādam,* the mercy of the Lord. Flowers, incense, the water, the food—everything you offer for the Lord's pleasure becomes spiritualized. The Lord enters into the offerings, and thus the remnants are nondifferent from Him. So you should not only deeply respect the things you've offered, but you should distribute them to others as well. Distribution of *prasādam* is an essential part of Deity worship.

Everyday Life: The Four Regulative Principles

Anyone serious about progressing in Kṛṣṇa consciousness must try to avoid the following four sinful activities:

1. Eating meat, fish, or eggs. These foods are saturated with the modes of passion and ignorance and therefore cannot be offered to the Lord. A person who eats these foods participates in a conspiracy of violence against helpless animals and thus stops his spiritual progress dead in its tracks.

2. Gambling. Gambling invariably puts one into anxiety and fuels greed, envy, and anger.

3. The use of intoxicants. Drugs, alcohol, and tobacco, as well as any drinks or foods containing caffeine, cloud the mind, overstimulate the senses, and make it impossible to understand or follow the principles of *bhakti-yoga*.

4. Illicit sex. This is sex outside of marriage or sex in marriage for any purpose other than procreation. Sex for pleasure compels one to identify with the body and takes one far from Kṛṣṇa consciousness. The scriptures teach that sex is the most powerful force binding us to the material world. Anyone serious about advancing in Kṛṣṇa consciousness should minimize sex or eliminate it entirely.

Engagement in Practical Devotional Service

Everyone must do some kind of work, but if you work only for yourself you must accept the karmic reactions of that work. As Lord Kṛṣṇa says in the *Bhagavad-gītā* (3.9), "Work done as a sacrifice for Viṣṇu [Kṛṣṇa] has to be performed. Otherwise work binds one to the material world."

You needn't change your occupation, except if you're now

engaged in a sinful job such as working as a butcher or bartender. If you're a writer, write for Kṛṣṇa; if you're an artist, create for Kṛṣṇa; if you're a secretary, type for Kṛṣṇa. You may also directly help the temple in your spare time, and you should sacrifice some of the fruits of your work by contributing a portion of your earnings to help maintain the temple and propagate Kṛṣṇa consciousness. Some devotees living outside the temple buy Hare Kṛṣṇa literature and distribute it to their friends and associates, or they engage in a variety of services at the temple. There is also a wide network of devotees who gather in each other's homes for chanting, worship, and study. Write to your local temple or the Society's secretary to learn of any such programs near you.

Additional Devotional Principles

There are many more devotional practices that can help you become Kṛṣṇa conscious. Here are two vital ones:

Studying Hare Kṛṣṇa literature. Śrīla Prabhupāda, the founder-*ācārya* of ISKCON, dedicated much of his time to writing books such as the *Bhagavad-gītā As It Is* and *Śrīmad-Bhāgavatam,* both of which are quoted extensively in *Beyond Illusion and Doubt.* Hearing the words—or reading the writings—of a realized spiritual master is an essential spiritual practice. So try to set aside some time every day to read Śrīla Prabhupāda's books. You can get a free catalog of available books and tapes from the BBT.

Associating with devotees. Śrīla Prabhupāda established the Hare Kṛṣṇa movement to give people in general the chance to associate with devotees of the Lord. This is the best way to gain faith in the process of Kṛṣṇa consciousness and become enthusiastic in devotional service. Conversely, maintaining intimate connections with nondevotees slows one's spiritual progress. So try to visit the Hare Kṛṣṇa center nearest you as often as possible.

In Closing

The beauty of Kṛṣṇa consciousness is that you can take as much as you're ready for. Kṛṣṇa Himself promises in the *Bhagavad-gītā* (2.40), "There is no loss or diminution in this endeavor, and even a little advancement on this path protects one from the most fearful type of danger." So bring Kṛṣṇa into your daily life, and we guarantee you'll feel the benefit.

Hare Kṛṣṇa!

Sanskrit Pronunciation Guide

The system of transliteration used in this book conforms to a system that scholars have accepted to indicate the pronunciation of each sound in the Sanskrit language.

The short vowel **a** is pronounced like the **u** in b**u**t, long **ā** like the **a** in f**a**r. Short **i** is pronounced as in p**i**n, long **ī** as in p**i**que, short **u** as in p**u**ll, and long **ū** as in r**u**le. The vowel **ṛ** is pronounced like the **ri** in **ri**m, **e** like the **ey** in th**ey**, **o** like the **o** in g**o, ai** like the **ai** in **ai**sle, and **au** like the **ow** in h**ow**. The *anusvāra* (**ṁ**) is pronounced like the **n** in the French word *bo***n**, and *visarga* (**ḥ**) is pronounced as a final **h** sound. At the end of a couplet, **aḥ** is pronounced **aha**, and **iḥ** is pronounced **ihi**.

The guttural consonants—**k, kh, g, gh,** and **ṅ**—are pronounced from the throat in much the same manner as in English. **K** is pronounced as in **k**ite, **kh** as in Ec**kh**art, **g** as in **g**ive, **gh** as in di**g h**ard, and **ṅ** as in si**ng.**

The palatal consonants—**c, ch, j, jh,** and **ñ**—are pronounced with the tongue touching the firm ridge behind the teeth. **C** is pronounced as in **ch**air, **ch** as in staun**ch-h**eart, **j** as in **j**oy, **jh** as in he**dgeh**og, and **ñ** as in ca**ny**on.

The cerebral consonants—**ṭ, ṭh, ḍ, ḍh,** and **ṇ**—are pronounced with the tip of the tongue turned up and drawn back against the dome of the palate. **Ṭ** is pronounced as in **t**ub, **ṭh** as in ligh**t-h**eart, **ḍ** as in **d**ove, **ḍh** as in re**d-h**ot, and **ṇ** as in **n**ut. The dental consonants—**t, th, d, dh,** and **n—**are pronounced in the same manner as the cerebrals, but with the forepart of the tongue against the teeth.

The labial consonants—**p, ph, b, bh,** and **m**—are pronounced with the lips. **P** is pronounced as in **p**ine, **ph** as in u**ph**ill, **b** as in **b**ird, **bh** as in ru**b-h**ard, and **m** as in **m**other.

The semivowels—**y, r, l,** and **v**—are pronounced as in **y**es, **r**un, **l**ight, and **v**ine respectively. The sibilants—**ś, ṣ,** and **s**—are pronounced, respectively, as in the German word *s***prechen** and the English words **sh**ine and **s**un. The letter **h** is pronounced as in **h**ome.

Glossary

A

Absolute Truth—the ultimate source of all energies.

Ācārya—an ideal teacher, who teaches by his personal eample; a spiritual master.

Acintya-bhedābheda-tattva—Lord Caitanya's doctrine of the "inconceivable oneness and difference" of God and His energies.

Age of Kali—*See:* Kali-yuga.

Arjuna—one of the five Pāṇḍava brothers. Kṛṣṇa became his chariot driver and spoke the *Bhagavad-gītā* to him.

Āśrama—one of four spiritual orders of life. *See also: Brahmacarya; Gṛhastha; Vānaprastha; Sannyāsa.*

B

Badas—deep-fried dhal dumplings in yogurt sauce.

Battle of Kurukṣetra—a battle between the Kurus and the Pāṇḍavas, which took place five thousand years ago and before which Lord Kṛṣṇa spoke the *Bhagavad-gītā* to Arjuna.

Bhagavad-gītā—the discourse between the Supreme Lord, Kṛṣṇa, and His devotee Arjuna expounding devotional service as both the principal means and the ultimate end of spiritual perfection.

Bhagavān—the Supreme Lord, who possesses all opulences in full.

Bhāgavata philosophy—the philosophy dealing with the Supreme Personality of Godhead, His devotees, and the process of devotional service.

Bhakti—devotional service to the Supreme Lord.

Bhaktivinoda Ṭhākura (1838–1915)—the great-grandfather of the present-day Kṛṣṇa consciousness movement. He was the spiritual master of Śrīla Gaurakiśora dāsa Bābājī and father of Śrīla Bhaktisiddhānta Sarasvatī, who was the spiritual master of Śrīla Prabhupāda.

Bharata Mahārāja—an ancient king of India from whom the Pāṇḍavas descended. A great devotee of the Lord, he developed an attachment causing him to take birth as a deer. In his next life, as the *brāhmaṇa* Jaḍa Bharata, he attained spiritual perfection.

Bourgeoisie—property owners.

Brahmā—the first created living being and secondary creator of the material universe.

Brahma-bhūta—the joyful state free of material contamination; liberation.

Brahmacārī—one in the first order of spiritual life; a celibate student of a spiritual master.

Brahmacarya—celibate student life; the first order of Vedic spiritual life.

Brahma-jijñāsā—inquiry into the Absolute Truth.

Brahman—(1) the individual soul; (2) the impersonal aspect of the Supreme; (3) the Supreme Personality of Godhead; (4) the *mahat-tattva,* or total material substance.

Brāhmaṇa—a person wise in Vedic knowledge, fixed in goodness, and knowledgeable of Brahman, the Absolute Truth; a member of the first Vedic social order.

Brahma-saṁhitā—a very ancient Sanskrit scripture recording the prayers of Brahmā to the Supreme Lord, Govinda.

Buddha—an incarnation of the Supreme Lord who, by bewildering the atheists, stopped them from misusing the *Vedas*.

C

Caitanya-caritāmṛta—a biography of Śrī Caitanya Mahāprabhu composed in Bengali in the late siteenth century by Śrīla Kṛṣṇadāsa Kavirāja.

Caitanya Mahāprabhu (1486–1534)—the Supreme Lord appearing as His own greatest devotee to teach love of God, especially through the process of congregational chanting of His holy names.

Caṇḍāla—an outcaste or untouchable; a dog-eater.

Capātī—a flat bread made from whole-wheat flour.

D

Deity of the Lord—the authorized form of Kṛṣṇa worshiped in temples.

Dhanur Veda—the section to the *Vedas* dealing with martial science.

Dharma—religion; duty; anything's intrinsic characteristic, which for living entities is the eternal propensity to serve.

Dhruva Mahārāja—a great devotee who as a child performed severe austerities to meet the Lord and get the kingdom denied him. He received an entire planet and God realization as well.

Droṇācārya—the military teacher of the Pāṇḍavas. He was obliged to fight against them in the Battle of Kurukṣetra.

E

Entelechy—a vital agent or force directing growth and life.

External energy—the Lord's material energy, consisting, in summary, of earth, water, fire, air, ether, mind, inelligence, and false ego.

F

False ego—the conception that "I am this material body."

G

Gopīs—Kṛṣṇa's cowherd girlfriends, who are His most surrendered and confidential devotees.

Gosvāmī—a controller of the mind and senses; the title of one in the renounced, or *sannyāsa,* order.

Gṛhastha—regulated householder life; the second order of Vedic spiritual life; one in that order.

Guru—a spiritual master.

H

Hare Kṛṣṇa mantra—the great chant for deliverance: Hare Kṛṣṇa, Hare Kṛṣṇa, Kṛṣṇa Kṛṣṇa, Hare Hare/ Hare Rāma, Hare Rāma, Rāma Rāma, Hare Hare.

Haridāsa Ṭhākura—a great devotee and associate of Lord Caitanya Mahāprabhu who chanted three hundred thousand names of God a day.

Haṭha-yoga—the practice of postures and breathing exercises for achieving purification and sense control.

Haṭha-yogī—one who practices *haṭha-yoga.*

I

Indra—the chief of the administrative demigods, king of the heavenly planets, and presiding deity of rain.

J

Jagāi and Mādhāi—two great debauchees whom Lord Nityānanda converted into Vaiṣṇavas.

Jīva (jīvātmā)—the living entity, who is an eternal individual soul, part and parcel of the Supreme Lord.

Jīva-tattva—the living entities, atomic parts of the Supreme Lord.

Jñāna-yogī—one who undertakes a speculative philosophical search for the Absolute Truth.

Jñānīs—one who cultivates knowledge by empirical speculation.

K

Kachoris—deep-fried stuffed savory pastries.

Kālī—the personified material energy and the wife of Lord Śiva.

Kali-yuga (Age of Kali)—the present age, characterized by quarrel. It is last in the cycle of four ages and began five thousand years ago.

Karma—(1) material action performed according to scriptural regulations; (2) action pertaining to the development of the material body; (3) any material action which will incur a subsequent reaction; (4) the material reaction one incurs due to fruitive activities.

Karmī—one engaged in karma, fruitive activity; a materialist.

Kṛṣṇa consciousness—the practices of devotional service to Lord Kṛṣṇa; the state of consciousness attained through such practices. *See also: Bhakti-yoga.*

Kṣatriya—a warrior or administrator in Vedc society; the second Vedic social order.

Kurus—the descendants of Kuru, especially the sons of Dhṛtarāṣṭra, who were enemies of the Pāṇḍavas.

M

Madhvācārya—a great thirteenth-century Vaiṣṇava spiritual master who preached the theistic philosophy of pure dualism.

Mahā-mantra—the great chant for deliverance: Hare Kṛṣṇa, Hare Kṛṣṇa, Kṛṣṇa Kṛṣṇa, Hare Harc/ Harc Rāma, Harc Rāma, Rāma Rāma, Hare Hare.

Manvantara-avatāras—special incarnations of the Supreme Lord who appear during the reign of each Manu.

Mathurā—Lord Kṛṣṇa's abode, surrounding Vṛndāvana, where He took birth and to which He later returned after performing His childhood pastimes in Vṛndāvana.

Māyā—the inferior, illusory energy of the Supreme Lord, which rules over this material creation; also, forgetfulness of one's relationship with Kṛṣṇa.

Māyāvāda—the impersonal philosophy propounding the unqualified oneness of God and the living entities and the nonreality of manifest nature.

Māyāvādīs—impersonalistic philosophers who conceive of the Absolute as ultimately formless and the living entity as equal to God .

Mūḍha—a foolish, asslike person.

Mukti—liberation from material bondage.

N

Nārada Muni—a pure devotee of the Lord who travels throughout the universes in his eternal body, glorifying devotional service. He is the spiritual master of Vyāsadeva and of many other great devotees.

Nārada-pañcarātra—Nārada Muni's book on the processes of Deity worship and mantra meditation.

Nārāyaṇa, Lord—the Supreme Lord in His majestic, four-armed form. An expansion of Kṛṣṇa, He presides over the Vaikuṇṭha planets.

Narottama Dāsa Ṭhākura—an exalted devotee of Lord Caitanya who lived in the sixteenth century and is known especially for his devotional songs, which are written in simple Bengali but contain the highest spiritual truths.

Nityānanda Prabhu—the incarnation of Lord Balarāma who appeared as the principal associate of Lord Caitanya.

P

Padma Purāṇa—one of the eighteen *Purāṇas,* or Vedic historical scriptures.

Pāṇḍavas—Yudhiṣṭhira, Bhīma, Arjuna, Nakula, and Sahadeva, the five warrior-brothers who were intimate friends and devotees of Lord Kṛṣṇa.

Paramātmā—the Supersoul, a Viṣṇu expansion of the Supreme Lord residing in the heart of each embodied living entity and pervading all of material nature.

Paramparā—a disciplic succession.

Parāśara—the great sage who narrated the *Viṣṇu Purāṇa* and was the father of Śrīla Vyāsadeva.

Parīkṣit Mahārāja—the emperor of the world who heard *Śrīmad-Bhāgavatam* from Śukadeva Gosvāmī and thus attained perfection.

Proletariat—the working class.

Prahlāda Mahārāja—a devotee persecuted by his demoniac father Hiraṇyakaśipu but protected and saved by the Lord in the form of Nṛsiṁhadeva (the half man, half-lion incarnation). He is one of the twelve *mahājanas,* great self-realized souls who are authorities on the science of Kṛṣṇa consciousness

Prakṛti—the energy of the Supreme; the female principle enjoyed by the male *puruṣa*.

Prasādam—the Lord's mercy; food or other items spiritualized by being first offered to the Supreme Lord.

Pṛthā—Kuntī, the wife of King Pāṇḍu, mother of the Pāṇḍavas, and aunt of Lord Kṛṣṇa.

Puruṣa-avatāras—the three primary Viṣṇu expansions of the Supreme Lord who are involved in universal creation.

R

Rādhārāṇī—Lord Kṛṣṇa's most intimate consort, who is the personification of His internal, spiritual potency.

Rājarṣi—a saintly king.

Rajo-guṇa—the material mode of passion.

Rāmānujācārya—a great eleventh-century spiritual master of the Śrī Vaiṣṇava *sampradāya*.

Rasagullā—a dessert consisting of small balls of soft-textured fresh cheese soaked in syrup.

Rūpa Gosvāmī—the chief of the six Vaiṣṇava spiritual masters who directly followed Lord Caitanya Mahāprabhu and systematically presented His teachings.

S

Śakty-āveśa avatāra—a living entity empowered by the Supreme Lord with one or more of His opulences.

Sampradāya—a disciplic succession of spiritual masters; the followers in that tradition.

Sanātana Gosvāmī—one of the six Vaiṣṇava spiritual masters who directly followed Lord Caitanya Mahāprabhu and systematically presented His teachings.

Sannyāsa—renounced life; the fourth order of Vedic spiritual life.

Sannyāsī—one in the *sannyāsa* (renounced) order.

Śāstras—revealed scriptures, such as the Vedic literature.

Sattva-guṇa—the material mode of goodness.

Śiva—the special incarnation of the Lord as the demigod in charge of the mode of ignorance and the destruction of the material manifestation.

Śrīmad-Bhāgavatam—the *Purāṇa,* or history, written by Śrīla Vyāsadeva specifically to give a deep understanding of Lord Kṛṣṇa, His devotees, and devotional service.

Śuddha-sattva—the spiritual platform of pure goodness.

Śūdra—a laborer; the fourth of the Vedic social orders.

Śukadeva Gosvāmī—the great devotee sage who spoke *Śrīmad-Bhāgavatam* to King Parīkṣit just prior to the king's death.

Summum bonum—the supreme good.

Svāmī—a controller of the mind and senses; the title of one in the renounced, or *sannyāsa,* order.

Śvetāśvatara Upaniṣad—one of the 108 *Upaniṣads*. It very clearly presents the truth concerning the Lord and the living entity.

T

Tamo-guṇa—the mode of ignorance.

Tapasya—austerity; accepting some voluntary inconvenience for a higher purpose.

V

Vaikuṇṭha—the spiritual world, where there is no anxiety.

Vaiṣṇava—a devotee of Lord Viṣṇu, or Kṛṣṇa.

Vaiṣṇavism—devotional service to Lord Viṣṇu, or Kṛṣṇa.

Vaiśya—a farmer or merchant in Vedic society; the third Vedic social order.

Vānaprastha—one who has retired from family life; the third order of Vedic spiritual life.

Varṇas—the four Vedic social-occupational divisions of society, distinguished by quality of work and situation in the modes of nature (*guṇas*). *See also: Brāhmaṇa; Kṣatriya; Vaiśya; Śūdra.*

Varṇāśrama-dharma—the Vedic social system of four social and four spiritual orders. *See also: Varṇas; Āśrama*

Vāsudeva—the Supreme Lord, Kṛṣṇa, son of Vasudeva and proprietor of everything, material and spiritual.

Vedānta-sūtra—the philosophical treatise written by Vyāsadeva consisting of aphorisms that embody the essential meaning of the *Upaniṣads.*

Vedas—the four original revealed scriptures (*Ṛg, Sāma, Atharva,* and *Yajur*).

Vedic—pertaining to a culture in which all aspects of human life are under the guidance of the *Vedas.*

Vena—the demoniac son of King Aṅga and father of King Pṛthu.

Viṣṇu-tattva—the status or category of Godhead; primary expansions of the Supreme Lord.

Vivekananda—an impersonalitic follower of Ramakrishna.

Vṛndāvana—Kṛṣṇa's eternal abode, where He fully manifests His quality of sweetness; the village on this earth in which He enacted His childhood pastimes five thousand years ago.

Vyāsadeva—the incarnation of Lord Kṛṣṇa who gave the *Vedas, Purāṇas, Vedānta-sūtra,* and *Mahābhārata* to mankind.

Y

Yāmunācārya—a great Vaiṣṇava spiritual master of the Śrī-sampradāya.

Yoga—spiritual discipline undergone to link oneself with the Supreme.

Yogi—one who practices yoga.

Index

Kṛṣṇa
surrender to (*continued*)
as culmination of knowledge, 199
immorality &, 94
by wise people, 3
will of, as all-powerful, 31
See also: Absolute Truth; God
Kṣatriya(s), 14, 22
hunting by, 15
See also: Varṇāśrama
Kṣetra-jñaṁ cāpi māṁ viddhi
verse quoted, 190

Leibnitz, 169
Lenin, Nikolai, 132, 146
"perfection" of, 133
Liberation
Bhagavad-gītā quoted on, 197
defined, 82
via Kṛṣṇa consciousness, 22, 58, 197, 199
Living entity (entities)
conditioned, as forgetful of relationship with Lord, 34
as dependent always, 156
as eternal, 3, 39, 59–60, 123–24
liberation of, via enlightenment, 36
Mill cited on immortality of, 123, 124
as servants always, 68
service as intrinsic nature of, 208
as sons of God, 35
spiritual body of, 36, 60
spiritual nature of, 154
suffering of, cause of, 35
See also; Bhagavad-gītā cited; *Bhagavad-gītā* quoted; Soul; Transmigration of soul
Logos, 34
Love
freedom necessary for, 95
for God, 88
as religion's essential characteristic, 80

Love
for God (*continued*)
varieties of, 80
vs. lust, 79
for Kṛṣṇa
Caitanya gives, 73
vs. lust, 94
surrender via, 94
in Vṛndāvana, 79–80

Madhvācārya, 32
Mahā-mantra. See: Hare Kṛṣṇa mantra
Malthus, Thomas, population theory of, 102
Māṁ hi pārtha vyapāśritya
verse quoted, 153
Man-manā bhava mad-bhakto
verse quoted, 73
Manuṣyāṇāṁ sahasreṣu
verse quoted, 126
Marx, Karl, 129
cited
on capitalism, 132
on classless society via communism, 131
on dialectical materialism, 129
on God as man's creation, 146
on means of production as supreme, 132
on religion, 143, 144
quoted
on human nature, 141
on religion, 143
Marxism, 209
Material life
via material desire & will, 90
misery via, 161
sex as basis of, 94, 161, 163
as unsatisfying, 133
Material nature
as agent of God for reformation of souls, 118
intelligence of Lord behind, 102
as mother of loving entities, 45, 177
See also: Material world

The International Society for Krishna Consciousness
Founder-Ācārya: His Divine Grace A.C. Bhaktivedanta Swami Prabhupāda

CENTERS AROUND THE WORLD

NORTH AMERICA

CANADA

Calgary, Alberta — 313 Fourth Street N.E., T2E 3S3/ Tel. (403) 265-3302
Edmonton, Alberta — 9353 35th Ave., T6E 5R5/ Tel. (403) 439-9999
Montreal, Quebec — 1626 Pie IX Boulevard, H1V 2C5/ Tel. & fax: (514) 521-1301
Ottawa, Ontario — 212 Somerset St. E., K1N 6V4/ Tel. (613) 565-6544
Regina, Saskatchewan — 1279 Retallack St., S4T 2H8/ Tel. (306) 525-1640
Toronto, Ontario — 243 Avenue Rd., M5R 2J6/ Tel. (416) 922-5415
Vancouver, B.C. — 5462 S.E. Marine Dr., Burnaby V5J 3G8/ Tel. (604) 433-9728
Govinda's Restaurant: Tel. (604) 433 2428

RURAL COMMUNITY

Ashcroft, B.C. — Saranagati Dhama (mail: P.O. Box 99, V0K 1A0, attn: Uttama Devi Dasi)/Tel. (250) 453-2397

U.S.A.

Atlanta, Georgia — 1287 South Ponce de Leon Ave. N.E., 30306/ Tel. (404) 378-9234
Austin, Texas — 807-A E. 30th St., 78705/ Tel. (512) 320 0372
Baltimore, Maryland — 200 Bloomsbury Ave., Catonsville, 21228/ Tel. (410) 744-4069 or 719-6738/ Tel. & fax: (410) 744-1624
Berkeley, California — 2334 Stuart Street, 94705/ Tel. (510) 540-9215
Boise, Idaho — 1615 Martha St., 83706/ Tel. (208) 344-4274
Boston, Massachusetts — 72 Commonwealth Ave., 02116/ Tel. (617) 247-8611
Chicago, Illinois — 1716 W. Lunt Ave., 60626/ Tel. (773) 973-0900
Columbus, Ohio — 379 W. Eighth Ave., 43201/ Tel. (614) 421-1661
Dallas, Texas — 5430 Gurley Ave., 75223/ Tel. (214) 827-6330
Denver, Colorado — 1400 Cherry St., 80220/ Tel. (303) 333-5461
Detroit, Michigan — 383 Lenox Ave., 48215/ Tel. (313) 824-6000
Gainesville, Florida — 214 N.W. 14th St., 32603/ Tel. (352) 336-4183
Gurabo, Puerto Rico — P.O. Box 1338, 00778/ Tel. (787) 737-3917
Hartford, Connecticut — 1683 Main St., E. Hartford, 06108/ Tel. & fax: (860) 289-7252/
Honolulu, Hawaii — 51 Coelho Way, 96817/ Tel. (808) 595-3947
Houston, Texas — 1320 W. 34th St., 77018/ Tel. (713) 686-4482
Kansas City, Missouri — Rupanuga Vedic College (Men's Seminary), 6309 McGee St., 64113/ Tel. (816) 361-6167 or (800) 340-5286
Laguna Beach, California — 285 Legion St., 92651/ Tel. (714) 494-7029
Long Island, New York — 197 S. Ocean Avenue, Freeport, 11520/ Tel. (516) 223-4909
Los Angeles, California — 3764 Watseka Ave., 90034/ Tel. (310) 836-2676
Miami, Florida — 3220 Virginia St., 33133 (mail: P.O. Box 337, Coconut Grove, FL 33233)/ Tel. (305) 442-7218
New Orleans, Louisiana — 2936 Esplanade Ave., 70119/ Tel. (504) 486-3583
New York, New York — 305 Schermerhorn St., Brooklyn, 11217/ Tel. (718) 855-6714
New York, New York — 26 Second Avenue, 10003 (mail: P. O. Box 2509, New York, NY 10009)/ Tel. (212) 420-1130
Philadelphia, Pennsylvania — 41 West Allens Lane, 19119/ Tel. (215) 247-4600
Philadelphia, Pennsylvania — 1408 South St., 19148/ Tel. (215) 985-9335
Phoenix, Arizona — 100 S. Weber Dr., Chandler, 85226/ Tel. (602) 705-4900
Portland, Oregon — 36312 SE Douglass Rd., Eagle Creek, 97022/ Tel. (503) 637-3891
St. Louis, Missouri — 3926 Lindell Blvd., 63108/ Tel. (314) 535-8085
San Diego, California — 1030 Grand Ave., Pacific Beach, 92109/ Tel. (619) 483-2500
San Jose, California — 2679 New Jersey Ave., 95124/ Tel. (408) 559-3197
Seattle, Washington — 1420 228th Ave. S.E., Issaquah, 98027/ Tel. (206) 391-3293
Spanish Fork, Utah — Krishna Temple Project & KHQN Radio, 8628 S. State Rd., 84660/ Tel. (801) 798-3559
Tallahassee, Florida — 1323 Nylic St., 32304/ Tel. & fax: (850) 681-9258/
Towaco, New Jersey — 100 Jacksonville Rd. (mail: P.O. Box 109), 07082/ Tel. & fax: (973) 299-0970
Tucson, Arizona — 711 E. Blacklidge Dr., 85719/ Tel. (520) 792-0630
Washington, D.C. — 1009 Noyes Dr., Silver Spring, MD 20910/ Tel. (301) 562-9662 or 765-8155
Washington, D.C. — 10310 Oaklyn Dr., Potomac, Maryland 20854/ Tel. (301) 299-2100

RURAL COMMUNITIES

Alachua, Florida (New Raman Reti) — P.O. Box 819, 32616/ Tel. & fax: (904) 462-2017
Carriere, Mississippi (New Talavan) — 31492 Anner Road, 39426/ Tel. (601) 749-9460 or 799-1354
Gurabo, Puerto Rico (New Govardhana Hill) — (contact ISKCON Gurabo)
Hillsborough, North Carolina (New Goloka) — 1032 Dimmocks Mill Rd., 27278/ Tel. (919) 732-6492

Moundsville, West Virginia (New Vrindavan) — R.D. No. 1, Box 319, Hare Krishna Ridge, 26041/ Tel. (304) 843-1600; Guest House, (304) 845-5905

Mulberry, Tennessee (Murari-sevaka) — Rt. No. 1, Box 146-A, 37359/ Tel. (615) 759-6888

Port Royal, Pennsylvania (Gita Nagari) — R.D. No. 1, Box 839, 17082/ Tel. & fax: (717) 527-4101

RESTAURANTS

Gainesville, Florida — Balaji Indian Cuisine, 2106 SW 34th St., 32608/ Tel. (352) 378-2955

San Juan, Puerto Rico — Gopal, 201B Calle Tetuan, Viejo San Juan, 00901/ Tel. (787) 724-0229

ASIA

INDIA

Agartala, Tripura — Assam-Agartala Rd., Banamalipur, 799 001

Ahmedabad, Gujarat — Sattelite Rd., Gandhinagar Highway Crossing, 380 054/ Tel. (079) 676-9827, 674-4944 or -4945

Allahabad, U.P. — Hare Krishna Dham, 161 Kashi Raj Nagar, Baluaghat 211 003/ Tel. (0532) 405294

Bangalore, Karnataka — Hare Krishna Hill, 1 'R' Block, Chord Road, Rajaji Nagar 560 010/ Tel. (080) 332-1956

Baroda, Gujarat — Hare Krishna Land, Gotri Rd., 390 021/ Tel. (0265) 310630

Belgaum, Karnataka — Shukravar Peth, Tilak Wadi, 590 006

Bhubaneswar, Orissa — N.H. No. 5, IRC Village, 751 015/ Tel. (0674) 453517, 453475 or 454283

Bombay — (see Mumbai)

Calcutta— (see Kolkata)

Chandigarh — Hare Krishna Dham, Sector 36-B, 160 036/ Tel. (0172) 601590 or 603232

Chennai, Tamil Nadu — 59, Burkit Rd., T. Nagar, 600 017/ Tel. (044) 434-3266

Coimbatore, Tamil Nadu — Padmam 387, VGR Puram, Alagesan Rd., 641 011/ Tel. (0422) 435978 or 442749

Dwarka, Gujarat — Bharatiya Bhavan, Devi Bhavan Road, 361335/ Tel. (02892) 34606

Guntur, A.P. — Opp. Sivalayam, Peda Kakani 522 509

Guwahati, Assam — Ulubari Chariali, South Sarania, 781 007/ Tel. (0361) 545963

Hanumkonda, A.P. — Neeladri Rd., Kapuwada, 506 011/ Tel. (08712) 77399

Haridwar, U.P. — Prabhupada Ashram, G. House, Nai Basti, Bhimgoda, 249401 (mail: P.O. Box 4)/ Tel. (0133) 422655 or 425849

Hyderabad, A.P. — Hare Krishna Land, Nampally Station Rd., 500 001/ Tel. (040) 474-4969 or -2018

Imphal, Manipur — Hare Krishna Land, Airport Road, 795 001/ Tel. (0385) 221587

Indore, M.P. — 101 Chetak Arch, 7 MG Rd./ Tel. (0731) 529665

Jaipur, Rajasthan —AB-95/96 Chanakya Marg, Nirman Nagar, 302019/ Tel. (0141) 399650 or 392437

Katra, Jammu and Kashmir — Srila Prabhupada Ashram, Srila Prabhupada Marg, Kalka Mata Mandir (Vashnov Mata), 182 101/ Tel. (01991) 33047

Kolkata, W. Bengal — 3C Albert Rd., 700 017/ Tel. (033) 247-3757 or 6075

Kurukshetra, Haryana — 369 Gudri Muhalla, Main Bazaar, 132 118/ Tel. (01744) 22806 or 23529

Lucknow, U.P. — 1 Ashak Nagar, Guru Govind Singh Marg, 226 018

Madras — (see Chennai)

Madurai, Tamil Nadu — 32 Chellatthamman Koil St. (Near Simmakkal), 625 001/ Tel. (0452) 627565

Mangalore, Karnataka — Hare Krishna Center (ISKCON), Hillgrove (R), Lady Hill, Chilimbi, Mangalore 6/ Tel. (0824) 450021 or 452626

Mayapur, W. Bengal — Shree Mayapur Chandrodaya Mandir, Shree Mayapur Dham, Dist. Nadia (mail: P.O. Box 10279, Ballyganj, Calcutta 700 019)/ Tel. (03472) 45239, 45240, or 45233

Moirang, Manipur — Nongban Ingkhon, Tidim Rd./ Tel. 795133

Mumbai, Maharashtra (Bombay) — Hare Krishna Land, Juhu 400 049/ Tel. (022) 620-6860

Mumbai, Maharashtra — 7 K. M. Munshi Marg, Chowpatty, 400 007/ Tel. (022) 369-7228

Mumbai, Maharashtra — Shrusthi Complex, Mira Road (E), opposite Royal College, Thane, 401 107/ Tel. (022) 881-7795 or 7796

Nagpur, Maharashtra — Sri Sri Radha Gopinath Mandir, Plot No. 1, Abhayankar Nagar Petrol Pump, Abhayankar Nagar, 440 010/ Tel. (0712) 224180 or 224787

New Delhi — Sant Nagar Main Road (Garhi), behind Nehru Place Complex (mail: P. O. Box 7061), 110 065/ Tel. (011) 623-5133

New Delhi — 14/63, Punjabi Bagh, 110 026/ Tel. (011) 541-0782

Noida, U.P. — B-40, Sector 56, 201301/ Tel. (0911) 858-3464

Pandharpur, Maharashtra — Hare Krsna Ashram (across Chandrabhaga River), Dist. Sholapur, 413 304/ Tel. (0218) 623473

Patna, Bihar — Rajendra Nagar Road No. 12, 800 016/ Tel. (0612) 50765

Pune, Maharashtra — 4 Tarapoor Rd., Camp, 411 001/ Tel. (0212) 667259

Puri, Orissa — Bhakti Kuthi, Swargadwar/ Tel. (06752) 23740

Secunderabad, A.P. — 27 St. John's Road, 500 026/ Tel. (040) 780-5232/ Fax: (040) 781-4021

Silchar, Assam — Ambikapatti, Silchar, Cachar Dist., 788 004

Siliguri, W. Bengal — Gitalpara, 734406/ Tel. (0353) 426619/ Fax: (0353) 526130

Sri Rangam, Tamil Nadu — 16A Thiruvadi Street, Trichy, 620 006/ Tel. (0431) 433945

Surat, Gujarat — Rander Rd., Jahangirpura 395 005/ Tel. (0261) 685516 or 685891

Surat, Gujarat — Bhaktivedanta Rajavidyalaya, Krishnalok, Surat-Bardoli Rd. Gangapur, P.O. Gangadhara, Dist. Surat, 394 310/ Tel. (0261) 667075

Thiruvananthapuram (Trivandrum), Kerala — T.C. 224/ 1485, WC Hospital Rd., Thycaud, 695 014/ Tel. (0471) 328197

Tirupati, A.P. — K.T. Road, Vinayaka Nagar, 517 507/ Tel. (08574) 30114 or 30009

Udhampur, Jammu and Kashmir — Srila Prabhupada Ashram, Prabhupada Marg, Prabhupada Nagar, 182 101/ Tel. (01992) 70298

Vallabh Vidyanagar, Gujarat — ISKCON, Opposite Polytechnic, 388 121/ Tel. (02692) 30796

Varanasi, U.P. — Annapurna Nagar, Vidyapith Rd., 221 001/ Tel. (0542) 362617

Vishakapatnam, A.P. — ISKCON, Plot 23, d. No. 50-

119-3/1, Northern Extension Seethammadhara, Vishakapatnam 530 013/ Tel. (0891) 710748

Vrindavana, U.P. — Krishna-Balaram Mandir, Bhaktivedanta Swami Marg, Raman Reti, Mathura Dist., 281 124/ Tel. (0565) 442-596 or 443-492

Warangal — Mulugu Road, Aiyappa Pidipally, 506007/ Tel. (08712) 26182

RURAL COMMUNITIES

Ahmedabad District, Gujarat (Hare Krishna Farm) — Katwada (contact ISKCON Ahmedabad)

Assam — Karnamadhu, Dist. Karimganj

Chamorshi, Maharashtra — 78 Krishnanagar Dham, Dist. Gadhachiroli, 442 603/ Tel. (0218) 623473

Hyderabad, A.P. — P. O. Dabilpur Village, Medchal Tq., R.R. Dist., 501 401/ Tel. 552924

Indore, M.P. (Krishna-Balarama Mandir) — Hare Krishna Vihar, Nipania Village/ Tel. (731) 572794

Karnataka (Bhaktivedanta Eco-Village) — Nagodi P.O., Vollur Valley, Hosanagar Taluq, Shivmoga District, 577 425 (mail: Garuda Guha, Kollur, D.K. District, 576 220)

Mayapur, West Bengal — (contact ISKCON Mayapur)

Puri, Orissa — Sipasurubuli Puri, Dist. Puri/ Tel. (06752) 24592 or 24594

Vrindavana, U.P. — Vrinda Kund, Nandagaon, Dist. Mathura, U.P.

RESTAURANT

Calcutta — Hare Krishna Karma-Free Confectionary, 6 Russel Street, 700 071

OTHER COUNTRIES

Cebu, Phillipines — Hare Krishna Paradise, 231 Pagsabungan Road, Basak, Mandaue City/ Tel. +63 (032) 345-3590

Chittagong, Bangladesh — Caitanya Cultural Society, Sri Pundarik Dham, Mekhala, Hathzari (mail: GPO Box 877)/ Tel. +88 (031) 225822

Colombo, Sri Lanka — 188 New Chetty St., Colombo 13/ Tel. +94 (01) 433325

Dhaka, Bangladesh — 5 Chandra Mohon Basak St., Banagram, 1203/ Tel. +880 (02) 236249

Hong Kong — 27 Chatham Road South, 6/F/ Tel. +852 (2) 739-6818/ Fax: +852 (2) 724-2186

Jakarta, Indonesia — P.O. Box 2694, Jakarta Pusat 10001/ Tel. +62 (021) 489-9646

Jessore, Bangladesh — Nitai Gaur Mandir, Kathakhali Bazaar, P. O. Panjia

Jessore, Bangladesh — Rupa-Sanatana Smriti Tirtha, Ramsara, P. O. Magura Hat

Kathmandu, Nepal — Budhanilkantha (mail: P. O. Box 3520)/ Tel. +977 (01) 371743

Kuala Lumpur, Malaysia — Lot 9901, Jalan Awan Jawa, Taman Yarl, off 5 1/2 Mile, Jalan Kelang Lama, Petaling/ Tel. +60 (03) 780-7355, 7360, or 7369

Manila, Philippines — 92 Champagnat St., Corner Narra St., Marakina Heights, Marikina City

Phnom Penh, Kampuchea — 49ZE Preah Sothearos St., Sankat Tunle Bassac, Khan Chamcar Mon

Taipei, Taiwan — (mail: c/o ISKCON Hong Kong)

Tel Aviv, Israel — 16 King George St. (mail: P. O. Box 48163, 61480)/ Tel. +972 (03) 528-5475 or 629-9011

Tokyo, Japan — 4-19-6 Kamatikada Nakano,1F Subarhu Bldg.,164 / Tel. +81 (03) 5343-9417 or 3811

Yogyakarta, Indonesia — P.O. Box 25, Babarsari YK, DIY

RURAL COMMUNITIES

Indonesia (Govinda Kunja) — (contact ISKCON Jakarta)

Malaysia — Jalan Sungai Manik, 36000 Teluk Intan, Perak/ Tel. +63 (032) 83254

RESTAURANT

Kuala Lumpur, Malaysia — Govinda's, 16-1 Jalan Bunus Enam, Masjid India/ Tel. +60 (03) 780-7355, 7360, or 7369

EUROPE

UNITED KINGDOM AND IRELAND

Belfast, Northern Ireland — Brooklands, 140 Upper Dunmurray Lane, BT17 OHE/ Tel. +44 (01232) 620530

Birmingham, England — 84 Stanmore Rd., Edgbaston, B16 9TB/ Tel. +44 (0121) 420-4999

Bristol, England — Alberta Cottage, Wraxhall Road, Nailsea, BS19 1BN/ Tel. +44 (01275) 853788

Cardiff, Wales — 18 Greenfield Place, Caerphilly, Mid Glamorgan/ Tel. +44 (01222) 831579

Cork, Ireland — Highland Cottage, 81, Lower Glanmire Road, Cork City/ Tel. (021) 552976

Coventry, England — Kingfield Rd., Radford, West Midlands (mail: 19 Gloucester St., CV1 3BZ)/ Tel. +44 (01203) 552822 or 555420

Glasgow, Scotland — Karuna Bhavan, Bankhouse Rd., Lesmahagow, Lanarkshire, ML11 0ES/ Tel. +44 (01555) 894790

Leicester, England — 21/21A Thoresby St., North Evington, LE5 4GU/ Tel. & fax: +44 (0116) 236-7723

Liverpool, England — 114A Bold St., Merseyside, L1 4HY/ Tel. +44 (0151) 708-9400

London, England (city) — 9/10 Soho St., W1V 5DA/ Tel. +44 (0171) 437-3662; (residential/pujaris/shop:) 439-3606; office, 437-5875; Govinda's Restaurant, 437-4928

London, England (country) — Bhaktivedanta Manor, Dharam Marg, Hilfield Lane, Watford, Herts, WD2 8EZ/ Tel. +44 (01923) 857244

London, England (south) — 42 Enmore Road, South Norwood, SE25/ Tel. +44 (0181) 656-4296 or 654-3138

Manchester, England — 20 Mayfield Rd., Whalley Range, M16 8FT/ Tel. +44 (0161) 226-4416/ Tel. & fax: +44 (0161) 860-6117

Newcastle upon Tyne, England — 304 Westgate Rd., NE4 6AR/ Tel. +44 (0191) 272-1911

Plymouth, England — 2 Windermere Crescent, Derriford, Devon, PL6 5HX/ Tel (01752) 776708

Romford, England — 3 Rowan Walk, Hornchurch, Essex, RM11 2JA/ Tel. +44 (01708) 454092

RURAL COMMUNITIES

Lisnaskea, Northern Ireland — Govindadvipa Dhama, ISKCON Inisrath Island, BT92 9GN, Co. Fermanagh/ Tel. +44 (013657) 21512 or 22682

London, England — (contact Bhaktivedanta Manor)

RESTAURANT

Dublin, Ireland — Govinda's Restaurant, 4 Aungier St., Dublin 2/ Tel. +353 (01) 475-0309

GERMANY

Abentheuer — Boecking Str. 8, 55767/ Tel. +49 (06782) 6494 or 2214

Berlin — Cuvrystrasse 1, 10997/ Tel. & fax: +49 (030) 536 98789
Cologne — Taunusstr. 40, 51105/ Tel. +49 (0221) 830-1241
Flensburg — Hoerup 1, 24980 Neuhoerup/ Tel. +49 (04639) 7336
Hamburg — Baernstrs. 67, 22765/Tel. +49 (040) 397602
Heidelberg — Forum 5/ App. 4, 69126/ Tel. +49 (06221) 384553
Munich — Wachenheimer Strasse 1, 81539/ Tel. +49 (089) 6880-0288
Nuernberg — Kopernikusplatz 12, 90459/ Tel. +49 (0911) 446-7773

RURAL COMMUNITY
Jandelsbrunn (Nava Jiyada Nrsimha Ksetra) — Zielberg 20, 94118/ Tel +49 (08583) 316

RESTAURANT
Heidelberg — Vegethali Restaurant, Mittelbadgasse 3, 69117/ Tel. +49 (06221) 830553

HUNGARY

Budapest — Mariaremetei ut. 77, 1028 II/ Tel. & fax: +36 (01) 275-8140
Debrecen — Szechenyi u. 55, 4025/ Tel. +36 (052) 413-370
Eger — Szechenyi u. 64, 3300/ Tel. +36 (036) 410-515
Szolnak — Baratsag u. 6, 5000/ Tel. +36 (056) 412-124

RURAL COMMUNITY
Somogyvamos — Krsna-völgy, Fö u. 38, 8699/ Tel. +36 (085) 340-185

ITALY

Asti — Frazione Valle Reale 20, 14018 Roatto (AT)/ Tel. +39 (0141) 938406
Bergamo — Villaggio Hare Krishna (from Medolago Road to Terno d'Isola), 24040 Chignolo d'Isola (BG)/ Tel. +39 (035) 494-0706
Bologna — Via Ramo Barchetta 2, Castagnolo Minore, 40010 Bentivogolio (BO)/ Tel. +39 (051) 863924
Milan — Centro Culturale Govinda via Valpetrosa 5, 20123/ Tel. +39 (02) 862417
Rome — Hare Krishna Forum, Piaza Campo de' Fiori 27, 00186/ Tel. +39 (06) 683-2660
Vicenza — Prabhupada-desa, Via Roma 9, 36020 Albettone (VI)/ Tel. +39 (0444) 790573/

RURAL COMMUNITIES
Florence (Villa Vrindavan) — Via Comunale Scopeti 108, 50026 San Casciano in Val di Pesa (FI)/ Tel. +39 (055) 820054

RESTAURANT
Milan — Govinda's, Via Valpetrosa 5, 20123/ Tel. +39 (02) 862417

POLAND

Gdynia — (mail:) P.O. Box 364/ Tel. & fax: +48 (058) 29-5188
Krakow — ul. Wyzynna 2, 30-617/ Tel. & fax: +48 (012) 654-5824
Warsaw — Mysiadlo, k. Warszawy, 05-500 Piaseczno, ul. Zakret 11 (mail: MTSK, 02-770, Warszawy 130, P.O. Box 257)/ Tel. +48 (022) 750-7797 or 8248
Wroclaw — ul. Bierutowska 23, 51-317 (mail: MTSK 50-900, Wroclaw 2, P.O. Box 858)/ Tel. & fax: +48 (071) 345-7981

RURAL COMMUNITY
Czarnow (New Santipura) — Czarnow 21, 58-424 Pisarzowice, gm. Kamienna Gora/ Tel. +48 (07574) 128 92

SPAIN

Barcelona — Plaza Reial 12, Entlo 2, 08002/ Tel. +34 (93) 302-5194
Madrid — Espíritu Santo 19, 28004/ Tel. +34 (91) 521-3096
Málaga — Ctra. Alora, 3, Int., 29140 Churriana/ Tel. +34 (95) 262-1038
Santa Cruz de Tenerife — C/ Castillo, 44, 4°, Santa Cruz 38003/ Tel. +34 (922) 241035
Tenerife — C/ La Milagrosa, 6, La Cuesta, La Laguna/ Tel. +34 (922) 653422

RURAL COMMUNITY
Guadalajara (New Vraja Mandala) — (Santa Clara) Brihuega/ Tel. +34 (949) 280436

RESTAURANT
Barcelona — Restaurante Govinda, Plaza de la Villa de Madrid 4–5, 08002/ Tel. +34 (93) 318-7729

SWEDEN

Göthenburg — Hojdgatan 22A, 431 36 Moelndal/ Tel. +46 (031) 879648
Grödinge — Korsnäs Gård, 14792/ Tel. +46 (8530) 29151
Lund — Bredgatan 28 ipg, 222 21/ Tel. +46 (046) 399500; Restaurant: +46 (046) 120413
Stockholm — Fridhemsgatan 22, 11240/ Tel. +46 (08) 654-9002
Uppsala — Nannaskolan sal F 3, Kungsgatan 22 (mail: Box 833, 751 08, Uppsala)/ Tel. +46 (018) 102924 or 509956

RURAL COMMUNITY
Järna — Almviks Gård, 153 95/ Tel. +46 (08551) 52050

RESTAURANT
Göthenburg — Govinda's, Viktoriagatan 2A, 41125/ Tel. +46 (031) 139698

SWITZERLAND

Lugano — Via ai Grotti, 6862 Rancate (TI)/ Tel. +41 (091) 646-0071
Zürich — Bergstrasse 54, 8030/ Tel. +41 (01) 262-3388

RESTAURANTS
Bern — Marktgasse 7, 301/ Tel. +41 (031) 312-3825
Zürich — Govinda's, Preyergrasse 16, 800/ Tel. +41 (01) 251-8859/

OTHER COUNTRIES
Aarhus, Denmark — Radio Krishna's Bogcafe, Thorvaldsensgade 32, 8000 Aarhus C/ Tel. +45 (08) 676-1545
Amsterdam, The Netherlands — Van Hilligaertstraat 17, 1072 JX/ Tel. +31 (020) 675-1404
Antwerp, Belgium — Amerikalei 184, 2000/ Tel. +32 (03) 237-0037
Bratislava, Slovak Republic — Za farou 12, 83107/ Tel. +0042 (17) 4371-2257

Copenhagen (Hillerød), Denmark — Baunevej 23, 3400 Hillerød/ Tel. +45 4828-6446
Den Haag, The Netherlands — Van Zeggelenlaan 76, 2524 AS/ Tel. +31 (070) 393-0750
Gutenstein, Austria — Vedisches Kulturzeutrum, Markt 58, 2770/ Tel. & fax: +43 (02) 634-7731
Helsinki, Finland — Ruoholahdenkatu 24 D (III krs) 00180/ Tel. +358 (0) 694-9879
Iasi, Romania — Stradela Moara De Vint 72, 6600
Kaunas, Lithuania — 37, Savanoryu pr./ Tel. +370 (7) 22-2574 or 26-8953
Lisbon, Portugal — Rua Dona Estefania, 91 R/C 1000/ Tel. & fax: +351(01) 314-0314
Ljubljana, Slovenia — Zibertova 27, 1000/ Tel. +386 (061) 131-2124
Oslo, Norway — Jonsrudvej 1G, 0274/ Tel. +47 (022) 552243
Paris, France — 31 Rue Jean Vacquier, 93160 Noisy le Grand/ Tel. +33 (01) 4304-3263
Plovdiv, Bulgaria — ul. Prosveta 56, Kv. Proslav, 4015/ Tel. +359 (032) 446962
Porto, Portugal — Rua de S. Miguel 19, 4050 (mail: Apartado 4108, 4002 Porto Codex)/ Tel. +351 (02) 200-5469
Prague, Czech Republic — Jilova 290, Praha 5 - Zlicin 155 21/ Tel. +42 (02) 5795-0391 or 0401
Pula, Croatia — Vinkuran centar 58, 52000 (mail: P.O. Box 10)/ Tel. & fax: +385 (052) 573581
Riga, Latvia — 56, K. Baron st., LV1011/ Tel. +371 (02) 27-2490
Rijeka, Croatia — Sv. Jurja 32, 51000 (mail: P.O. Box 61)/ Tel. +385 (051) 543 055
Sarajevo, Bosnia-Herzegovina — ISKCON, Gornjo Vakufska 12, 71000/ Tel. +387 (071) 201530
Septon-Durbuy, Belgium — Chateau de Peá!te Somme, B-6940/ Tel. +32 (086) 322926
Skopje, Macedonia — Vvz. "ISKCON," Roze Luksemburg 13, 91000/ Tel. +389 (091) 201451
Sofia, Bulgaria — (mail: Sofia 1000, P.O Box 827)/ Tel. +359 (02) 981-0478
Split, Croatia — Cesta Mutogras 26, 21312 Podstrana (mail: P.O. Box 290, 2100)/ Tel. +385 (021) 651137
Tallinn, Estonia — Luise Street 11a, 10142/ Tel. +372 6460047
Timisoara, Romania — ISKCON, Porumbescu 92, 190/ Tel. +40 (961) 54776
Vienna, Austria — Bhaktivedanta-Zentrum Wien, Roetzergaase 34/3, 117/ Tel. & Fax: +43 (01) 481-9212
Vilnius, Lithuania — 23-1, Raugiklos st., 2024/ Tel. +370 (2) 23-5218/
Zagreb, Croatia — (mail: P.O. Box 68, 10001)/ Tel. & fax: +385 (01) 3772-643

RURAL COMMUNITIES

Czech Republic — Krsnuv Dvur c. 1, 257 28 Chotysany/ Tel. +420 (0602) 375978/
France (Bhaktivedanta Village) — Chateau Bellevue, F-39700 Chatenois/ Tel. +33 (03) 8472-8235
France (La Nouvelle Mayapura) — Domaine d'Oublaisse, 36360, Lucay le Mâle/ Tel. +33 (02) 5440-2395

RESTAURANTS

Copenhagen, Denmark — Govinda's, Nøerre Farimagsgade 82, DK-1364 Kbh K/ Tel. +45 3333-7444
Oslo, Norway — Krishna's Cuisine, Kirkeveien 59B, 0364/ Tel. +47 (02) 260-6250
Prague, Czech Republic — Govinda's, Soukenicka 27, 110 00 Prague-1/ Tel. +420 (02) 2481-6631 or 2481-6016
Prague, Czech Republic — Govinda's, Na hrazi 5, 180 00 Prague 8-Liben/ Tel. +420 (02) 683-7226
Presov, Slovak Republic — Govinda's, Hlavna 70, 08001/ Tel. +0042 (191) 722 819
Tallinn, Estonia — Damodara, Lauteri Street 1, 10114/ Tel. +372 6442650
Vienna, Austria — Govinda, Lindengasse 2A, 1070/ Tel. +43 (01) 522-2817

C. I. S.

RUSSIA

Chita — 27, Kurnatovskogo st./ Tel. +7 (30222) 23-4971 or 0911
Ekaterinburg — 620078, G. Ekaterinburg, per. Otdelniy 5DK VOG/ Tel. +7 (3432) 74-2200 or 49-5262
Irkutsk — st. Krimskaya 6A/ Tel. (3952) 38-71-32 or 3240-62
Kazan — 13, Sortirovochnaya st, pos.Yudino/ Tel. +7 (8432) 55-2529 or 42-9991
Krasnodar — 418, Stepnaya st., selo Elizavetinskoye, Krsnodarski krai/ Tel. +7 (8612) 50-1694
Kurjinovo — 8, Shosseinaya st., pos. Ershovo, Urupski region, Karachayevo-Cherkessia
Moscow — 8/3, Khoroshevskoye sh. (mail: P.O. Box 69), 125284/ Tel. +7 (095) 255-6711/ Tel. & fax: +7 (095) 945-3317
Moscow — Nekrasovsky pos., Dmitrovsky reg., 141700/ Tel. +7 (095) 577-8543, -8601, or -8775
Murmansk — 16, Frolova st. (mail: P.O. Box 5823)/ Tel. +7 (8152) 58-9284
Nijny Novgorod — 14b, Chernigovskaya st./ Tel. +7 (8312) 30-5197 or 25-2592/
Novorossiysk — 117, Shillerovskaya st./ Tel. +7 (86134) 38-926 or 51-415
Novosibirsk — 18/2 Kholodilnaya st., 630001/ Tel. +7 (3832) 46-2655 or -2666
Omsk — 664099, 42 10th Severnaya st. (mail: P.O. Box 8741)/ Tel. +7 (3812) 24-6310 or 41-4061
Perm — 12, Verhnekuryinskaya st., 614065/ Tel. +7 (3422) 33-5740 or 27-0681
Rostov-Na-Donu — 84/1, Saryana st., 344025 (mail: P.O. Box 64, 344007)/ Tel. & fax: +7 (8632) 51-0456
Samara — 122, Aeroportovskoye sh., Zubchininovka/ Tel. +7 (8462) 97-0318 or -0323
Simbirsk — 10, Glinki st., 432002/ Tel. +7 (8422) 21-4016
Sochi — 81a, Lesnaya st., Bytha/ Tel. +7 (8622) 98-5639/ Tel. & fax: +7 (8622) 97-2483
Ulan-Ude — 670013, Prirechnaya str. 23/ Tel. +7 (3012) 30-795
Vladimir — 60000, Nikolo-Galeyskaya st. 56/25/ Tel. +7 (0922) 32-6726
Vladivostok — 5-1, Rudneva st., 690087/ Tel. +7 (4232) 23-6685

RESTAURANTS

Ekaterinburg — Sankirtana, 33 Bardina st./ Tel. +7 (3432) 41-2737
St. Petersburg — Govinda's, 58, Angliysky pr., 190008/ Tel. +7 (812) 113-7896
Vladivostok — Gopal's, 10/12, Oleansky pr./ Tel. +7 (4232) 26-8943

UKRAINE

Dnepropetrovsk — Kalininskiy spusk 39/ Tel. +73 (0562) 42-3631 or 45-4709
Donetsk — 22, Rubensa st., Makeyevka 339018/ Tel. +380 (0622) 94-9104 or 3140
Kharkov — 43, Verhnegiyovskaya st., Holodnaya Gora, 310015/ Tel. +380 (0572) 20-2167 or 72-6869
Kiev — Dmitrievskaya, 21-13/ Tel. +380 (044) 219-1041 or -1042/ Tel. & fax: +380 (044) 244-4934
Kiev — 16, Zorany per., 254078/ Tel. +380 (044) 433-8312, or 434-7028 or 5533/
Lvov — 4, Aurora st., Bldg. No. 4, 290032/ Tel. +380 (0322) 33-3106 or 72-8756
Nikolaev — 5-8, Sudostroitelny per., 327052/ Tel. +380 (0510) 35-1734
Vinnica — 5, Chkalov st., 28601/ Tel. +380 (0432) 32-3152

OTHER COUNTRIES

Almaty, Kazakstan — 5, Kommunarov per., 480022/ Tel. +7 (327) 235-3830 or 3930
Baku, Azerbaijan — 2, Zardobi per., Uzbekistan st., pos. 8th km. 370060/ Tel. +994 (12) 21-2376
Bishkek, Kirgizstan — 5, Omsky per., 720007/ Tel. +7 (3312) 24-2230 or 44-3776
Dushanbe, Tadjikistan — 38, Anzob st., 734001/ Tel. +7 (3772) 27-1920 or -3990
Kishinev, Moldova — 13, A. Popovich st., 277022/ Tel. +373 (2) 55-8099 or 76-9254
Minsk, Belarus — 11, Pavlova st., 220053/ Tel. +375 (172) 13-0629/
Sukhumi, Georgia — st. Pr. Mira d 274/ Tel. +995 (8122) 2-9954
Tashkent, Uzbekistan — 54, Chervyakova st., 700005/ Tel. +7 (3712) 93-0352 or 34-4612
Tbilisi, Georgia — 16, Kacharava st., Avchalskoye sh., 380053/ Tel. +995 (32) 62-3326 or 98-5812

RESTAURANT

Almaty, Kazakstan — 4, Zalomova st., 480037/ Tel. +7 (327) 235-1444

AUSTRALASIA

AUSTRALIA

Adelaide — 227 Henley Beach Rd., Torrensville, SA 5031/ Tel. +61 (08) 8234-1378
Brisbane — 95 Bank Rd., Graceville (mail: P.O. Box 83, Indooroopilly), QLD 4068/ Tel. +61 (07) 3379-5455
Canberra — 117 Hawksbury Crescent, Farrer, ACT 2607/ Tel. +61 (02) 6290-1869
Melbourne — 197 Danks St., Albert Park (mail: P.O. Box 125), VIC 3206/ Tel. +61 (03) 9699-5122
Perth — 144 Railway Parade (mail: P.O. Box 102), Bayswater, WA 6053/ Tel. +61 (08) 9370-1552
Sydney — 180 Falcon St., North Sydney, NSW 2060 (mail: P.O. Box 459, Cammeray, NSW 2062)/ Tel. +61 (029) 9959-4558

RURAL COMMUNITIES

Bambra (New Nandagram) — Oak Hill, Dean's Marsh Rd. VIC 3241/ Tel. +61 (052) 887383
Millfield, NSW — New Gokula Farm, Lewis Lane (off Mt. View Rd., near Cessnock [mail: P.O. Box 399, Cessnock]), NSW 2325/ Tel. +61 (049) 981800
Murwillumbah (New Govardhana) — Tyalgum Rd., Eungella, via Murwillumbah (mail: P.O. Box 687), NSW 2484/ Tel. & fax: +61 (02) 6672-6579 or 3047

RESTAURANTS

Adelaide — Hare Krishna Food for Life, 79 Hindley St., SA 5000/ Tel. +61 (08) 8231-5258
Brisbane — Govindas, 1st Floor, 99 Elizabeth St., QLD 4000/ Tel. +61 (07) 3210-0255
Brisbane — Hare Krishna Food for Life, 190 Brunswick St., Fortitude Valley, QLD/ Tel. +61 (07) 3854-1016
Melbourne — Crossways, 1st Floor, 123 Swanston St., VIC 3000/ Tel. +61 (03) 9650-2939
Melbourne — Gopals, 139 Swanston St., VIC 3000/ Tel. +61 (03) 9650-1578
Perth — Hare Krishna Food for Life, 200 William St., Northbridge, WA 6003/ Tel. +61 (08) 9227-1684
Sydney — Hare Krishna Food for Life, 529b King St., Newtown, NSW 2042/ Tel. +61 (02) 9550-6524

NEW ZEALAND, FIJI, AND PAPUA NEW GUINEA

Christchurch, NZ — 83 Bealey Ave. (mail: P.O. Box 25-190)/ Tel. +64 (03) 366-5174
Labasa, Fiji — Delailabasa (mail: P.O. Box 133)/ Tel. +679 812912
Lautoka, Fiji — 5 Tavewa Ave. (mail: P.O. Box 125)/ Tel. +679 664112/ Fax: +679 663039
Port Moresby, Papua New Guinea — Section 23, Lot 46, Gordonia St., Hohola (mail: P.O. Box 571, POM NCD)/ Tel. +675 259213
Rakiraki, Fiji — Rewasa (mail: P.O. Box 204)/ Tel. +679 694243
Suva, Fiji — Joyce Place, Off Pilling Rd., Nasinu 7^1/2 miles (mail: P.O. Box 2183, Govt. Bldgs.)/ Tel. +679 393 599
Wellington, NZ — 105 Newlands Rd., Newlands (mail: P.O. Box 2753)/ Tel. +64 (04) 478-1414

RURAL COMMUNITY

Auckland, NZ (New Varshan) — Hwy. 28, Riverhead, next to Huapai Golf Course (mail: R.D. 2, Kumeu)/ Tel. +64 (09) 412-8075

RESTAURANTS

Auckland, NZ — Gopal's, Civic House (1st floor), 291 Queen St./ Tel. +64 (09) 303-4885
Christchurch, NZ — Gopal's, 143 Worcester St./ Tel. +64 (03) 366-7035
Labasa, Fiji — Hare Krishna Restaurant, Naseakula Road/ Tel. +679 811364
Lautoka, Fiji — Gopal's, Corner of Yasawa St. and Naviti St./ Tel. +679 662990
Suva, Fiji — Hare Krishna Vegetarian Restaurant, 18 Pratt St./ Tel. +679 314154
Suva, Fiji — Hare Krishna Vegetarian Restaurant, Dolphins FNPF Place, Victoria Parade/ Tel. +679 314154
Suva, Fiji — Hare Krishna Vegetarian Restaurant, Terry Walk, Cumming St./ Tel. +679 312295

AFRICA

GHANA

Accra — Samsam Rd., Off Accra-Nsawam Hwy., Medie, Accra North (mail: P.O. Box 11686)
Kumasi — P.O. Box 101, U.S.T
Nkawkaw — P.O. Box 69
Sunyani — South Ridge Estates, P.O. Box 685
Takoradi — New Amanful, P.O. Box 328

Tarkwa — State Housing Estate, Cyanide

RURAL COMMUNITY

Eastern Region — Hare Krishna Farm Community, P.O. Box 15, Old Akrade

NIGERIA

Abeokuta — Ibadan Rd., Obanatoka (mail: P.O. Box 5177)
Benin City — 108 Lagos Rd., Uselu/ Tel. +234 (052) 247900
Enugu — 56, Destiny Layout, Old Abakaliki Rd., Near Enugu Airport, Emene (by Efemeluna Bus stop)
Ibadan — 700 meters from Iwo Rd., Ibadan-Lagos Express Way (mail: UIPO Box 9996)
Jos — Airforce Base, Abattoir Rd., by Nammua, Ginrng Village (mail: P.O. Box 6557)
Kaduna — Federal Housing Estate, Abuja Rd. (mail: P.O. Box 1121), Goningora Village
Lagos — 12, Gani Williams Close, off Osolo Way, Ajaoo Estate 7/8 Bus stop, International Airport Rd. (mail: P.O. Box 8793, Marina)/ Tel. & fax +234 (01) 876169
Port Harcourt — Umuebule 11, 2nd tarred road (mail: P.O. Box 4429), Trans Amadi
Warri — Okwodiete Village, Kilo 8, Effurun/Orerokpe Rd. (mail: P.O. Box 1922)

SOUTH AFRICA

Cape Town — 17 St. Andrews Rd., Rondebosch 7700/ Tel. +27 (021) 689-1529
Durban, South Africa — 50 Bhaktivedanta Swami Circle (mail: P.O. Box 56003), Chatsworth, 4030/ Tel. +27 (031) 403-3328
Johannesburg — 40 Impala Crescent, Ext. 5 (mail: P.O. Box 926), Lenasia, 1820 South Africa)/ Tel. +27 (011) 854-1975/ Tel. & fax: +27 (011) 852-3176
Port Elizabeth — 15 Whitehall Court, Western Road 6000/ Tel. & fax +27 (041) 534330
Pretoria — 1189 Church St., Hatfield 0083 (mail: P.O. Box 14077, Hatfield 0028)/ Tel. & fax: +27 (12) 342-6216

OTHER COUNTRIES

Abidjan, Cote D'Ivoire — AICK-CI, 01 B.P. 8366
Gaborone, Botswana — P.O. Box 201003/ Tel. +267 307768
Kampala, Uganda — Bombo Rd., near Makerere University (mail: P.O. Box 1647)
Kisumu, Kenya — P.O. Box 547/ Tel. +254 (035) 42546/ Fax: +254 (035) 43294
Marondera, Zimbabwe — 6 Pine Street (mail: P.O. Box 339)/ Tel. +263 (028) 887-7801
Mombasa, Kenya — Hare Krishna House, Sauti Ya Kenya and Kisumu Rds. (mail: P.O. Box 82224)/ Tel. +254 (011) 312248
Nairobi, Kenya — Muhuroni Close, off West Nagara Rd. (mail: P.O. Box 28946)/ Tel. +254 (02) 744365/ Fax: +254 (02) 740957
Phoenix, Mauritius — Hare Krishna Land, Pont Fer (mail: P. O. Box 108, Quartre Bornes)/ Tel. +230 696-5804/ Fax: +230 686-8576
Rose Hill, Mauritius —13 Gordon St./ Tel. +230 454-5275

RURAL COMMUNITY

Mauritius (ISKCON Vedic Farm) — Hare Krishna Rd., Vrindaban/ Tel. +230 418-3955
Uganda — 9 Dewington Rd. (mail: P.O. Box 1647), Kampala/ Tel. +256 (041) 232302

LATIN AMERICA

BOLIVIA

Cochabamba, Bolivia — Av. Heroinas E-435 Apt. 3 (mail: P. O. Box 2070)/ Tel. & fax: +591 (042) 54346
La Paz, Bolivia — Pasaje Jauregui, 2262 Sopocachi/ Tel. +591 (02) 721945/
Santa Cruz — Calle 27 de Mayo No. 99 esq. Justo Bazan/ Tel. & fax: +591 (03) 345189

RESTAURANTS

Cochabamba, Bolivia — Restaurant Gopal, calle España N-250 (Galeria Olimpia)/ Tel. ,i91 (042) 34082
Cochabamba, Bolivia — Restaurant Govinda, calle Mexico #E0303/ Tel. +591)d42) 22568
Cochabamba, Bolivia — Restaurant Tulasi, Av. Heroinas E-262
La Paz, Bolivia — Restaurant Imperial, Calle Sagarnaga No. 213
Oruro, Bolivia — Restaurant Govinda, Calle 6 de Octubre No. 6071
Santa Cruz, Bolivia — Snack Govinda, Calle Bolivar esq. Av. Argomosa (primer anillo)/ Tel. +591 (03) 345189
Sucre, Bolivia — Restaurant Sat Sanga, Calle Tarapacá No. 161/ Tel. +591 (64) 22547

RURAL COMMUNITY

Bolivia — Contact ISKCON Cochabamba

BRAZIL

Belém, PA — Av. Almirante Tamandari, 1012, Centro, CEP 66023 000/ Tel. +55 (091) 243-0558
Belo Horizonte, MG — R. Amotiota, 818, Prado, CEP 30410 420/ Tel. +55 (031) 332-8460
Campina Grande, PB — R. Verancio Neiva, 136, Centro
Curitiba, PR — Alameda Cabral, 670, Centro, CEP 80410 210/ Tel. +55 (041) 277-3176
Florianópolis, SC — R. Cesar Augusto de Souza, 319, Careanos, CEP 88047 440
Fortaleza, CE — R. José Lourenço, 2114, Aldeota, CEP 60115 228 / Tel. +55 (085) 264-1273
Manaus, AM — Av. 7 de Setembro, 1599, Centro, CEP 69005 141/ Tel. +55 (092) 232-0202
Natal, RN — Praia de Serinhaem, 2254, Ponta Negra, CEP 55092 180
Porto Alegre, RS — R. Tomás Flores, 331, Bonfim, CEP 90035 201/ Tel. +55 (051) 233-1474
Recife, PE — R. Demóclitos de Souza Filho, 235, Madalena, 50001 970
Ribeirão Preto, SP — R. Carlos Gomes, 2315, Campos Elásios, CEP 14085 400/ Tel. +55 (016) 628-1533
Rio de Janeiro, RJ — (contact ISKCON Teresopolis)
Salvador, BA — R. Alvaro Adorno, 17, Brotas, 40225 460/ Tel. +55 (071) 382-1064
São Carlos, SP — R. Emilio Ribas, 195, Centro, CEP 13563 060
São Paulo, SP — Av. Angelica, 2583, Santa Cecilia, CEP 01227 200/ Tel. +55 (011) 259-7352

RURAL COMMUNITIES

Parati, RJ (Fazenda Goura Vrindavana) — CP 62, Serto

Śrī Śrī Rukmiṇī-Dvārakādhīśa—Presiding Deities of ISKCON Los Angeles (New Dvārakā)

Idaiatuba, CEP 23970 020

Pindamonhangaba, SP (Fazenda Nova Gokula) — CP 108, Bairro Ribeiro Grande, CEP 12400 000/ Tel. +55 (012) 982-9036

Teresopolis, RJ (Vrajabhumi Dhama) — CP 92430, Varzea, CEP 25951 970/ Tel. +55(021) 262-8208

RESTAURANT

Caxias do Sul, RS — R. Itália Travi, 601, Rio Branco CEP 95097 710

MEXICO

Guadalajara — Pedro Moreno No. 1791, Sector Juarez, Jalisco/ Tel. +52 (3) 616-0775

Mexico City — Tiburcio Montiel 45, Colonia San Miguel, Chapultepec D.F., 11850/ Tel. & fax: +52 (5) 271-1953

Monterrey — Av. Luis Elizondo No. 400, local 12, Col. Alta Vista/ Tel. +52 (8) 387-3028

Saltillo — Blvd. Saltillo No. 520, Col. Buenos Aires/ Tel. +52 (84) 178752

Tulancingo — (mail:) Apartado 252, Hildago/ Tel. +52 (775) 34072

RURAL COMMUNITIES

Guadalajara — Contact ISKCON Guadalajara

Veracruz — Mail: Jesus Garcia 33, Col. Ferrocarril, Cerro Azul

ADDITIONAL RESTAURANT

Veracruz — Restaurante Radhe, Sur 5 No. 50, Orizaba, Ver./ Tel. +52 (272) 57525

PERU

Lima — Carretera Central Km. 32 (frente a la curva que baja a la Cantuta) Chosica/ Tel. & fax: +51 (014) 491-0250

Lima — Schell 634 Miraflores/ Tel. +51 (014) 444-2871

Lima — Av. Garcilaso de la Vega 1670/ Tel. +51 (014) 433-2589

RURAL COMMUNITY

Correo De Bella Vista — DPTO De San Martin

ADDITIONAL RESTAURANT

Cuzco — Espaderos 128

OTHER COUNTRIES

Asunción, Paraguay — Centro Bhaktivedanta, Mariano R. Alonso 925/ Tel. +595 (021) 480-266
Bogotá, Colombia — Calle 46 BIS, 3-27, Chapinero Alto/ Tel. & fax +57 (01) 288-4680/ Tel. +57 (01) 288-6692
Buenos Aires, Argentina — Centro Bhaktivedanta, Andonaegui 2054 (1431)/ Tel. +54 (01) 523-4232
Cali, Colombia — Avenida 2 EN, #24N-39/ Tel. +57 (023) 68-88-53
Caracas, Venezuela — Avenida Berlin, Quinta Tia Lola, La California Norte/ Tel. +58 (02) 225463
Chinandega, Nicaragua — Edificio Hare Krsna No. 108, Del Banco Nacional 10 mts. abajo/ Tel. +505 (341) 2359
Essequibo Coast, Guyana — New Navadvipa Dham, Mainstay
Georgetown, Guyana — 24 Uitvlugt Front, West Coast Demerara
Guatemala, Guatemala — Calzada Roosevelt 4-47 tercer nivel, Zona 11
Guayaquil, Ecuador — 6 de Marzo 226 or V. M. Rendon/ Tel. +593 (04) 308412 or 309420
Montevideo, Uruguay — Centro de Bhakti-Yoga, Mariano Moreno 2660/ Tel. +598 (02) 477919
Panama, Republic of Panama — Via las Cumbres, entrada Villa Zaita, casa #10, frente a INPSA, (mail: P.O. Box 6-1776, El Dorado)/ Tel. +507 231-6561
Pereira, Colombia — Carrera 5a, No.19-36
Rosario, Argentina — Centro de Bhakti-Yoga, Paraguay 556 (2000)/ Tel. +54 (041) 252630 or 264243/ Fax: +54 (041) 490838
San José, Costa Rica — (mail:) Apartado 166, 1002, Paseo de los Estudiantes/ Tel. +506 227-4505/ Fax: +506 226-0685
San Salvador, El Salvador — (mail:) Apartado Postal 1506/ Tel. +503 78-0799
Santiago, Chile — Carrera 330/ Tel. +56 (02) 698-8044
Santo Domingo, Dominican Republic — Calle San Francisco de Asis No. 73, Ensanche Ozama
Tegucipalpa, Honduras — Apartado Postal 30305/ Tel. +504 32-3172/ Fax. +504 34-7806
Trinidad and Tobago, West Indies — Orion Drive, Debe/ Tel. +1 (809) 647-3165
Trinidad and Tobago, West Indies — Prabhupada Ave., Longdenville, Chaguanas

RURAL COMMUNITIES

Argentina (Bhaktilata Puri) — Ciudad de la Paz 3554 (1429) Capital Federal/ Tel. & fax: +54 (01) 523-8085
Colombia (Nueva Mathura) — Cruzero del Guali, Municipio de Caloto, Valle del Cauca/ Tel. 612688 en Cali
Costa Rica (Nueva Goloka Vrindavana) — Carretera a Paraiso, de la entrada al Jardin Lancaster (por Calle Concava), 200 metros al sur (mano derecha) Cartago (mail: Apdo. 166, 1002)/ Tel. +506 551-6752
Ecuador (Nueva Mayapur) — Ayampe (near Guayaquil)/
El Salvador — Carretera a Santa Ana, Km. 34, Canton Los Indios, Zapotitan, Dpto. de La Libertad
Guyana — Seawell Village, Corentyne, East Berbice

RESTAURANTS

Buenos Aires, Argentina — Jagannath Prasadam, Triunvirato 4266 (1431)/ Tel. +54 (01) 521-3396
Buenos Aires, Argentina — Restaurante Tulasi, Marcelo T. de Alvear 628, Local 30/ Tel. +54 (01) 311-0972
Cuenca, Ecuador — Govinda's at "Posada's del Sol," S.Bolivar 5-03 y Mariano Cueva
Guatemala, Guatemala — Callejor Santandes a una cuadra abajo de Guatel, Panajachel Solola
San Salvador, El Salvador — 25 Avenida Norte 1132

ISKCON Los Angeles (New Dvārakā)

GREAT
VEGETARIAN DISHES

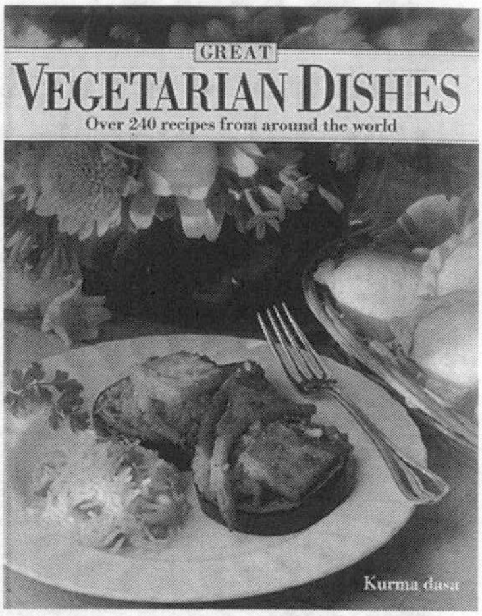

Featuring over 100 stunning full-color photos, this book is for spiritually aware people who want the exquisite taste of Hare Krishna cooking without a lot of time in the kitchen. The 240 international recipes were tested and refined by the author, world-famous Hare Krishna chef Kūrma dāsa.

240 recipes, 192 pages, coffee-table-size hardback

US: $19.95 #GVD

THE HARE KRISHNA BOOK OF
VEGETARIAN COOKING

This colorfully illustrated, practical cookbook by Ādirāja dāsa not only helps you prepare authentic Indian dishes at home but also teaches you about the ancient tradition behind India's world-famous vegetarian cuisine.

130 kitchen-tested recipes, 300 pages, hardback

US: $11.50 #HKVC

BEYOND BIRTH AND DEATH

What's the self? Can it exist apart from the physical body? If so, what happens to the self at the time of death? What about reincarnation? Liberation? In *Beyond Birth and Death* Śrīla Prabhupāda answers these intriguing questions and more.

Softbound, 96 pages

US$1.00 #BBD

THE HIGHER TASTE

A Guide to Gourmet Vegetarian Cooking and a Karma-Free Diet

Illustrated profusely with black-and-white drawings and eight full-color plates, this popular volume contains over 60 tried and tested international recipes, together with the why's and how's of the Krishna conscious vegetarian life-style.

Softbound, 176 pages

US$1.50 #HT

LIFE COMES FROM LIFE

In this historic series of talks with his disciples, Śrīla Prabhupāda uncovers the hidden and blatantly unfounded assumptions that underlie currently fashionable doctrines concerning the origins and purpose of life.

Softbound, 96 pages

US$1.50 #LCFL

CIVILIZATION AND TRANSCENDENCE

In this book Śrīla Prabhupāda calls the bluff of modern materialistic culture: "Modern so-called civilization is simply a dog's race. The dog is running on four legs, and modern people are running on four wheels. The learned, astute person will use this life to gain what he has missed in countless prior lives—namely, realization of self and realization of God."

Softbound, 90 pages

US$1.00 #CT

Order Form

Make check or money order payable to The Bhaktivedanta Book Trust and send to:

The Bhaktivedanta Book Trust
Dept. BID-H
3764 Watseka Avenue • Los Angeles, CA 90034

Name ______________________________
Please Print
Address ______________________________
City ____________________ ST ______ Zip __________

Code	Description	Qty.	Price	Total

Subtotal US $ __________
CA Sales Tax 8.25% US $ __________
Shipping 15% of Subtotal (minimum $2.00) US $ __________
TOTAL US $ __________

To Place a Credit Card Order Please Call

1-800-927-4152

VISA MasterCard